THEATRE AND ALCHEMY

Theatre and Alchemy

by
Bettina L. Knapp

*Hunter College
and the
Graduate Center of the
City University of New York*

**Wayne State
University Press**

Detroit, 1980

Library of Congress Cataloging in Publication Data

Knapp, Bettina Liebowitz, 1926–
  Theatre and alchemy.

  Bibliography: p.
  Includes index.
  1. Drama—History and criticism. 2. Alchemy in
literature. I. Title.
PN1650.A42K6   809.2′9356   80-17438
ISBN 0-8143-1656-5

TO CHARLES

CONTENTS

FOREWORD

In every culture in which we find alchemy, it is always intimately related to an esoteric or mystical tradition: in China to Taoism; in India to Yoga and Tantrism; in hellenistic Egypt to Gnosis; in Islamic countries to hermetic and esoteric mystical schools; and in the western Middle Ages and Renaissance to Hermetism, Christian and sectarian mysticism, and kabbalah. All alchemists proclaim their art to be an esoteric technique, pursuing a goal similar or comparable to that of the major esoteric and mystical traditions. The main objects of the alchemical quest were health and longevity, transmutation of base metals into gold, and production of the elixir of immortality.[1]

In the last decades a number of historians have demonstrated the importance of Hermetism and alchemy not only in the Middle Ages, the Italian Renaissance, and the Reformation period, but also among some of the great scientists of the seventeenth century.[2] In brief, these earlier thinkers believed that a world reform could be achieved through the spiritual powers released by occult—especially alchemical—powers. Such was the conviction of the famous mathematician and alchemist John Dee (b. 1527) and of Elias Ashmole, who, like many of their contemporaries, considered alchemy and natural magic to be the savior of the sciences of their day. Alchemy, not astronomy, was thought to be the key that would unlock the secrets of heaven and earth. Alchemy had a divine significance. Since the Creation was understood as an alchemical process, both earthly and celestial phenomena were interpreted in chemical terms. Thus Robert Fludd, a fellow of the Royal College of Physicians and an adept of mystical alchemy, gave a chemical description of the circulation of the blood which paralleled the circular motion of the sun.

The Hermetists and the "chemical philosophers" were expecting—some of them actively expecting—a radical and general reform of all religious, social, and cultural institutions. The first, indispensable stage of this universal *renovatio* was the reform of learning. In his *Christianopolis* (1619), Jonathan Valentin Adreae suggested that a proper community of scholars be formed in order to elaborate a new method of learning based on "chemical philosophy." In that utopian city Christianopolis, the center for such studies would be the laboratory; there the "sky and earth are married together," and the "divine mysteries impressed upon the land are discovered." Robert Fludd stated that it was impossible for anyone to attain the highest knowledge of natural philosophy without serious training in the occult sciences.

More recently, Professor Betty J. Teeter Dobbs made a careful investigation of Newton's alchemical manuscripts. According to Dobbs, Newton probed in his laboratory "the whole vast literature of the older alchemy as it has never been probed before or since." Newton sought in alchemy the structure of the small world to match his cosmological system. When he began to work seriously on the dynamics of orbital motion, he applied his ideas of chemical attraction to the cosmos. He did not reject the principle of transmutation, the basis of all alchemies. "Newton's alchemical thoughts were so securely established on their basic foundations that he never came to deny their general validity, and in a sense the whole of his career after 1675 may be seen as one long attempt to integrate alchemy and the mechanical philosophy."[3]

As has been shown by many historians of culture and by literary critics, such passionate interest in alchemy and Hermetism (demonstrated also by the tremendous success of the Rosicrucian movement) did not fail to influence a number of European and English poets, playwrights, and artists of the sixteenth and seventeenth centuries.[4] In her competent and meticulous analysis of nine dramas selected from the universal history of theatre—from *Shakuntala* to Claudel's *Break of Noon*—Professor Bettina Knapp did not look for the actual familiarity of their authors with an alchemical tradition. (As a matter of fact, only Strindberg was deeply involved in alchemical experiments.) She chose a more promising approach, namely the path opened by C. J. Jung when he noticed that the unconscious undergoes processes which express themselves in alchemical symbolism and which bring forth a psychic renewal corresponding to the results of hermetic operations.[5]

In the last two generations, many critics have endeavored to identify initiation scenarios in various literary works, ancient or modern. As we well know, *opus alchemicum* constitutes an initiatory process par excellence. In some cases—Maud Bodkin's *Archetypal Patterns in Poetry* (1934), for instance—the authors utilized Jung's hypothesis and vocabulary in their exegesis. But there are also a number of critics who, without directly applying Jung's method, investigated the initiation scenarios in such works as Gérard de Nerval's *Aurélie,* Herman Melville's *Moby Dick,* Henry David Thoreau's *Walden,* and Mark Twain's *Huckleberry Finn,* as well as in the novels of James Fenimore Cooper, Henry James, Sherwood Anderson, F. Scott Fitzgerald, Thomas Wolfe, and William Faulkner.[6] More recently, researches into the *imagination créatrice* in general and into the literary imagination in particular have disclosed the same traditional patterns of initiation in the entire oeuvre of Jules Verne, in such "realist" novels as *The Magic Mountain* of Thomas Mann, and even in the structure of the novel as such or of poetic creativity.[7]

At the very beginning of her book, Professor Knapp quotes this line from Antonin Artaud: "There is a mysterious identity of essence between the principle of theatre and that of alchemy." As far as I know, no literary critic nor historian of culture until now has envisaged a systematic analysis of the alchemical process underlying the entire dramatic literature. This is the first and foremost merit of Professor Knapp's work. The "specialists" will judge, from case to case, the success of her exegesis. But the significance of *Theatre and Alchemy* cannot be minimized: it discloses a deep and hidden spiritual dimension of the theatre in world literature.

Mircea Eliade
University of Chicago

Notes

1. See my book *The Forge and the Crucible: The Origins and Structures of Alchemy,* 2d ed. (Chicago, 1978) and the article "The Myth of Alchemy," *Parabola* 3 (August 1978):6–23.
2. See, inter alia, Allen G. Debus, *The Chemical Dream of the Renaissance* (Cambridge, 1968); Peter French, *John Dee* (London, 1972); Frances A. Yates, *The Rosicrucian Enlightenment* (Chicago, 1972); John Warwick Montgomery, *Cross and Crucible: Jonathan Valentin Andreae, Phoenix of the Theologians* (The Hague, 1973).
3. Betty J. Teeter Dobbs, *The Foundation of Newton's Alchemy* (Cambridge, 1975), pp. 88, 230.

4. See, for instance, the secondary sources quoted by Frances A. Yates in her books *Shakespeare's Last Plays* (London, 1975) and *The Occult Philosophy in the Elizabethan Age* (London, 1979).
5. See my essay "C. G. Jung and Alchemy," in *Forge and the Crucible,* pp. 221–26.
6. See the references in my essay "Initiation and the Modern World," reprinted in *The Quest* (Chicago, 1969), pp. 112–26, particularly pp. 123ff.
7. See, for example, Simone Vierne, *Jules Verne et le roman initiatique* (Paris, 1973) and *Rite, roman, initiation* (Grenoble, 1973); Max Bilen, *Écriture et initiation* (Lille-Paris, 1977); and the eight volumes of *Circé: Cahiers de recherches sur l'imaginaire* (Paris, 1970–79).

ACKNOWLEDGMENTS

I would like to thank Tobey Gittele for her editorial assistance and for preparing the index, and my research assistant, Simone Guers-Martynuk of the City University of New York, for her help in this project. I would also like to record my deep gratitude to the City University of New York for the Faculty Research Award given to me for this book.

Thanks are also due to the following for permission to republish material which first appeared in their pages in a somewhat different form: to *par rapport* for "Castle, Cave, and Cauldron: Strindberg's Alchemical Tinctures in *A Dream Play* 1 (Summer 1978):87–100; to the *Stanford French Review* for "Michel de Ghelderode's *Escurial*: The Alchemist's *Nigredo*" 2 (Winter 1978):405–17; to *Educational Theatre Journal* for "An Alchemical Brew: From *Separatio* to *Coagulatio* in Yeat's *The Only Jealousy of Emer*" 30 (December 1978):447–65; to *Symposium* for "Stanislaw Ignacy Witkiewicz's *Kurda Wodna*: 'Perform No Operation 'till All Be Made of Water' " 33 (Spring 1979):5–24; to *L'Esprit Créateur* for "Adam/Axël/Alchemy" 18 (Summer 1978):24–41; and to the *Journal of Altered States of Consciousness* for *"The Dybbuk*: 'The Spagyric Marriage' " 4, no. 3 (1978–79):253–76, © 1979, Baywood Publishing Co., Inc.

Introduction: *Solve et Coagula*

Alchemy is a science, a psychology, and a metaphysics. It is also theatre. Antonin Artaud wrote:

There is a mysterious identity of essence between the principle of theatre and that of alchemy. Where alchemy, through its symbols, is the spiritual Double of an operation which functions only on the level of real matter, the theatre must also be considered as the Double, not of this direct, every day reality of which it is gradually being reduced to a mere inert replica . . . but of another archetypal and dangerous reality, a reality of which the Principles, like dolphins, once they have shown their heads, hurry to dive back into the obscurity of the deep.[1]

A relationship also exists between alchemy and psychology, declared C. G. Jung.

The entire alchemical procedure . . . could just as well represent the individuation process of a single individual, though with the not unimportant difference that no single individual ever attains to the richness and scope of the alchemical symbolism. This has the advantage of having been built up through the centuries, whereas the individual in his short life has at his disposal only a limited amount of experience and limited powers of portrayal.[2]

The alchemist transmutes his metals. The dramatist projects his yearnings and fantasies onto his play (his double) and, in so doing, alters their form and reality. In the psychological sphere, the un-

1

conscious delineates its contents in dreams, visions, hallucinations, and free associations, in the form of archtypal images and symbols of all types. In each of these domains the realm of the unknown is encountered; it enters into being, acquires dimensionality, and becomes a dynamic force with which the creative individual must contend.

Alchemy offers many of its riches in the written records kept by ancient scientists: in iconographic representations, symbols, ciphers, and diagrams. Alchemists believed in the original unity of matter and in the possibility of its transformation and differentiation. What was of import to them was their ability to change impure leaden metal to a higher and more perfect Golden Essence. A parallel existed between their scientific activities and their metaphysical beliefs; as metals could be purified, so humankind could be elevated from dross to its spiritualized essence. Mystical notions concerning primordial unity, diversity in the manifest world, and the theory of correspondences and reincarnation were expressed in scientific terms—that is, in conjunction with chemicals and metals. First viewed as distinct substances, chemical combinations were observed to recombine under certain conditions and, interpreted from a mystical point of view, indicated a *coniunctio*, a union of opposites, an integration of antagonistic forces. Once opposing polarities were welded together, everything within the cosmos formed a cohesive whole, enabling a *renovatio*, a renewal, to take place.

The psychotherapist seeks to encounter the unconscious, to understand some of its contradictions and antagonisms as well as its creative élan. To transform what is negative into a positive and fruitful orientation or ruling principle of the personality is his goal. In so doing, the psychotherapist is elevating unregenerate matter (a leaden condition) or chaos into a new golden sphere or cosmos. If therapy is successful, the individual may work in harmony with himself and the world about him; he may remain independent despite functioning as a member of a collective society.

The dramatist also experiences a transmutation: from the uncreated (amorphous) idea which lies buried within his unconscious to the externalized incarnation which is his play; from the alchemical integration of disparate forces on the physical stage (actors, director, sets, lighting, sound effects, and more) to the realization of a new unity in the dramatic spectacle.

The term "alchemist" as used in this book does not refer to the "puffers" or "goldmakers," as certain charlatans were called, nor even to the "common gold" of existential man who, like Midas, so frequently identified with this metal and became possessed by it. Rather, I will concentrate in these pages on the "invisible" or "incorporeal" Philosopher's Gold, a symbol for the higher spiritual, psychological, and aesthetic values.

Alchemy—or the "Great Work" (*Ars Magna*), another term frequently used—was said to have originated in Egypt with the Egyptian god Hermes (Thoth) Trismegistus, who was the alleged founder of both the arts and the sciences. Hence alchemy is sometimes called the "hermetic" or "secret" art. It was said that Hermes Trismegistus was the author of the "Emerald Table" (*Tabula Smaragdina*) upon which the foundations of alchemy had been written in ancient Phoenician. Legend tells us that Alexander the Great found it in the tomb of Hermes Trismegistus in a cave near Hebron. It stated in part:

Thou shalt separate the earth from the fire, the subtle from the gross, gently, with great industry. It rises from earth to heaven, and it receives the power of things above and of things below. By this means shalt thou obtain the glory of the whole world, and all darkness shall depart from thee. It is the strong power of every power, for it will overcome all that is subtle and penetrate all that is solid. Thus the world was created.[3]

The fourth-century mystic and alchemist, Father Zosimos of Panoplis, declared that alchemy was God-given. According to the kabbalah, certain angels fell in love with mortal women and came down to earth. They taught the women the secrets of nature and as a result were condemned and exiled from heaven. From the cohabitation of angels and mortals was born a race of giants. According to Genesis 6:4, "There were giants in the earth in those days; and also after that, when the sons of God came in unto the daughters of men, and they bare children to them, the same became mighty men which were of old, men of renown." In the Book of Enoch, it is written that Cain built Enochia, an underground city which he named after his son Enoch; Genesis 4:22 records that his descendant, Tubal-cain, was "an instructor of every artificer in brass and iron." It was in this dwelling place beneath the earth's surface that man was taught the art of metallurgy. Alchemists were convinced, after hearing about the wonders revealed in the Book of Enoch, that ores were conceived and matured within the earth as the embryo in the mother's womb. Their goal was to wrest nature's secrets from her, to hasten the process of perfection within the earth's womb through their art.

According to Arab tradition, the mysteries of alchemy were given to Moses and Aaron by God. Other sources suggest that Shem, Noah's son, indoctrinated some of his contemporaries into the occult teachings dealing with the art of melting and smelting metals. Considered a sacred, royal, evil, and magic art and science, alchemy was developed in Alexandria around the third century A.D. and spread to Egypt, Greece, and Rome. Practiced by Christians, Jews, Muslims, and polytheists, it spread to Byzantium, the Arab world, England, and the European continent during the Middle Ages.

Alchemy is not only an occidental phenomenon, but was also practiced in China as far back as 4500 B.C. The Taoists were the greatest practitioners of the art. They experimented with water, fire, wood, metals, and earth, but were more interested in questions of immortality than in creating gold. *K'i* was believed to be the vital essence which existed prior to the division of the cosmos into *yang*, associated with the male principle (representing light, heat, activity) and *yin*, related to the female principle (symbolized by darkness, cold, passivity). Each struggled to unite with the other. It was Pao P'u Tzu who, in the fourth century A.D., outlined three processes for the creation of liquid gold and an elixir of long life. Hindu alchemy, interwoven with the complex spiritual techniques of hatha and tantric yoga, was called by Madhava, the fourteenth-century Vedantic sage, "the science of mercury."

Etymologically, "alchemy" is derived from the Egyptian *khem-ein*, meaning "the preparation of the black ore or powder," or from *kême*, signifying "the black land," the appellation given Egypt in ancient days. The addition of the prefix *al* ("the") to the Greek *khyma* ("smelting" or "casting") was the basis for the word "alchemy"; denoting that black, sacred, divine art which has fascinated man since earliest times.[4]

Alchemical theory in general is based on the notion of transmutation: nothing disappears in the cosmos; it merely alters in form and texture. Alchemists contend that everything which emerges from the ground, whether animal, mineral, or vegetable, is composed of some primitive matter or *prima materia*. In Plato's *Timaeus*, it is defined as a substance common to all things and capable of taking on any form during the course of earthly or manifest existence. The idea of it was formulated by Xenophanes, who believed in a primal unity from which all creation emerged. Thales of Miletus also posited a monistic theory, suggesting that all things emanated from water, which he defined as "the foundation of the world" and which alchemists term *aqua permanens*, or primordial waters. Such concepts were not unknown to the Egyptians, who were convinced that Osiris was water and that all things came from and were enclosed within him. Anaximander went a step forward when he declared that opposites develop from an original or primal substance. Such polarity, which is part of alchemical belief, was expressed by the Babylonians in terms of the sun (associated with gold, the masculine principle, the godhead) and the moon (the earthly, female, silvery entity, always in a state of flux and dependent upon another element for life). Empedocles went on to note the conflict inherent in primordial indestructible atoms, which were animated by either love or hatred, attraction or repulsion, and so introduced the law of opposites basic to the universe. Heraclitus assumed that the cosmos was in a state of becoming and that its essence was fire. The conflict of opposites, introduced by Anaximander and elaborated by Empedocles and Heraclitus, created an energetic and dynamic condition leading directly to tension. When Heraclitus spoke of fire, whether emerging from the human, mineral, or vegetable world, it was not to be understood merely as physcial combustion, but rather as the fire within a being or thing. In man it was associated with feeling. For the alchemist it indicated a philosophical fire—hence the expression "philosophy by fire" (*philosophus per ignem*) to describe alchemy.[5]

Although the techniques used by the alchemists varied, they had a common goal: to divest the baser elements with which they were working of their impurities by means of a series of experiments which they hoped would take them from primal unity to the creation of the Philosopher's Stone. As Eirenaeus Philalethes, an alleged sixteenth-century alchemist, wrote: "All metallic seed is the seed of gold: for gold is the intention of Nature with regard to all metals. If the base metals are not gold, it is only through some accidental hindrance: they are all potentially gold."[6]

From a metaphysical point of view, the Philosopher's Stone was defined as a substance from which the All emanates as a new unity (the Self or God). Such oneness is encompassed in the phrase "the alpha and the omega," used by Christ to describe himself and implying universality. It is also referred to by the Hebrew kabbalists as the "creative point," the beginning in divinity, and by the Hindus in their mandalas as the *shri-yantra*, the "spiritual center." Within the center, suggested Michael Maier, the seventeenth-century alchemist, exists "the invisible point" which can never be destroyed and which is eternal.[7] The alchemist not only wanted to transform the imperfect into the perfect—to purify matter—but also to raise man to the paradisiac state he had known prior to his alienation from God. Metaphysically, the alchemist attempted to redeem his metals, humankind, and himself as well. He longed to become reintegrated into the primordial unity he had known before his earthly existence.

As C. G. Jung explained in *Psychology and Alchemy* (1944), the alchemist usually led an isolated existence. He spent long hours in front of his athanor (oven), inhaling the toxic gases and fumes which emanated from it. He had to be endowed with or to develop special character traits: perseverance, patience, humility, and basic calmness. Never could he yield to anger or discouragement; to do so would defeat his purpose. Important, too, was the fact that the later alchemist was a learned man who usually had studied at a university and was familiar with the works or at least the commentaries of Aristotle, Hippocrates, Galen, and other ancient scientists and philosophers. Strict secrecy had to be maintained over his experiments for fear that the information he discovered might be used and misused by others; secrecy was also a protective device, since the Catholic church punished alchemists, believing their discoveries might in some way lessen its authority. The alchemists, generally speaking, had faith in their mission and believed that they were truly accomplishing God's wishes.

As the alchemist worked on his experiments, he was continuously facing mysterious chemical substances, which he looked upon as living and dynamic forces. Whenever man is faced with a mystery, he fills the void with unconscious contents or psychological projections (fantasies). In so doing, the alchemist attributed all sorts of virtues and philosophical concepts to his observations, thereby indicating a corresponding activity within his own psyche. His attempt to understand the mystery of matter may be considered as a manifestation of work going on within him, an individual desire to discover meaning in his own subliminal world. Jung wrote:

Although their labours over the retort were a serious effort to elicit the secrets of chemical transformation, it was at the same time . . . the reflection of a parallel psychic process which could be projected all the more easily into the unknown chemistry of matter since that process is an unconscious phenomenon of nature, just like the mysterious alteration of substances. What the symbolism of alchemy expresses is the whole problem of the evolution of the personality . . . the so-called individuation process.[8]

While the alchemist was responding to his own unconscious notions or to the creative energy emerging from his confrontation with his own depths, he projected a variety of human characteristics onto the substance with which he was dealing. Sulfur and mercury, two opposing material polarities, were always attracted to one another within the earth the alchemist posited. Each was given a sex, character traits, and a spiritual existence. Sulfur was masculine, active, hot, and fixed, and corresponded to the soul; mercury (or quicksilver) was feminine, passive, cold, and volatile, and corresponded to the spirit. Sulfur and mercury were looked upon as the father and mother of other metals, while salt was regarded as the vital spirit which unites mercury and sulfur and corresponds to the force that links body and soul.

Since, according to the alchemists, everything emerges from divinity or the One, becomes differentiated when entering the manifest world, and returns to its undifferentiated state after death, everything that is incarnated must necessarily follow the death/rebirth sequence. Metals, once functioning in the world, are living and breathing substances, as are all other things in the cosmos. Their modalities and stages of evolution are what distinguish mineral, vegetable, and animal. Life, therefore, involves a complex series of transformations from the minutest particles to the largest of entities, continuous and contiguous within deity.[9] Everything alters through adaptation.

Alchemists lived in a world of analogies and parallels and were forever enlarging the scope of their vision. For example, they believed that the principles of sulfur, mercury, and salt corresponded to the body, spirit, and soul of the human being, as well as to God, nature, and man, and to the archetypal world, the macrocosm, and the microcosm. According to the alchemist, the elements of fire, water, air, and earth emerged from the All and were synthesized in the six-pointed Star of Solomon. In the *Timaeus*, Plato stated that each element except earth could become the other.[10]

fig 1

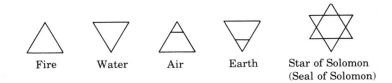

Fire   Water   Air   Earth   Star of Solomon
(Seal of Solomon)

Adding the four elements to the three principles produces seven, a significant number for the alchemist. It indicates not only the days of the week, the notes of the scale, and the alchemical operations, but also the planets. The alchemists also found analogies between the constellations and the metals. The two perfect metals, gold and silver, corresponded to the sun and the moon respectively; the other metals were imperfect, and corresponded to the planets as follows: mercury/Mercury, tin (pewter)/Jupiter, iron/ Mars, copper/Venus, and lead/Saturn. The sun and moon and each of the planets were humanized by the alchemist and took on a variety of personality traits, as did the metals with which they corresponded. Lead, for example, was heavy and took on the saturnine or melancholy disposition, and a person associated with this planet was said to be given to despair.

During the course of his experiments, the alchemist endowed the substance with which he was working with the names and sexes of people and animals. The fire he used to cook his metals was considered masculine; it inseminated matter, which was feminine; the athanor was compared to a womb. God, hermaphroditic before the Creation, afterwards became divided into opposites: masculine as the sun, feminine as the earth (also incarnated in the moon). The green lion, according to the system of alchemical ciphers, was green vitriol (sulfur and mercury after conjunction); the wolf was antimony; the dog was sulfur or gold. A dog devoured by a wolf indicated purification of gold through antimony. A swan stood for whiteness and purity. Metals and chemicals, therefore, were considered living entities in various stages of development.

The path leading to the creation of the Philosopher's Stone (or Gold, also called "congealed light," or the "Earth's Sun") was arduous and consisted of four steps before the fifteenth century and three stages thereafter. These steps were described by the alchemist in terms of color. Three different psychological stages in the development of the human personality correspond, Jung wrote, to the three-part alchemical process.

Nigredo, the blackening process, was comparable to chaos, the *massa confusa* that existed before the separation of the elements; it is a state in which matter is reduced to an almost liquid condition or has become a "quality of the *prima materia*."[11] Lead corresponds to this stage. Psychologically, the *nigredo* phase has been compared to man's primitive nature, to the state of unconsciousness. He is unaware of his conflicts, needs, and desires, and either lives in a state of paradisiac ignorance or is overcome by his troubles and is a perpetual prey to inner chaos and turmoil. The Gnostic symbol of the *uroborus*, the serpent eating his own tail, symbolizes the first stage, before the child has severed himself from his world parents (or personal parents), prior to his experiencing himself as an individual. Such a state, depending upon its acuteness, leads to a lowering of mental capacity, and in some cases may make a person virtually helpless. The "Primal Darkness" of the Gnostic, Jung's "collective unconscious," and Goethe's "Realm of the Mothers" may all be associated with *nigredo*: the undifferentiated and unknowable realm within which the arcane substance in all matter exists.

Albedo, the whitening stage, comes into being with the washing of the elements or metals in question, their *ablutio* or baptism in the *aqua permanens*. Since this phase has been called the "silver" or "moon" condition, it coincides with the metal silver. Psychologically, *albedo* implies the birth of duality and with it a deepening self-knowledge. The individual has cut himself loose from the rest of nature and his world (or personal parents) and has become conscious of his inner conflicts. "Light dawns," as the saying goes; daybreak emerges. With the birth of consciousness, a concomitant separation of the various facets of the personality occurs. Jung's four functions (thinking, feeling, sensation, and intuition) may become evident at this point.

Rubedo, the reddening phase, comes into being when the fire with which the alchemist tests his elements and their "genuineness" or "incorruptibility" rises to its most powerful intensity. It is at this time that the reddened metals have reached a state of purity, that the union of opposites comes to pass and the Philosopher's Stone emerges. The notion of the Philosopher's Stone varied with each alchemist. For some it contained the elixir of life; for others it was gold or the *prima materia* out of which gold could be produced. It was capable of bringing happiness, health, and equilibrium to its creator and to those who came in contact with it. It was also looked upon as a spiritual or mystical substance from which the new man, the *homunculus*, would be molded. Referred to by the Gnostics as *Anthropos* or "divine original man," the homunculus was capable of transcending the old divisions of time, space, birth, and death, thereby uniting with a higher form. Gold is associated with this stage.

Psychologically, the *rubedo* phase implies a union of opposites, a free-flowing relationship between conscious and unconscious spheres. The *coniunctio* has come into being, not because the individual has become unconscious of his conflicts as he had been in the *nigredo* stage, but because of his very knowledge and understanding of them. Man in this phase has been delivered from the domination of his instincts but has not rejected them; his physical and spiritual halves are working in harmony. He has understood what has been happening within him and has assimilated the component parts and polarities into his psyche. The *rubedo* stage is comparable to man's highest earthly spiritual state, the quintessential element born out of the purification of the four elements composing the physical nature of man. It is in the *rubedo* stage that the individuation process is most marked; the "transcendental totality" (the Philosopher's Stone), or the Self, becomes integrated, bringing equilibrium and harmony to the disjointed and antagonistic. The psychological *coniunctio* corresponds to the alchemist's mystical coitus or spagyric marriage.[12]

The *nigredo*, *albedo*, and *rubedo* sequence may be broken down into seven alchemical operations which also have metaphysical and psychological associations. In this series, the sick metals or personalities are put through difficult operations and will suffer trituration, dismemberment, corrosion, putrefaction, and other painful experiences in the course of the healing process. If the results are successful, the perfect metal and the sound personality will become operative.

Calcinatio, the fire operation, implies the burning off of all impurities and the drying out of all moisture. Only ashes remain. Jung suggested that an affinity exists between the *calcinatio* condition and libido (psychic energy): the inner fire or emotion within the personality which seared the old and unproductive ways allows a fresh ruling principle to emerge. Burning also implies negative conditions: hellfire, damnation, frustration, anguish, and turmoil: extreme conditions of friction and tension which may lead to an impasse.

Solutio, the water operation, solves and dissolves. The unsolvable problem vanishes in this phase. The former stumbling block in the psychotherapeutic process has been liquefied, as is sugar or salt when placed in a bowl of water. A smoother or more objective and comprehensive attitude may therefore come into being. Problems are viewed from a distance and with more perspective. The whole, rather than merely the particular, comes into consideration. The negative condition of *solutio* leads to drowning; a regression, loss of identity, or depression ensues.

Coagulatio, the earth condition, represents a hardening, fixing, or solidifying of the previous liquid attitude. Notions have congealed and a realistic point of view or ruling principle, now more broadly based, has emerged. An adaptability between unconscious and conscious contents is experienced. With an overly fixed relationship to the earth element or to reality, however, one may become anchored in one view or fixated.

Sublimatio corresponds to the air operation. Here the previously solid ruling principle becomes gaseous; earth is transformed into spirit; the coarse has become refined; the liquid has evaporated and has become distilled. Psychologically, it implies spiritual growth, an ability to abstract and conceptualize problems and to divest them of earthly entanglements. *Sublimatio*, therefore, implies height, spirituality, flight, an amorphous condition. If one soars to too great a height, contact with reality may be diminished to a dangerous point.

Separatio requires the separation of the whole into its component parts; solid is divested of its liquidity. At this stage the undifferentiated becomes differentiated. The process of evaluation and discrimination is used to face problems. The alchemist is said to cut, torment, and incise his metals, implying in the psychological sphere that duality, ambivalence, and conflict between subjective and objective approaches is present. This stage corresponds to the Creation as described in Genesis: God separated light from darkness. Aristotle's four elements, Jung's four functions, and Galen's four humors are included in this sequence. Fragmentation and

fig 2

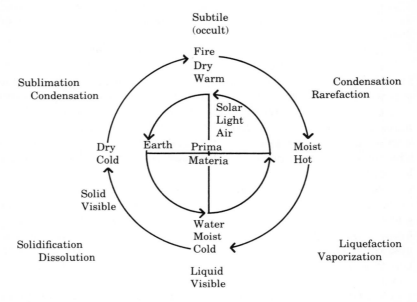

The four elements according to Aristotle, from Serge Hutin, *L'Alchimie* (Paris: Presses Universitaires de France, 1971), p. 72. By permission.

splintering of the personality in the *separatio* process, if carried to the extreme, may lead to disorientation and an inability to focus on a given problem or view.

    Putrefactio and *mortificatio* reduce everything to its *prima materia*. The alchemist tortures his materials, changing their textures and forms. This stage implies rotting, decomposition, and disintegration. When the conscious ruling principle is no longer productive and degeneration has set in, destruction of the fixed is in the offing. The ritual slaying of the king in myths belongs to this category. Such death/rebirth rituals occur when the collective (or personal) libido proves inadequate and can no longer fulfill the life function. John 12:24 reads: "Verily, verily, I say unto you, Except a corn of wheat fall into the ground and die, it abideth

Elements	Nature	Temper-ament	Color	Taste	Odor	Sex
Fire	hot-dry	bilious	red	bitter	penetrating	masculine
Air	hot-moist	sanguine	yellow	sugary	perfumed	masculine
Water	cold-moist	lymphatic	white	insipid	weak	feminine
Earth	cold-dry	melancholy (spleen)	black	sour	fetid	feminine

The four humours according to Galen, from Wilhelm Ganzenmüller, *L'Alchimie au moyen âge* (Verviers, Belgium: Bibliothèque Marabout, 1974), p. 110. By permission.

alone: but if it die, it bringeth forth much fruit." Dismemberment, mutilation, crucifixion, and killings are all symptomatic of this stage of evolution. Important at this juncture are the operative notions of sin and guilt. Rot and disintegration may spread and infect the entire personality. In this case, real death or insanity could follow.

Coniunctio is a unification on a higher plane of conflicting polarities within the psyche. It implies a condition of harmony and gnosis; the individuation process is pursuing its course; the integration of the human personality and the conditions necessary for the birth of the Philosopher's Stone have come into being.

Jung's cyclical concept of psychological evolution parallels the alchemist's view of the perfection of metals. To experience the unconscious during the seven alchemical/psychological operations enables the individual to transform chaos into cosmos. The previously unadapted conscious attitude has now been transformed into a productive view in which the whole of the psyche operates as an integrated force.

The dramatist also believes in *solve et coagula*—"separate and coagulate." His trajectory is equally difficult, laborious, and excoriatingly painful. The play he hopes to see performed must be extracted from his unconscious, his *prima materia*, where it lives in a dormant and amorphous state. He too must experience the three alchemical steps.

Nigredo: the play (its themes and characters) lies buried in the unconscious, in an undifferentiated state. It exists as a blackened mass, somnolent in unfathomable and opaque matter.

Albedo: the separation or cleansing process requires the dramatist to cut himself loose from his double (the play) and allow its component parts to grow individually (the protagonists, voices, situations, scenes, sets, decor, and so forth).

Rubedo: the libido (or energy) experienced by the dramatist in the course of the creative process has enabled him to pull the disparate parts of the spectacle together. The work of forming his protagonists, of endowing them with stage life has caused the dramatist friction, fire, tension. Each force encountered during his travail (plot or plotlessness, characterizations or diffusion of personalities, conflicts, suspense, and so forth) now has to be welded together into a harmonious whole, bringing the completed work of art or Philosopher's Stone into existence.

The three alchemical and psychotherapeutic principles also have parallels in the theatrical domain: sulfur corresponds to the dramatist; mercury corresponds to the double (play); salt corresponds to the spirit behind the work which serves to unite the polarities.

Sulfur	masculine	active	hot	fixed	Dramatist
Mercury	feminine	passive	cold	volatile	Double (play)
Salt	quintessence				Spirit (élan)

The four elements are equally important to the dramatist in the creation and perfection of his work.

Fire: the energy (libido) expended by the dramatist in the creation of his play. The amalgams with which he works must be heated, their courses and alterations traced and vivified. The actors go through a similar process as they begin to live out their stage personalities.

Air: the mysterious, spiritual, and occult factors involved in the transformation process within the dramatist's psyche are in full progress from idea to reality, spirit to body. The same alteration occurs in the actors' approach to their portrayals.

Water: the fluidity and malleability of the dramatist's élan has been expressed in the birth of the various parts of his play. The double now lives as an entity unto itself: the characterizations and the emotions derived from them, arouse the dramatist, compelling him to act and react. A similar relationship exists between the actors and the personalities they have now created on stage. Each is confronted with a double; the emotional and physical needs of the actor and his creation now take on reality.

Prima materia: source of all things, unique, inde-structible: God, the Uncreated, the Unconscious, the World *in potentia*	Fire (occult, subtile state) Air (occult, gaseous state)	Inspiration (energy) Play (amorphous, un-created state)
	Water (visible, liquid)	Birth of the play (separation of drama-tist and his creation)
	Earth (visible, solid state)	Stage performance

Earth: the playwright's work has become concretized. He sees it alive on the stage before him: acting and reacting to the theatrical conventions of sets, costumes, lights, vocalizations, gestures, sound effects, and so forth. The same may be said of the actor as he portrays his role, injecting it with a life of its own, attracting and repelling those forces which live around him—the audience in particular.

The theatre has metaphysical ramifications similar to those found in alchemy and psychology. Artaud suggested that author, actor, director, spectator, objects, color, sound, gesture, movements, rhythms, and words in the theatrical arena must be looked upon as differentiations or parts of the cosmic whole. Space, therefore, is to be seen as something alive, full, and active—as part of the cosmic flow and not distinct from it.[13] The alchemist's seven operations therefore have equivalents in the theatrical field. *Calcinatio* coincides with the dramatist's fire, courage, and patience to do away with peripheral or extraneous material. Only the purest and finest of substances must remain. *Solutio* corresponds to the immersion of all aspects of the playwriting procedure into one receptacle. From such a vantage point (all factors equalized) the play may be considered from a distance and with objectivity, thus disentangling the dramatist from his work and allowing a free-flowing attitude to emerge. *Coagulatio* indicates the fixing process. The dramatist's ideas have been set. He begins the writing phase, endowing his characters with life, personalities, bodily structures. The physical stage properties may also come into consideration at this point. *Sublimatio* concentrates on the distillation of all preceding steps: the ventilation and reassessing of ideas and concepts, thus allowing greater perspective: reflection and conceptualization may be used with felicity. *Separatio* implies a new objectivity and renewed power. The dramatist must have the courage to cut, delete, and evaluate the play as a whole; each aspect of the play must be examined as if under a microscope. Unity no longer exists. Change in form and cohesiveness is required: from inertia to movement. The playwright must be ruthless as he looks at his work.

To mutilate or dismember what was whole leads to a condition of *putrefactio*: the killing of unregenerate or unadaptable material. Events, situations, and characterizations must be plowed back into the unconscious. With this return to the womb only the most vital aspects of the spectacle as a unit are offered. Thus the play emerges redeemed, and the *coniunctio* or integrations of the disparate parts forms a harmony of opposites.

The plays I have selected for discussion in this book are not well known to everyone, yet each is unique in its own way. My choice of a Strindberg work rather than one by Ibsen, of a Yeats play instead of one by Synge, and so forth, was strictly intuitive. Any play may be interpreted alchemically. The field, therefore, is limitless. *Theatre and Alchemy* (which may be read as one work or as individual essays) has been divided into the three alchemical phases: *nigredo*, *albedo*, and *rubedo*. Although the individual plays transcend the categories under which they have been placed and are intimately connected with the other two operations, their ruling principles or prevailing dominant motivated my positioning of them.

"Solve et coagula," said the alchemist, and Goethe responded in *Faust*.

> Begin the play. . . .
> Let these our walls disclose the mysteries hidden.
> Hindrance there's none, for magic is our aim,
> The arras shrivels up, as if in flame;
> The wall is cleft, folds back, and has become
> The vista of a theatre, deep, inviting,
> Embracing us in its mysterious lighting.[14]

Nigredo

Purge the horrible darknesses of our mind.
>   *Aurora Consurgens*

1

A Dream Play:
Castle, Cave, and Cauldron

August Strindberg called *A Dream Play* (1902) "My most beloved drama, the child of my greatest pain."[1] The dramatic expression of conflicts and torments, *A Dream Play* is also a spiritual and psychological probing, an initiation ritual—a trial by fire and water—rendered in alchemical terms.

Theatre and alchemy are rituals of transformation and projections of inner states onto matter. Just as the alchemical process is composed of numerous and seemingly disconnected sequences and operations, *A Dream Play* is likewise divided into disparate images which give form and substance to intangible and invisible thoughts and feelings. The events delineated in Strindberg's drama, although autobiographical for the most part, live in an eternal or cyclical time scheme, when past, present, and future fuse, alternate, and diffuse. "Anything can happen; everything is possible and probable. Time and space do not exist," claimed Strindberg in his "Preliminary Note" (p. 33). Nor are his characters flesh and blood. They are symbols, archetypal images, fantasy figures, instincts, functions, essences—all reminiscent of alchemical representations and personifications to be found in the manuscripts of medieval and Renaissance scientists. Like hostile metals, corrosive chemicals, and seared matter, which eventually blend back into the universal solvent within the crucible or retort, so Strindberg's incarnations live their brief interludes upon the stage, hacking themselves to death or carving out their existences at the expense of the other protagonists, after which they disintegrate and flow back into the author's psyche. "The characters split, double, multiply, dissolve, condense, float apart, coalesce," Strindberg concludes, using alchemical terminology (p. 33).

That *A Dream Play* should have alchemical analogies is not surprising. From his student days at Uppsala University, Strindberg had been fascinated by the mystery of matter. The unknown, the invisible, those darkened realms hidden behind the phenomenological world, haunted his existence and aroused his imagination. When he moved to Berlin in 1892, he pursued his scientific studies, concentrating on alchemy and astrology, with forays into the occult. His small room was filled with books, chemical apparatus, an easel, an athanor, porcelain crucibles, alembics, retorts, tongs, and sulfur. He was determined to prove that sulfur was not an element impossible to decompose; rather, it was an entity which could be broken down into component parts. His move to Paris in 1894, after his marriage to Frida Uhl, a young journalist, did not impede his research. His wife left him, however, because she was unable to stand the odor of burning sulfur issuing from the fireplace converted into a smelting furnace, the clutter in their small apartment, the poverty to which his work had reduced them, or his mystical excursions into the world beyond.

Alone, he focused all of his energies on his work. He set up two ovens in his rooms and sealed his retorts and vials with putty, hoping to prevent foreign matter from entering his mixtures and spoiling his work. Finally he proved to his satisfaction that sulfur could be decomposed and contained "a special base" which he had not yet isolated. In "Inferno," he wrote:

Night fell, the sulfur burned with hellish flames, and toward morning I observed a pure element, sulfur. And with this observation I supposed myself to have solved a great problem, destroyed the prevailing chemical theory, and won the only immortality allowed mortal man.[2]

Strindberg's experiments were so successful that in 1895 *Le Temps*, *Le Moniteur*, and *Le Figaro* published his essays describing his experiments. He was also invited to use the Sorbonne laboratory to further his research on sulfur and iodine. So seriously were his experiments considered by a German company that it was suggested he take out a patent for the manufacture of synthetic iodine.

Since Strindberg had neglected to take proper precautions when working with chemicals and metals, his already delicate hands became infected. For years he had been plagued with psoriasis. Now, however, the large clusters of eruptions turned into bleeding boils which became so painful that he could no longer button his clothes. When his arms began to swell in January 1895, he went to the Hôpital Saint-Louis, where he remained until the acute phase of the infection subsided. His physical state and extreme poverty added to his already despairing frame of mind. He suffered several psychotic crises. He began hallucinating. His paranoia grew more intense. He was convinced that evil beings were trying to destroy him and that his psoriasis had been divinely sent: a stigmata. In a better mood, later on in the year, the dramatist in him prevailed, and when he was interviewed by a journalist, he played up the incident, adding mystery and excitement to the experiments he had undertaken and to his physical condition. He declared that he had "suffered blood poisoning" as a result of protracted work with explosives.[3]

Meanwhile, Strindberg's debts mounted. He was obliged to move into a small pension for monks and students, the Hôtel Orfila. The works of the chemist Mateo Orfila (1787–1853), after whom his new lodgings were named, inspired him with unflagging ardor. Strindberg's own records of his scientific probings (*Antibarbarus*, 1894; *Sylva Sylvarum*, 1896; "Inferno," 1896; *Hortus Merlini*, 1896–97) detailed not only his scientific pursuits but his metaphysical and psychological experiences: the pain of loneliness, extreme depression, and feelings of intense guilt, resulting in part from his Pietist upbringing, which plagued him unceasingly. He was haunted by delusions of persecution, bouts of frenzied jealousy, and obsessive hatreds. "Life was a penal colony," he wrote. "A zone of silence and solitude was set up around me."[4] In *Jacob Wrestles* (1896), he blamed cosmic powers for his sordid existential plight. His readings, which included the works of Sören Kierkegaard, Emanuel Swedenborg, and Honoré de Balzac, helped him find only momentary solace from his earthly afflictions. In *Madman's Defense* (1887–88), he plunged more deeply and inextricably into occult spheres. He described the altar he had arranged in his room, reminiscent of those places of worship which the alchemists had set up to aid them in their work. Strindberg dedicated his experiments to his secret cult of the Ma-

donna with Child. His dreams, which he reported in detail, re-
volved around severed heads and birds pecking at his flesh. Por-
tents, premonitions, and cataclysms (cloudbursts and cyclones)
plagued his existence and strengthened his belief that "someone
was tampering" with his destiny.[5] A slow paralysis had invaded
his being, he claimed. Noxious fumes were sent to destroy him
and electric currents, which coursed through his body like so
many sharp blades, were aimed his way to torture him. Strindberg was convinced that he was the butt of sorcerers and a victim
of demonic powers. In his despair, he went to consult Dr. Papus
(Gérard Encausse, 1865–1916), the contemporary high priest of
Paris occultism and the editor of the famous journal *Initiation*.

Nothing seemed to help Strindberg. Restless, uncomfortable,
haunted by increasing anxiety, it was not unusual for him to fall
into trances. During these moments he felt that his spirit was
departing from his body. He also foresaw future events and in so
doing experienced even greater hopelessness. "The earth is hell—a
prison so constructed by a superior intelligence that I cannot take
a single step in it without treading on the happiness of others, and
in which my cell mates cannot remain happy without making me
suffer."[6]

Philosophically, spiritually, and scientifically, Strindberg considered himself to be a hylozoist, a mystic, and a monist. Nature
for him had now taken on a new vitality. As a hylozoist, he believed that all phenomena are alive. Plants had nerves and reacted
to both stimulants and narcotics. Since matter was dynamic, memory, he declared, existed in everything on a variety of levels. In his
essays "The Sighing of Stones" and "The Intelligence of Animals
and Plants" (1888), he suggested that animals and plants were
endowed with their own types of memory, judgment, methods of
deduction, and reflection. As a mystic and monist, he believed that
All is in All. "I am a transformist like Darwin and a monist like
Spencer and Haeckel."[7] Along with Schopenhauer, Goethe, and Mo-
ritz Hartmann, he felt that everything in the universe, whether
organic or inorganic, was a manifestation of a *prima materia*. In
Antibarbarus, he declared:

In my capacity as a monist, I have committed myself . . . to the assumption
that all elements and all forces are related. And if they derive from one
source, then they sprang into existence by means of condensation and
attenuation, of copulation and cross-breeding, of heredity and transforma-

tion, of selection and struggle, addition and substitution—and whatever else one wants to suggest.[8]

If Darwin was correct in stating that all animal life comes from one source, Strindberg believed, then the same reasoning could be applied to chemistry: the material world may be condensed or dissolved into a *prima materia*.[9] In fact, Strindberg did not err. The basic premise of alchemy, that of the transmutability of matter into a single or universal entity, which Antoine Lavoisier had rejected, was proved possible through subatomic transformation. Nineteenth-century chemists were convinced that elements were not decomposable. Only after the experiments of Ernest Rutherford and Frederick Soddy in 1902, which demonstrated that elements could be transformed by certain types of radioactive decay, and after the quantum theory showed that particles are waves, were those ancient scientists proved correct.[10] Strindberg was instinctively right, as had been the alchemists of old, despite their unscientific reasoning and their primitive methods.

Strindberg experienced the cosmos as a living entity. He inserted the following anecdote in "Graveyard Reveries" (1897): "A child once asked me: 'How is it that flowers, which are so pretty, don't sing like birds?' They do sing, I replied, but we don't know how to hear them."[11] The same may be said for *A Dream Play*. It may be heard in a variety of ways since it possesses its own dramatic and alchemical language. *A Dream Play* is a drama of corrosion and torment, the product of a creative individual who sought to rid himself of his distaste for life, and for himself. It begins with a descent from celestial spheres to earth, an embodiment into a physical condition, and concludes with the ultimate transformation: a dissolution of matter and an ascension. The prologue and the three acts which compose *A Dream Play* have alchemical equivalents, thereby endowing the drama with broad psychological and philosophical ramifications which expand its scope and pave the way for greater insights into its mysterious teachings.

Prologue: *Albedo/Sublimatio*

Both visually and dramatically, the prologue sets the stage for the alchemical operations of *albedo/sublimatio*. The scene has a background of clouds, cliffs, constellations, and distant ruins. The

Hindu god Indra, a cosmic force empowered to wield thunderbolts, unleash lightning, liberate waters, split mountains, and fecundate the earth, is heard speaking to his daughter. He is going to send her to earth to discover the meaning and reasons for humanity's perpetual lamentations.

For the alchemist, the *albedo*, or whitening, phase of his experiments exists when all impurities in the matter with which he is working are absent; then, he reasons, light and sacrality reign. White represents an absence as well as unlimited color: a world *in potentia*. Psychologically, *albedo* refers to an ideal, a spiritualized or undifferentiated attitude where things are viewed from remote and distant areas as collective items and not as specific situations. *Sublimatio* occurs when, for example, the alchemist takes a solid substance such as sulfur and heats it in his alembic; it disappears from the bottom of the vessel and collects at the top as distilled, condensed, and "sublimated" gas. *Albedo/sublimatio* implies purity of spirit, immaculateness of being, impalpability, and incorporeality: a vaporous state where body is made spiritual.

At the outset of *A Dream Play*, ethereal climes, lightness, airy spatialities, and rarefied regions are Indra's Daughter's habitat. She is all spirit. Her vertical trajectory casts her down to earth, to the world of matter. A Christ figure, she will act as a mediator trying to pave the way for a dialogue between heaven and earth, perfect and imperfect, abstract and concrete. As she drifts down from above into man's world, soul becomes body; idea is transformed into act.

Act 1: *Citrinitas/Separatio*

As Indra's Daughter steps onto the stage, the alchemical condition alters. *Citrinitas*, or the yellowish condition, prevails: the purity of celestial spheres has now blended with the impurities of matter. *Separatio*, the passage from abstract regions where earthly problems are viewed as collective entities, gives way to the phenomenological and differentiated realm where particulars gain in importance. The decor mirrors the change in focus and atmosphere. A "Growing Castle," so named because it is "still growing up out of the earth," is visible (p. 39). A chrysanthemum bud sits on its highest tower. Giant hollyhocks (pink, white, purple, violet, and "sulphur-yellow") surround it. Nearby, straw covers "manure and litter from the stables" (p. 39).

Citrinitas is a mysterious condition. Within its being resides a spirit of sanctity and cleanliness, according to the alchemist, who referred to it as "holy water" and spread it about his laboratory to cleanse and purify the atmosphere. Owing to its color, the spirit of gold is present (that purest of metals), as well as fire (combustion as in the sun). The alchemist pointed to the hot sulfur springs to support his argument; these are continuously igniting and thus prove to his satisfaction "that there is in [*citrinitas*] a great affinity for fire."[12]

For Strindberg, as for alchemists, *citrinitas* has cosmic significance. It is a visual expression of the Daughter's descent into matter. As she takes on body, she yields her ideal condition as a unified force and darkens progressively as she enters the earth below: tainted, yellowed, differentiated. In her earthly form she becomes mortal and subject to life and death or perpetual transformation, to seasonal changes, when late summer turns into autumn and nature yellows, while greens vanish and growth gives way to stasis and death. Since the Daughter is semidivine, she reflects the yellow light of nature in the form of the sun's rays: she is brilliant, exciting, violent, ardent, glaring in effect, and cutting in temperament.

When the abstract becomes concrete and the general becomes the particular, the *separatio* process is required. The individual alchemist or dramatist must distinguish himself from the others, as must the child from the parent, the ego from the Self, or the I from the Thou. Consciousness is born and with it the process of evaluation. The unified vision of the prologue gives way to differentiation on stage. A castle, hollyhocks, manure, and litter—each takes on significance for both the alchemist and the playwright.

The castle is a mysterious force; a secret domain which acts as an entrance to a world beyond. It is a *complexio oppositorum* ("complex of opposites"), being sinister and beautiful, light and dark, protective and imprisoning. In *A Dream Play*, it spells excitement, terror, awe, and admiration. It has a hauntingly hypnotic quality about it. Hollyhocks, and flowers in general, represent beauty, perfection, and the ephemerality of worldly existence. Hollyhocks are slender and spirelike, and as such may be said to depict man's longing for celestial spheres and his need to escape from worldly conflicts. ("This notion is reinforced by the root of the word, the

Middle English *holi*, "holy.") In that hollyhocks are perennials, they stand for the cycle of life, the death and rebirth ritual implicit both in alchemical beliefs and in the circular pattern of *A Dream Play*, which begins with the Daughter's descent into matter and concludes with her ascent into heavenly spheres.

The manure and litter surrounding the castle reinforce the play's verticality, the air/earth interplay. Manure and litter were not considered negative forces by the alchemist. On the contrary, excrement was vital to experimentation: it was a fecundating and nourishing force. The Earth Mother blends with these agents, thereby adding the dynamism necessary for life to pursue its course, allowing a development and fulfillment to ensue. Beauty emerges from soil in the form of flowers, trees, and grass, adding aesthetic appeal to the picture.

The Glazier is the first person the Daughter meets. For the alchemist who worked with vials, crucibles, and alembics, glass was of utmost importance. Glass was considered incorruptible and was associated with "the glorified body" and with salt crystals and was called the "virgin and pure earth." Since glass was made in fire, it was considered as pure as solidified water or air and, therefore, synonymous with spirit. The Glazier is a type of angelic figure (angels are similarly made of fire and air); he is a messenger of sorts, comparable to the Daughter. It is no wonder then that they understand each other and that he is able to answer her questions. Why do flowers grow up from dirt? What separates beauty from ugliness, purity from impurity? "Since they don't like to be in the dirt, [flowers] hurry up into the light as fast as they can—to bloom and die" (p. 40). Equally at home in both worlds, the Glazier informs the Daughter of the polarities in worldly existence, of the dichotomies and divisiveness in life, of man's need for escape into spiritual spheres, and of the cyclical process in nature.

The Daughter, no longer able to view earthly conditions from above and remain uninvolved, must confront specific situations and relate to them. Almost at once she voices her discomfiture. She feels stifled. She cannot breathe. She is ill at ease and considers human relationships awkward and unpleasant. The *separatio* process has already begun to take effect. The Daughter must adjust to her new surroundings and live as an individual because she has been cut off from her father's domain, where spirit prevailed. The fluidity and multiplicity of the scenes which follow compel the

Daughter to develop her discriminatory capacities, to evaluate and
to create a hierarchy of values to which she can refer during her
earthly sojourn.

An Officer is seated on a chair in the next scene. He strikes a
table with his sabre. He has a dual function as a member of the
military: he destroys the enemy and preserves his nation. His condition in this regard is reminiscent, symbolically, of Lord Siva's
role in the pantheon of Hindu gods. He represents power, discipline, structure, and order. The sword he holds, an alchemical symbol, is a weapon designed to cut obscurity, differentiate problems,
and dismember large and collective situations into specific acts.
The sword is a masculine image and is associated in the western
world with solar heroes such as Roland, Tristan, and Siegfried; it
belongs to a person who takes a stand in difficult situations and
acts overtly to protect his ideas. Only in the world of matter, however, must problems be thus cut up and situations examined according to their component parts: chemicals must be reduced to
their smallest particles. In the rarefied atmosphere of the spirit,
earthly contentions are sublimated; the concrete vanishes; the disparate is unified and the breaking up or *separatio* process is not in
order.

The Officer speaks to the Daughter and addresses her as
"Agnes." In Latin, *agnus* ("lamb") is associated with a sacrificial
agent and spells purity, innocence, and meekness. *Agnus Dei*, "the
Lamb of God," has come as a helping force to the Officer in the
form of Indra's Daughter. She is not passive, particularly when her
name is linked with the god of fire, Agni, who causes combustion,
an activity which is one of the most important factors in the process of transformation for the alchemist. In *A Dream Play*, Agnes is
a composite of opposites. A sacrificial and self-abnegating creature,
she is also a catalyst. She is an energetic or fiery principle capable
of paving the way for illumination, altering dark and tenebrous
concepts. A representative of both passivity and aggressivity as a
fire principle, she acts throughout the play as a conductor of souls
to the afterworld, a psychopomp in the manner of Virgil in Dante's
Inferno. It is she who encourages the Officer to complete his destiny and not to remain in the static condition in which he is found
at the outset of the play. The Officer tells Agnes that he used to
long for freedom but now fears the thought of liberation, since it
will surely entail additional suffering. Indra's Daughter repri-

mands him. "It's your duty to find your way to light," she maintains. The Officer replies: "Beauty itself, the harmony of the universe. There are curves and lines in your form and features that can't be found anywhere else except in the orbits of the planets, in the strings that vibrate with music, in the trembling pulsations of the light. . . . You've come from heaven" (p. 41).

Separatio works its way into the next scene. A screen is now removed on stage. The Mother sits at a table. The Father brings her a shawl. She is about to die and asks to see her son. The Officer walks forward. A spokesman for organized religion, the Mother attempts to imitate Christ and take her family's pains and sins unto herself. First she asks her son not to question God's ways, although he may grow angry because of the torments inflicted upon him. Then she asks her husband's forgiveness for whatever wrongs she might have perpetrated during their years together. "We've tortured each other" (p. 43), she declares, indicating her awareness of the destructive side of marriage. (Alchemists refer to metals "torturing" each other during the *separatio* process.)

The scene changes. A wall with a gate in the center opens onto an alleyway: a bright green area becomes visible, in the midst of which grow colossal blue monkshood. The Doorkeeper's lodge is visible. The Officer arrives on the scene with a bouquet of roses. He wants to enter a building which houses some sort of theatre or concert hall where his beloved Victoria is singing. The Doorkeeper informs him that Victoria is on stage and cannot be disturbed. He is not to be discouraged. He asks where the door with the cloverleaf air hole leads. It is this object which separates him from his Victoria. Each of the symbols in this scene (door, gate, alleyway, the Doorkeeper, shawl, and plant) are used in initiation procedures. They represent difficulties with which the alchemist or dramatist must contend before being able to transmute his metals into the goal of his search, the Philosopher's Stone.

The gate, door, and alleyway give access to another area, state, or level of consciousness and chemical condition: from light to darkness, the known to the unknown. Meister Johannes Eckhart believed the gate to be that force which separates inner from outer man. In Hebrew and Christian symbolism, the gate and door prevent free access to revelation, knowledge, and illumination (Ps. 24:7; Matt. 6:6). These impediments must be removed before a hierophant may reach the alleyway leading to greater knowledge and to the next stage of his development.

A doorkeeper is a protective and powerful figure in various mythologies. Cerberus watched the passage leading to Hades for the Greeks; Saint Peter was the keeper of the doors of heaven for the Christians. In Strindberg's drama, a woman embodies this staying force. Although she is old and sick and wears a shawl representing the sorrows of the world, her task is to remain alert at all times. Awareness and readiness for action is incumbent upon her despite her condition. She protects the treasure which lies hidden behind the door: the mystery of life which is its spiritual wealth. This maternal figure, like the alchemist's queen, protects discoveries from the rabble who might misunderstand their import and unwittingly destroy them. The Doorkeeper represents those powers gathered together prior to spiritual evolution, growth, and progress. She is the guardian of the threshold, who must be overcome before an initiation may be completed. As a feminine principle, she stands for the feeling function which must be activated in a male-dominated society (she is particularly relevant to Strindberg's Pietist upbringing, with its patriarchal emphasis) so that harmony between the extremes may be achieved.

In this scene the color green stresses what alchemists term spermatic and procreative tinctures. Alchemists described the Holy Ghost who inseminated Mary as green. The color is thus a composite of spiritual and physical elements. The Greeks associated Venus with green, adding beauty, sensuality, and erotic characteristics. Arnold of Villanova, the fourteenth-century alchemist, stated that within the component particles of green there existed a substance of "total perfection" and that "green is quickly turned into the truest gold."[13] Rather than the sulfur yellow of the previous scene, signifying death and decline, green now invades the stage with its chlorophyll, its earthly qualities which lead to joy and hope. Mention must be made in this regard of a fishing net with a green handle which rests on one of the stage walls. Fish stand for food from the deep for the alchemist, for the unsuspected riches and compounds imprisoned in retorts or crucibles; psychologically, fish indicate unconscious contents which have not yet been fished out and brought to the light of consciousness. Fish symbolize Christ, thereby injecting a spiritual value to an already earthy and richly endowed stage happening.

The blue of the monkshood is a celestial color. It enables alchemists to underscore man's attempt to transcend his flesh, to live in mystical or higher spheres. The flower itself contains dual symbolism: it is beautiful, arched, and possesses a hoodlike sepal; it is aesthetically and spiritually appealing, although poisonous. It is used for medicinal purposes by doctors and alchemists and for hunting and making war by American Indians, who rub a bit of the poison on their arrows. In that the *separatio* process is being enacted at this juncture in *A Dream Play,* it is incumbent upon the protagonists to look at situations, people, and symbols from several rather than from a single point of view, thereby evaluating, sifting, and using the thinking principle to remedy their ills. Only then will they transcend their condition and take on the blueness of spiritual climes.

The Officer declares that he had seen monkshood when he was seven years old: and that he has been waiting for the Doorkeeper to open the door for the past seven years. Numerology, for the alchemist and for Strindberg, who was well versed in the subject, was of vital importance. Numbers are endowed with the plenitude of being. They are archetypal in dimension and possess their own energy, which acts and reacts upon anything with which they come into contact. Numbers represent an ordered way of explaining that which surpasses man; they translate into finite terms the world of the infinite. Everything in the universe, Pythagoras stated, has a numerical equivalent. It is man's task to discover its meaning, characteristics, personality, and depth. In *A Dream Play,* the number seven takes on great value: it represents the alpha and omega of life. One remembers that the alchemical operation included seven stages; that God created the world in seven days; that the ancients believed in the existence of seven planets; and that seven branches grew from the cosmic tree. The number seven contains four (the number of the soul according to Pythagoras, and also the number of seasons, directions, and character types) and three (the trinities in Egyptian, Hindu, and Christian religions), thereby binding and unifying important cosmic principles: the microcosm blending into the macrocosm.

Despite the Officer's supplications, the audience knows that he will not succeed in going beyond the door. Because seven is a complete entity and therefore static, it does not possess the energetic charge necessary to force entry into another world or to begin the alchemical operation anew. Something is missing in the Officer's initiation ritual. He will not succeed in uniting with Victoria, his beloved and ideal woman. He waits in vain. The military man, representing earthly power, is not at ease with the feminine principle, and therefore its full import remains hidden from view. The Officer regresses into his past. He complains that when his maid took him visiting as a child, he never went beyond the kitchen. Alchemically, then, the Officer has never experienced the world beyond his mixtures, concoctions, blends, and utensils. He has never penetrated the mysteries which lie behind the phenomenological world. He knows only form, the ritual but not its mystery; his initiation remains incomplete.

Time passes. Cyclical and linear time are expressed in natural ways on stage. The trees have lost leaves; the monkshood is dead; the green has turned to autumn brown and yellow; the Officer's hair is gray; his clothes are soiled and shabby; the roses have fallen from his bouquet. He worries about Victoria. Has she vanished? No, he is told. "Victoria never leaves." The anima figure—that is, his unconscious idealization of woman—is fixed within his psyche just as the notion of the Philosopher's Stone remains buried deep within the alchemist's being.

Singers from *Die Meistersinger* and extras for *Aïda,* who had been performing within the building, emerge on stage and gather around the door, along with the Glazier and other members of the cast. The Policeman now forbids entry. The mystery must remain intact. Meanwhile, the Lawyer's office becomes visible. Once an idealist, the Lawyer has grown ugly, reflecting the "hideous crimes and sins" required of his profession (p. 61). He has found it difficult to earn a living and feels victimized by society. In desperation and rage, he tells Agnes that he wants to burn the white shawl she has now donned. Not just yet, Agnes replies, whereupon she places a crown of thorns on his head. The stage is blackened.

Fingal's Cave comes into view. It is a grotto with occasional drops of falling water which represent mankind's tears. The waves wash against the basalt pillars in rhythmic and contrapuntal beats, producing a chorus of sounds. The Daughter and Lawyer attempt to solve society's problems, to find a *solutio,* as had the alchemists of old, who resolved problems by washing away impurities, cleansing difficulties, and lightening the atmosphere.

Act 2: *Nigredo/Mortificatio*

The *solutio,* or water, in act 1 was not sufficiently powerful to cleanse worldly conditions. To wash away and dissolve what is fixed, and in so doing to alter man's one-sided views, takes more potent acids. Neither the alchemist nor the protagonists in *A Dream Play* have the force necessary to pass the test; they have not encountered sufficient hardships to pass beyond them, nor have they endured the hostility of the elements and risen above them. A continued earth-bound and therefore painful situation is still required. The alchemist's *nigredo* condition must be experienced: chaos and a *massa confusa.* It is in this state of saturnine blackness ushering in an atmosphere of melancholia that fear and wretchedness gain the upper hand; lostness invades and the dark night of the soul is experienced. The alchemist's *mortificatio* or death condition occurs before resurrection can be accomplished. The protagonists, therefore, must be subjected to the rigorous severities of life just as the alchemist must torture and brutalize his compounds. Only after such an ordeal can transformation occur and the guilt and self-torture be purged.

It is during the *nigredo/mortificatio* operation that the characters return to a kind of preformal darkness, the undifferentiated condition of the *prima materia.* It is not the celestial spheres of the prologue, but rather the abysmal depths where matter is reabsorbed unto itself, where elements are broken up and mortified, then to reblend and emerge anew. Just as Satan was necessary to Yahweh (see the books of Genesis and Job) and the anti-Christ to Christ, so the *nigredo/mortificatio* condition is indispensable to the alchemist in order to complete his Great Work. Torment and pain, the destructive forces in life, compelled Strindberg to express his agony in his dramatic ritual.

The experience of worldly corruption, commonly alluded to as decay, darkness, and differentiation, is tantamount to what the Greeks called a *katabasis* ("inward journey"): it constitutes an exploration of one's inner world during which decomposition precedes the new synthesis. The next scene features a room adjacent to the Lawyer's office containing a bed, small stove, and pots and pans. The Lawyer is now married to Agnes. They have a baby. They reasoned that two intelligent people could marry and live happily. They did not foresee that economic difficulties might trigger emotional distress. Christine, the maid, spends her time sealing the windows of the room. "I am pasting and sealing" (p. 69), she tells Indra's Daughter and the Lawyer, and in so doing she hermetically shuts the room, preventing the outside world from entering the inner domain, just as the alchemists had closed off their vessels with putty in order to keep out impurities. The Daughter, however, rebels against this claustrophobic condition. She feels stifled by Christine, who, as the first syllable of her name indicates, is a Christ figure. Christine represents the Pietist's inability to accept the outer world with all of its positive and negative attributes. The situation grows increasingly unhealthy because of her constricting attitude: guilt, remorse, sorrow, and bereavement come to the fore. The Daughter, however, as a representative of Hindu tradition, believes physical joy to be as important as spirituality. Without the body, ugliness pervades existence. "I think I could stand anything, if only I could have some beauty in my home" (p. 72). She wants to break the bonds of her mundane world. Marriage, domesticity, and organized religion add stress and distress to her life. "It is hard to be a human being," she concludes (p. 74). Two hostile forces, the Daughter and the Lawyer, are sealed in the room, reminiscent of corrosive metals locked in a crucible and heated in an athanor. Combustion is sure to ensue.

The following scene confirms the *nigredo/mortificatio* condition. Foul Strand, a type of hell, is featured on stage. Charred hills are covered with red brush and black and white stumps, the remains of a forest fire (p. 78). There are pigstys, an open air gymnasium for invalids, exercise machines which resemble instruments of torture, a quarantine station with boilers, a complicated system of pipes, and furnaces ready to disinfect all impurities. Fair Haven, a heavenly sphere, lies beyond this den of turmoil. It is a beautiful area with docks, flags, boats, gardens, villas, and marble statues.

A Medical Inspector dressed as a blackamoor informs the visitors to Foul Strand that a cholera epidemic is raging. The Poet makes his voice heard. He has been condemned to Foul Strand because "He's got his head in the clouds so much he gets homesick for the mud" (p. 81). He is compared to pigs whose skin is toughened by wallowing in the mud. The Poet must similarly strengthen himself against the gadflies who, like ignorant rabble, sting and mutilate his delicate covering. As had the alchemist of old, he understands man's need for the blackness and richness of earth. Mud is imperative for growth and transformation.

Out of clay the god Ptah created man on a potter's wheel. . . . Out of clay
the sculptor creates his more or less imperishable masterpieces—Out of
Clay are created the world's kitchens and pantries those indispensable
vessels known under the generic name of pots, plates. . . . In its liquid
state, it's called mud.

(P. 82)

Mud, the representative of the telluric domain, is the point of departure for the creation of objects and, according to many mythologies, humanity. Both object and man are molded into a blend of
earth and idea; man evolves via a combination of additives, formulas, and ferment. Once his shape has been stabilized, he breathes,
bubbles, and begins to live on his own.

Foul Strand, although a place of iniquity, punishment, and
pain, must be experienced in the life process; it is an important
factor in the alchemical operation. It is in the darkness of *nigredo*
that the *massa confusa* of chemicals are blended and that polarities
fuse, their components to be evaluated at some future time, sifted,
and separated. The Medical Inspector informs two new visitors—
He and She—that forty days and forty nights must be spent in
Foul Strand. Just as seven was important in the case of the Officer,
so the number forty determines the length of the initiation in Foul
Strand. It is reminiscent of the forty years the Israelites spent in
the desert in order to rid themselves of their slave mentality, of the
forty days of the Flood, of the forty days of Jesus's temptation and
of the forty hours of his entombment before his resurrection. The
alchemist's forty is fundamental in the creation of the Philosopher's Stone.

Blackness pervades. Decay and putrefaction invade the atmosphere. In a spirit of levity, the Poet mocks Christianity with its
simplistic answer to life's problems: "Love conquers everything."
Then he adds, talking to the Medical Inspector, "including sulphur
fumes and carbolic acid" (p. 86). It is Christianity's rejection of the
notion of evil as adumbrated by Saint Augustine that has caused
the greatest turmoil within man's soul and has inseminated his life
with excoriating feelings of guilt.

Music invades the scene. Fair Haven comes into view. Here
too, despite its beauty, unhappiness reigns. Ugly Edith, who repels
men because of her distorted features, is playing Bach's Toccata
con Fuga. In the next room, dancers are swaying to the beat of a
waltz. Bach's music, however, dominates the proceedings. The

waltz is soon silenced, and the guests leave the hall to gather around Edith and her piano, just as the heavenly music of Orpheus moved rocks.

Music was frequently used by alchemists in their experiments. It was a means of expressing feeling, mood, and rhythms. It can also be a way of defining chemicals. The complicated numerological schemes which govern some Renaissance and Baroque polyphony have alchemical equivalents. In the seventeenth century, the alchemist Michael Maier composed a musical score, *Atlanta Fugiens,* with subtle analogies to alchemical sciences.[14] Frequently alchemists would begin their work with hymn-singing or dances of all types, thereby calling to themselves the cosmic forces and spirits in the form of tones, rhythms, and vibrations.[15]

Ugly Edith is playing a toccata and fugue. *Toccata* means "to be touched," and, indeed, she succeeds in touching the dancers in the next room by the quality she instills in her playing, the feeling in her tone. The toccata stresses free fantasy in contrast to the strict counterpoint of Renaissance music. In Bach's work, rhapsodic passages are included as well as brilliantly figurative ones. Although repulsive, Edith has the capacity to attract through feeling, touch, and emotion—not through the brash beats of the waltz, but through very imaginative passages of Bach's deeply moving work. The guests gather around her and the waltz is silenced.

Indra's Daughter realizes that the only happy persons living in Fair Haven are newlyweds, and even they realize that pain is soon to follow their euphoria. One of the coal haulers of Foul Strand comments about their world: "This is Hell. Hundred and twenty in the shade" (p. 103). Heat. Blackness. Fumigation is necessary. Elements therefore are cooked, dissolved, mortified. "Time to bring out the guillotines and operate," he exclaims. In act 1 the sword cut through matter, breaking it down into individual particles; the guillotine now takes precedence: dismemberment. Divisiveness ushers in a reexamination of the *nigredo* condition which is the matrix of all potentialities.

Act 3: *Solutio/Calcinatio*

Fingal's Cave again comes into view in act 3. When Felix Mendelssohn wrote his Overture to *Fingal's Cave,* he incorporated into his music the wild country of the Inner Hebrides, the screaming of the birds, the whistling of the winds, and the sea roaring in the caverns. Strindberg accomplished a similar feat. Nature comes to life on stage under his baton: remote, awe-inspiring, fearsome, exciting. Audiences hear the music of the wind and waves as a kind of giant cosmic awakening, a creation, an epiphany.

Water dominates the first part of the act. One of the most important additives in alchemy, water acts as a dissolving agent; it disperses and makes certain chemicals disappear. Just as salt vanishes when placed in water, so specific problems may be dispersed when placed in a more comprehensive frame of reference. When perspectives alter, one-sided attitudes become all-inclusive. The *solutio* process has its negative side as well. It can lead to regression into an unconscious state, loss of identity, and drowning in despair. It leads to the disappearance of the chemical components one seeks to solidify.[16]

In *A Dream Play,* the water sequence represents the purification ritual which began in act 2 but never succeeded in bettering the condition of *mortificatio.* The water now abounding in Fingal's Cave is able to wash away the stagnant, sluggish elements. It liberates and agitates, thus bringing new attitudes and insights to the fore. Hardened and concrete entities are now dispersed. Water is also a connecting factor. In Hindu philosophy, water is believed to circulate throughout nature in the form of rain, milk, sap, and blood. It is vital to life and preserves it. Pilgrims bathe in the Ganges and, in so doing, rid themselves of their sins. After cremation, their ashes are strewn in these beatific waters. In Christian ritual, baptism washes away man's original sin. Miracles occur on water: Christ walked on the sea (Mark 6:48) and the Israelites walked across the Red Sea (Exod. 14). Water facilitates cleansing, rejuvenation, harmony, and communicability among things and people.

Water had further significance for Strindberg. As a Neptunist, he believed, as had the Hindus, that all is born from water and returns to it. In his novel *By the Open Sea* (1890), he wrote that water is "the universal mother, from whose womb the first spark of light was lighted, the inexhaustible well of fertility, of love, life's origin and life's enemy."[17] In "The Basic Elements of Matter" (1898), he stated:

Water, which appears to be the primordial element, does not consist of oxygen and hydrogen, but from water one can derive oxygen and hydrogen—along with all other elements, which are concentrations that either approach the negative (hydrogen pole) or the positive (oxygen pole).[18]

In 1889, Strindberg declared in *Antibarbarus:*

Water is the transition between the colloids (organic) and the crystalloids (nonorganic), for when the bottom of the sea freezes, it gelatinates and ejects plantlike forms in the pattern of the frozen crystals (ice ferns).[19]

The creatures of Strindberg's fantasy, particularly those who have passed through Foul Strand, seem overwhelmed with a sense of sin and paralyzed with guilt, and therefore desperately in need of cleansing. As Pontius Pilate publicly washed his hands after Jesus's condemnation and declared his innocence (Matt. 27:24), so Strindberg's creatures seek rebirth into innocence in the *solutio* sequence.

Indra's Daughter has brought the Poet to Fingal's Cave. The atmosphere tingles with excitement and expectation. As Venus was born from the waters and with her came the emergence of love, sensuality, and a sense of renewal, so the protagonists in *A Dream Play* seek to be reborn. The music of the waves and of the winds utter man's lamentations in symbolic terms. The stage directions state that the grotto, called "Indra's ear," is located on the "outermost edge of the world and the sea." It is there that "the god of the skies and sovereign of the heavens listens to the pleas and petitions of mortals" (p. 108). The waters take on spiritual significance in Fingal's Cave; upper and lower waters blend and reflect the sun's brilliance and the moon's night rays, shedding illumination throughout the universe.

Caves and grottos, the abodes of hermits, oracles, and deities, are cult sites in most religions. They contain, protect, conceal, and frequently imprison. Psychologically, they represent the unconscious. Their darkness is reminiscent of the womb. The cave may be looked upon as a nourishing area where the seed is implanted and germinates, where the idea in the unconscious develops and emerges into consciousness, and where life takes on tangibility and reality. The maternal matrix or cave stands for a passageway leading down into the earth as well as up to light. When Demeter descended into Hades through a cavern to see her daughter, Persephone, she became a linking agent, bringing upper and lower worlds together: two stages in psychological development. In his allegory of the cave, Plato defined such an area as a darkened state reflecting ignorance. Humanity is severed from illumination.

Strindberg's cave is a composite of ideas. It spells light, since the world at large is visible and the music of the winds and waves is audible, and it is also a fecundating area where the Poet draws his food/inspiration, thus enabling him to create his own symphonic tone poem. The cave spells distress and pain because both the Poet and the Daughter (and humanity at large) are held captive within its limitations or walls. The creative individual is prevented from making the ideal real or the abstract concrete; the alchemist will never create his Philosoper's Stone. Perfection exists only in the world of the absolute and is therefore incompatible with earthly existence.

The wind and watery mist spray their songlike lamentations in bold sonorities and rhythms.

> Life is not clean,
> Life is not kind;
> Man is not evil,
> Neither is he good.

> (P. 109)

> We, we are the waves,
> cradling the winds,
> lulling the winds
> to sleep.

> Green cradles that rock and wave . . .

> (P. 111)

The Daughter castigates the waves. They are "faithless" and "false," cruel and earth-eaters. The Poet has written about the elements and the cosmos, life in its various manifestations. "What is poetry?" the Poet asks the Daughter. "Not reality," she answers, but a kind of metareality. It consists of flashes of intuition divinely inspired, enlightenment and not of dreams, which emanate from the unconscious. The person who has not been fully initiated into the higher spiritual spheres of poetry or into the mysteries of matter cannot perceive the wondrous things with which the universe is filled. The Poet seeks; he wants to know and discover the world beyond. The Daughter remains adamant. She will not reveal cosmic secrets. She will depart from earth and return to the celestial domain, "As soon as I have burned away the ashes that cling to me, for not all the water in the world can wash me clean" (p. 113).

Burning and ash are the alchemical factors in *calcinatio*. Burning means purification through combustion, calcination, and incineration. Flame alters the chemical components of metals or bodies. It recycles matter, light, energy, and darkness. The fifteenth-century *Rosarium* states:

Sublime with fire, until the spirit which thou wilt find in it [the substance] goeth forth from it, and it is named the bird or the ash of Hermes. . . . Despise not the ashes, for they are the diadem of thy heart, and the ash of things that endure.[20]

The alchemist alluded to the burning process as a "baptism in fire," thus uniting what is seemingly in opposition. In the Roman Catholic ritual of baptism, the priest plunges a burning candle into the font, saying, "He shall baptize you with the Holy Ghost, and with fire" (Matt. 3:11). The mystery of baptism has an alchemical equivalent: the *solutio* or dissolution of that which is imperfect within the holy water. Similarly, the Daughter's burning at the play's finale leaves a residue or ash, an element of whiteness and purity.

Ashes, when associated with the death of the human body, represent man reduced to atomized particles, helpless without his god. The Christian prayer which begins "Pulvis es et in pulverem reverteris" is said on Ash Wednesday, the first day of Lent, indicating man's repentance. Ashes stand for his suffering and desire for forgiveness: "Wherefore I abhor myself, and repent in dust and ashes" (Job 42:6). Hindu yogis rub ashes on their bodies in imitation of Lord Siva who, in his ascetic period, wears ashes as a symbol of renunciation. It was from the ash that the alchemist attempted to create an incorruptible glorified body which would evolve into *albedo* and could never be subject to decay. The Daughter alludes to ash as superior in cleansing power to water; it is the only agent enabling her to divest herself of the darkness of matter, her earth condition.

The Daughter is, nevertheless, not yet ready to undergo her supreme metamorphosis. The trial by water has not yet been completed. The sea begins to rise. A ship is visible in the distance. It belongs to the Flying Dutchman, who must sail the seas eternally as punishment for his infidelities.[21] A white glow appears on the waters, which is reminiscent of Christ walking on the sea. The Flying Dutchman and Christ are now associated, each having been condemned by "honest, straight-thinking people" (p. 118).

The Officer, dancers, actors, and the Dean of the Four Faculties come on stage. Each in his own way and according to his own understanding seeks to have the door opened and to discover the mysteries behind it. Indra's Daughter, guardian of the secrets, stands firm, as had the alchemists of old. She refuses to reveal the knowledge behind the door, since it is too vast and too important to be comprehended by man's limited mentality. Only those initiated into the mysteries of matter and of being can understand the infinite nature of the cosmos. "The time has nearly come when with the help of the fire I shall rise and return to the heaven of ether. This is what you call death and what you approach with fear in your hearts" (p. 131).

The castle seen in act 1 reappears. The windows are lit from the inside. The Daughter enters. Music is sounded. The rear of the stage is aflame. It is not the punitive fire of the Last Judgment; rather, it is the apocalyptic flame leading to the Daughter's ascension and reintegration into the abstract cosmic principle. The chrysanthemum bud at the top of the castle bursts into bloom, and with it the spirit of rebirth comes into being.

Strindberg, whose fascination with alchemy had led him to conduct his own experiments in sulfur and coal, also accomplished an alchemical feat in *A Dream Play,* which moves from a descent and incarnation to ascent and disembodiment. Reflecting a phase of being, a psychological condition, a feeling state, and replete with its own images, motifs, rhythms, tensions, and discordant and harmonious tonalities, *A Dream Play* gathers unto itself the spirit of air, earth, water, and fire in one symphonic orchestration. Strindberg's subtle alchemical transmutations have succeeded in stilling time, stretching space, illuminating darkness, and sensing the mysteries of matter.

2

Escurial: God, Father, Senex

Alchemy, frequently referred to as the "black art," requires the condition of *nigredo* before illumination or rebirth can ensue. In Michel de Ghelderode's *Escurial* (1927), only the first stage of the alchemical process is experienced: *nigredo,* with its accompanying phases of *mortificatio* and *putrefactio*. No *renovatio* follows. There is no cleansing operation, no purification. Darkness hovers over the stage proceedings. The finale is as sinister and fetid as the outset of this dramatic ceremony.

Alchemists have made analogies between the *nigredo* phase of their operation and the seed implanted in the darkness of the earth. Each paves the way for creativity: the seed roots in the soil and the idea in the brain. Each feeds on surrounding nutritive agents, developing and enacting a specific role or function. Each battles its way into the light of day or consciousness, the manifest world. Rather than burgeoning and offering positive alchemical blends, however, Ghelderode's phantasms in *Escurial* remain embryonic. Like the seed which rots in the earth, so Ghelderode's creatures are stuck in the *massa confusa* of a dark and regressive atmosphere.

Escurial, a one-act play, is an alchemical drama, as are all of Ghelderode's plays. They delineate different phases involved in the decomposition of personalities, exposing in the process the nuances of decay. Few if any of Ghelderode's characters are endowed with

41

vision; fewer still have the strength to battle for their ideas and to pave the way for inner evolution. Their feeble natures and unhealthy psyches and the insalubrious conditions surrounding them impede normal growth. Their world is black, but it is not the rich blackness which offers a full range of harmoniously blended nutrients. Ghelderode's mixtures breed ghouls and gnomes, monsters with distorted souls. His creatures befoul the air they breathe, revel in their own decay, delight in their sadomasochistic rounds, copulate with larvae and fungi, grimace and screech; all rejoice in their sexual perversions. Reminiscent of the emanations of a Bosch, Grünewald, Brueghel, or Ensor, or of Goya's excoriating depictions of crazed beings, Ghelderode's excrescences are stunted, malformed, degenerate creatures who have never grown beyond the *nigredo* phase.

In all of his plays, Ghelderode's monsters turn and churn, disrupt and disorient, but never resolve the chaos in their hearts. Instead, each brings further deterioration, greater ruin and despair. The central character in *The Death of Doctor Faustus* (1925) is not Goethe's Faust, a man whose descent culminates in redemption, but instead is an antihero who fails religiously, philosophically, and socially. A neurasthenic, Ghelderode's Faust sees no positive way in life and takes no affirmative stand. Life is absurd. To experience one's reality and individuality is impossible, he concludes. "Only microbes" exist in *Don Juan* (1928). Love is based on the lie. It is an illusion created by man to help him escape the horrors of life. *Christopher Columbus* (1927) dramatizes the plight of the idealist-poet who dreams of adventure and beauty and instead becomes the prey of a jealous, covetous, and ungrateful populace dominated by political and religious fanatics. Christopher Columbus is imprisoned. When death finally beckons, he does not fear it. On the contrary, he welcomes that other realm. He says that he "loved adventure too deeply not to love death." *Barabbas* (1928) demonstrates the futility of sacrifice. Nothing positive can come to man through sacrifice. Nothing can stop humanity's lust for maiming and killing.

We haven't been able to alter anything of all that we found baneful, sickening, and hateful. And after our useless death, Justice will still not be done, and untruth will reign no less supremely than it has reigned since human beings have existed. That is what drives this man to despair, and that is what drives me to despair also. The festivities are beginning.

Listen to the bands. The crowd is merry. And have they really a reason for making merry? The time is about to come. Soon nothing will remain of what we are. There is nothing more to do than to wait and to offer no resistance, just as he is offering no resistance.[1]

Revolt is useless. Whether composed of the weak or the powerful, the collective always wins. *Pantagleize* (1929) dramatizes the fate of the creative person; the sensitive and innocent poet is devoured by society. *Chronicles of Hell* (1929) focuses on death: a poisoned host, a noxious idea, individuals and societies killed. The miser's saga unfolds in *Red Magic* (1931). Gold, around which the spiritual and physical revolve, absorbs Ghelderode's hero, who finally couples with his shekels. Unlike Plautus's or Molière's misers, who are finally punished for their possessive natures, Ghelderode's protagonist is defeated because he decides to become generous. *Lord Halewyn* (1934) delineates the antics of an impotent man who pleasures in blood and gore.

Ghelderode situates *Escurial,* named after a palace built near Madrid by Philip II, in sixteenth-century Spain. In 1557, after having defeated the French at Saint Quentin, Philip's armies had inadvertently destroyed a church dedicated to the third-century Saint Lawrence. Philip built Escurial in his honor. It housed a rich library, paintings by El Greco and others, a convent, and a college. The monarch also had an iron grill installed over glowing coals in memory of the saint's martyrdom. Philip II lived in only one of the rooms in Escurial. It was virtually devoid of furniture. It opened on two alcoves: a study and a bedroom with a slit in the wall which allowed the monarch to follow from his bed the religious services held in an adjoining chapel. Philip II died in Escurial.

Ghelderode had always been absorbed by the past. His father, a clerk at the General Archives in Brussels, encouraged him to study ancient documents, genealogies, history books, and engravings of all types. His fascination with the past also may have resulted in part from a bout with typhus in 1915, which necessitated his withdrawal from school at the Institut Saint-Louis in Brussels. Deep-seated introversion followed and became a hallmark of Ghelderode's character for the rest of his life. Desultory studies at the Conservatoire royal de musique and the writing of articles for the financial weekly *Mercredi-Bourse* allowed him to earn a meager living, but in no way prevented him from spending his leisure time haunting the marionette theatres. He was mesmerized by the wooden puppets, and these "supernatural" beings fired his imagination. During his teens he wrote short stories in which one senses the presence of marionettes as well as of a living past, and in his first play, *Death Looks in at the Window* (1918), Poelike gravity and tremulous sensations make inroads onto the stage happenings.

Renaissance Spain provided a setting that in many ways reflected Ghelderode's penchant for the lugubrious; it concretized certain unregenerate forces within his subliminal world. Philip II was a formidable monarch. A colossal worker, he was endowed with a powerful personality. Somber and introverted, he surrounded himself with darkness; he even clothed himself in black. His shadow spread death and ruin wherever it was cast. Although the Holy Inquisition was first established in Spain by Ferdinand and Isabella in 1492, Philip II had been instrumental in furthering its power. He had encouraged the clergy and the military to seek out Jews, Moors, or anyone accused of heresy, either to convert them or to burn them at the stake. Death, murder, and horror marked his reign. It was Ghelderode's interest in this kind of atmosphere that inspired *Escurial*.

As *Escurial* begins, the curtains part on a dimly lit room. Barking dogs are heard. The King cups his ears to shut out the deafening sounds and the message they convey of the Queen's imminent death. The King is anguished and calls for Folial, his buffoon. He orders him to make him laugh. Folial, who loved the Queen and was loved by her, feels his pain too acutely even to pretend to amuse his master. The King threatens him with death unless he obeys. Folial acquiesces and suggests they enact a farce together. In Belgium, farces are traditionally performed during the Lenten season. Someone is chosen to assume the power and authority of a great monarch. When he is fully bloated with pride, the populace uncrowns and deflates him. The merriment of such a ritual is derived from the destruction of the powerful ruling force in the community.

The farce begins. Folial grabs the King's crown and scepter and assumes a regal stance. He then wraps his hands around the monarch's neck. His grip tightens. The King's strident cackle disorients him, and Folial loosens his grip. The King is delighted. He has enjoyed the game. He suggests they carry it a step further. He asks Folial to don his vestments while he puts on the jester's. Folial walks up to the throne. The King, playing the role of the buffoon, confesses his suffering and the jealousy he experienced when discovering his wife's love for Folial. He tells him also that his wife has been poisoned. "The farce is over."[2]

The King asks Folial to return his crown and scepter, his identity. Folial refuses. A monk enters and informs the King of his wife's death. Folial is stunned. Taking advantage of his shock, the King grabs the symbols of authority. He calls for the Executioner. "After the farce, the tragedy," he says (p. 84). The Executioner, dressed in scarlet and wearing a hood which allows only his eyes and nose to be seen, enters and strangles Folial. The King bursts out in hysterical laughter.

Blood Sacrifice: *Mortificatio* and *Putrefactio*

Ghelderode's King, like Philip II, is a lonely being. Solitude helps the creative effort. "It is a purification, a hygiene of the soul," Ghelderode wrote in "The Ostend Interviews."[3] A "night spirit" with a shadow personality, Philip II's smile resembled that of a satiated vampire (p. 14). So Ghelderode's King was also cruel. He was rigid in his ways and sinful in the sense that he was absorbed by possessiveness, intransigence, and hatred, never varying the stranglehold he had on those whom he considered his enemies. Ghelderode's genius lies in his ability to dramatize the King's subliminal world—to bring his myopic creatures into the open and compel his audiences to experience their chaos and *nigredo*. To increase the tension required for a theatrical spectacle, Ghelderode divided the King into two beings, each representing facets of the monarch's character: the King, the old man, a Senex figure, and Folial, the young man, the Puer. *Escurial* enacts a blood sacrifice (Folial's immolation) and the death of those functions (love and feeling) that he represents. The ruling principle, in the form of the King, survives: it is based on anger, hatred, and repression.

Blood sacrifice, symbolically speaking, is part of the alchemical operation and the focal point of Ghelderode's dramatic ritual. According to Mircea Eliade, blood sacrifices were practiced when society changed from agriculture to metallurgy, when a "spiritual universe," with its "heavenly god," was "ousted by the strong God, the fertilizing Male, spouse of the terrestrial Great Mother." At this level of man's development, "the notion of creatio ex nihilo was replaced by the idea of creation by hierogamy and blood sacrifice."[4] Life, then, came into being only after another life had been sacrificed. In Babylonian religious tradition, this idea was exemplified when Marduk conquered the sea monster Tiamat and then brought the universe into being, finally killing himself in order to create man.[5] Marduk said: "I shall make my blood solid, I will make my bones there from, I shall raise up Man, indeed, Man will be. . . . I shall construct man, inhabitant of the earth."[6] Parallel sacrificial rituals are to be found in totem meals, Mithraic bull sacrifices, and in the Christian communion when the blood of Christ is shed. Blood, the most precious of all elements, spells life.

Just as God was a builder, so the metallurgist replicated deity's gesture each time he struck his anvil. So did the alchemist when blending his metals and elements in the heated athanor, and the playwright each time he molded his creatures and constructed his situations. On a psychological level, sacrifice implies the obliteration of a limited view of things in favor of a broadening of vision. The ego must die symbolically or sink into the Self (the collective factor which exists prior to the ego). With the obliteration or dispersion of the ego, the narrow conscious orientation, as represented by the ego personality, is reshuffled; its parts are reblended into the entire personality (the Self). When the conscious orientation once again emerges, new factors are constellated; fresh views are synthesized in a new and more expanded view of things.

The word "sacrifice" means "to make sacred." It requires the relinquishing of that object, or feeling, or thought with which one identifies: the "mineness." It is man's way of offering something that belongs to him (himself, if need be) to that which transcends his offering. To sacrifice that which is secure and comfortable, what eventually may engender a condition of stasis, is both a threat and a challenge to the ego personality. It can be attempted only if the ego is strong and healthy. Theseus and Peirithous descended into hell; their ego personalities were eclipsed.[7] When they returned—that is, when consciousness functioned—they were renewed. They had fed on the nutritive agents embedded in the collective unconscious and were ready to struggle and forge ahead with fresh ideas. Many religious and literary heroes who have undergone such experiences and returned possess the treasure hard to attain, self-knowledge. Others have been less fortunate. Submersion in some cases has resulted in drowning, as with

Gérard de Nerval and Antonin Artaud. The ego never surfaced again: they lived in their schizophrenic realm. Sacrifice requires a willingness on the part of the initiate to advance into darkness and face the unknown, terrifying regions of the psyche where archaic forces live and breed.[8]

The alchemist has a dual view of sacrifice. It occurs on a physical plane as he cooks his metals in his athanor. It also takes place in the spiritual sphere, when he transcends what he calls his base, or leaden, instinctual condition and attempts to ascend the ladder by which he hopes to attain the golden or purest of states. When blending, burning, and reshaping his metals, the alchemist destroys the present combinations of the *prima materia* with which he is working in order to form the *ultima materia*. He sacrifices what is to bring about what could be, to move from the earthly to the celestial sphere, from the vulgar to the noble state.

Analogies to Christ are inherent in alchemical dicta. According to Thomist doctrine, the Catholic mass was not a real immolation of the body of Christ, but a representation of his sacrificial death.[9] According to the alchemists, his descent from the heavenly sphere to the earthly domain meant a *coagulatio* into flesh. Once Christ had accepted incarnation, he also accepted corruption: man's finitude, his shadow, and more. Christ's descent was expressed by the alchemist as *nous* fallen into *physis*, spirit into matter, the immortal into the mortal domain. The alchemist's goal was to imitate Christ, not only with regard to his chemicals, but also with respect to his own inner evolution. The alchemist took it upon himself to bring about his own redemption by extracting the *anima mundi* in matter. To accomplish such a goal required strength and courage, a symbolic journey into death. "Visita interiora terrae; rectificando invenies occultum lapidem" ("Visit the interior of the earth; through purification thou wilt find the hidden Stone").[10] Such a rite of passage allowed the alchemist to experience the terrors of the unknown and, in so doing, to transcend his limitations and be reborn into clarity and understanding.

Ghelderode's King is a God-Father-Senex figure. Since the alchemist kills to vivify, the King should have been sacrificed, as was the case in ancient times when the old king (or the old year) was ceremoniously killed, thus insuring seasonal fertility. With the King's demise a separation of the prevailing conscious attitude would have given way to new blendings, new solutions. Such did not come to pass. The old stayed, and limited views prevailed. As a Senex figure, Ghelderode's King is identified with both the planet and the god Saturn and with lead, their metallic equivalent. In *Escurial*, the King is in conflict with his double Folial, who represents new ways and ideas and is reminiscent of the alchemist's Mercury, the Son, and the Puer. But Folial, that aspect of the King which loves and which relates to others, is weak. Relegated to a starvation diet, he cannot thrive in a climate of secrecy and terror. With his death, the positive elements are strangled by sinister forces. Hate smothers love. Youth is destroyed, while old age pursues its narrow and negative course.[11]

Ghelderode's King is sick. He suffers from spiritual and physical sterility. He has reached an impasse. Viewed according to Christian dogma, to which Ghelderode was forever drawn in an ambivalent love-hate embrace, the King symbolizes God; Folial is Christ. Unlike Christ's crucifixion, which had been predicted and accepted, Folial's sacrifice went counter to his desire. Indeed, it was no sacrifice at all. It was murder. Folial was psychologically unwilling to relinquish his emerging ego, the feeling principle which manifested itself in his love for the Queen. Whereas Christ's death resulted in his resurrection and the birth of new ideas and philosophies, thus compensating for the one-sided ruling principle of the time, Folial's murder merely prolonged an already decomposed atmosphere. By destroying Folial, the King was further repressing his love instinct, sacrificing kindness for cruelty, relatedness for hatred, and understanding for authority.

King/Senex/Saturn figures are depicted in alchemical documents as carrying scythes, sickles, and sometimes hourglasses. In alchemical tracts, Saturn is pictured as an old man with a scythe cutting off Mercury's feet, thus attempting to fix and immobilize potential developments.[12] The scythe and the sickle are symbols of dismemberment by shearing, pruning, and other methods. To prune a tree helps conserve its vitality; it forces back the nutritive agents from the branches into the trunk and roots. Cutting or cutting off, then, takes on a positive connotation in this regard. The hourglass carried by Saturn identifies him with time, the great destroyer, the harbinger of death and *putrefactio*, the spreader of saturnine melancholia and the darkness of the soul. For the alchemist, to experience such a condition paves the way to *albedo*, the cleansing and whitening process. Alchemists, therefore, most always sought to "purge the horrible darkness of [the] mind."[13] But the King, like Saturn, is caught up in his own bile. He suffers, agonizes, and is the victim of his own limited vision. He tends only to the needs of his inflated ego; nothing else exists.

Alchemists identify Senex-Saturn (the god) with the Titan Kronos. The Titans were primeval beings invested with anthropoid psyches. Ghelderode's King also lives on an instinctual level and is incapable of evaluating situations and people. More important was the fact that Kronos, fearful that his children would overthrow him, swallowed them. Such fear indicates an inability to accept the natural process of death and rebirth. Nature, however, in the form of Kronos's wife, Rhea, hid her son, Zeus, and replaced his body with a stone which alchemists allude to as the Philosopher's Stone. Rhea forced Kronos to regurgitate the other children, thus bringing new life and blood to the land and restoring to nature what was rightfully hers. The Senex figure then weakened progressively.[14] No such outcome takes place in *Escurial*. The King kills Folial and there is no restitution to nature. On the contrary, nature is impoverished. The loss adds to an already imbalanced situation.

Since King-Saturn-Senex-Kronos was associated with lead, the basest of all metals, he was incapable of bringing the light of consciousness to his acts. Like lead when exposed to moist air, his dark and somber personality traits became more obvious; their blackness and bleakness permeated the atmosphere. He was weighted down in every respect by the heaviness of the metal and its accompanying lugubrious tones. According to pseudo-Democritus, lead generates other metals and was used by the Egyptians and Babylonians to produce a variety of metallic substances; such reblendings resulted in the formation of fresh alloys. It could be said, then, that the King had the potential to create but failed in his endeavor. There were no new mixtures. Only lead remained. With prolonged contact, lead may act as a poison. The King represents the noxious side of this element, destroying everything and everyone with whom he comes into contact.

Ghelderode accentuates the destructive and negative inner climate in *Escurial* through his lighting effects and decor. The stage directions call for an eerie "subterranean" light to emanate from the proscenium (p. 71); the funereal hangings draped about the stage are perpetually in motion, mirroring both the King's fear of being overthrown and his horror of sterility and impotence. Even the rugs are worn and holey, further stressing the outdated and unregenerate ruling principle. The stage room takes on the contours of a cave. Cave cults, let us recall, were popular in ancient times. Sybils and oracles inhabited these dark and remote regions and from them predicted events. Initiates performed rituals (as in Eleusinian mysteries) in caves to earn redemption and inner transformation.[15] Many Christian martyrs found serenity in such protective areas. In them nature and man worked together; symbiotic relationships helped the maturation process. Mineral gestation, the alchemists believed, also took place in subterranean areas. The cave, like the Earth Mother, permitted the contents of her uterus to grow and burgeon.[16] The King's room, however, was unhealthy. No air was allowed to flow; his mephitic realm led to further decomposition, ugliness, and decadence.

Folial, the buffoon, is mercury. Alchemists referred to mercury as "Saturn's child."[17] Folial is a life force representing those traits, the feeling principle and the capacity to love, that are so weakly developed in the King. Although Folial's dress as a buffoon is colorful, his entire demeanor mirrors the hue of pain. Yet, when in love, he had experienced an inner change—he had known the heat and fire of passion. The intensity of his inner fire was comparable to the alchemical operations needed to complete the *hieros gamos*, or union with the Queen. It is he who is the catalyst, who alters circumstances and moods, fermenting constantly. It is he who forces the King's adventure to its climax. Yet it is he also who, had things been so organized, could have brought the events to a joyful conclusion and created a new orientation, a new center of gravity. As the *Rosarium* states: "At the end of the work the king will go forth for thee, crowned with his diadem, radiant as the sun, shining like the carbuncle . . . constant in the fire."[18] Yet the King cut him down.

Folial, the son of the King, failed. The root of his name indicates "fool" or "madman" (*fou, fol* in French). He lacked the necessary mental attributes to compel a concerted effort. His momentary exchange of identity with the King was not sufficient to establish a new ruling principle. The thinking function, so well developed in the King, was dormant in Folial. His feelings were forever surging forth and disconcerting him at the most inappropriate moments. Since they had been experienced only on a subliminal level, in secret, dark, and remote corners of the palace, and thus on unconscious rather than conscious levels, they remained undeveloped, infantile, and ineffective. Twice Folial could have killed the King; twice his feelings intruded and prevented him from completing his act. He loosened his grip around the King's neck when he heard his strident laughter and when he was told of the Queen's death. Rather than attempting to understand Folial's contempt for what he represents, the King enjoys his buffoon's game of strangulation. He delights in his hatred of him and admires the power in his hands. In time, he muses, Folial could even become a good executioner.

When Folial fails to strangle him, however, the King loses respect for the buffoon. He derides the fact that Folial's feelings dominate and not his reason. "Worry, anguish, despair" appear on his face and not on the King's, where they rightfully belong. Folial is so weakly structured that when attired in the King's vestments and ordered to mount the throne, he barely has the strength to walk up the few steps. The crown and scepter weigh too heavily upon him. The love and beauty he had once known, and which had helped him find momentary fulfillment, no longer exist. The "beautiful, pure, and holy" things in life were dead, killed by the "silence and tenebrous nature of the palace" (p. 82).

It is not surprising that Folial should have been chosen as the sacrificial victim. Throughout history, jesters have been associated with goats, which for many people were incarnations of evil. In the iconography of the Middle Ages, the devil was frequently portrayed as a goat. Louis Claude de Saint-Martin, the eighteenth-century mystic philosopher, identified the goat with putrefaction and iniquity. There was also the scapegoat: after evils were heaped upon him, this animal was ejected from the tribe, thus purging the community of sin and assuring its fertility and well-being. The goat was a tragic figure. Indeed, the word "tragedy" is derived from *tragōidia*, meaning "the song of the goat." Members of the chorus appeared as goats during Greek dramatic performances. In *The Bacchantes* of Euripides, the goat was divinity's choice victim and thus the perfect sacrificial agent. During certain religious ceremonies, Dionysus himself was metamorphosed into a goat. God became animal, with all of the negative implications and tragedy such a condition implies. As a devote of Aphrodite, the goat also represented instinct, sensuality, libido, and desire—those traits which religious ascetics considered unclean and worthy of destruction. "Love is forbidden in this palace," the King declares (p. 83).

That Folial should have suggested the enactment of a farce which included an exchange of identities was appropriate. The farce is the supreme vehicle for the expression of bitterness, black humor, and iconoclasm. In Ghelderode's play, as in *The Chairs* of Eugene Ionesco and *The Birthday Party* of Harold Pinter, anger and hatred spurt and gush. Ghelderode's farce derides the concept of royalty and authority by pointing out the King's narrow views and his failures. Important truths are spoken in the spirit of banter. The sacred is demeaned and ridiculed. Rather than to the happy-go-lucky prankster of a Plautus or a Molière, Ghelderode introduces audiences to an exhausted and despairing jester who laughs with the rictus of pain, like the nineteenth-century Pierrot.

When the King in Folial's disguise announces the Queen's death by poison and pursues his chatter in the most cavalier manner, informing Folial that another wife will be found with great ease, he prances about the stage and admits he was really born to be a clown. "I grimace naturally; I am perfidious and dissimulate, like women in this respect" (p. 81). His abandon seems complete. The King begins to whirl about like "an old satyr" (p. 82). He is decidedly comfortable in the role he plays. "My business is to wound," he declares. Indeed, his métier is to kill, and he does.

Symbols: Dramatic and Alchemical

Just as the alchemist wrote his formulas in complex symbols, thereby hiding them from the vulgar who might not only misunderstand but also seek to destroy the material, so the playwright inserts signs into his drama that only the initiate may penetrate.

Escurial opens to the sound of barking dogs. The King cups his hands to shut out the sounds and the reality they force upon him: the Queen is about to die. The fear, horror, and torment leading up to the event is unbearable. He forbids the sounds. Once the Queen's death has occurred, however, the situation has become acceptable to the King, who finally allows the baying of the dogs.

In most mythologies, dogs are associated with the underworld. They are chthonic spirits (Anubis, Tien-k'uen, Cerberus). Their function is to guide man to the realm of the dead and to protect the underworld. Garm, in German mythology, guards the entrance to Nifleheim, a cold and tenebrous realm. In *Escurial*, dogs are the harbingers of death and not the positive and faithful creatures associated with Saint Roch or the Dominican order (*Domini canes*, "dogs of the Lord"). As creatures of the night and, according to alchemical dictum, theriomorphic forms of spirit and the soul, dogs also serve to blend with, and prolong, the *nigredo* atmosphere implicit in the play. Because they are identified with the night, a state which preceded light (Gen. 1:2), they do not belong to the ego personality, but are "supraordinate" to it.[19] Their collective quality allows them to precede events, to see into them, to intuit feelings and situations.[20]

Alchemists associate the dog with Hecate and the moon—that is, with the unconscious or the transpersonal sphere. Dark, quixotic, and volatile, Hecate is depicted in drawings and paintings with a cortège of terrifying barking dogs, roaming about tombs and graveyards and calling up the ghosts of the departed.[21] Pico della Mirandola considered the moon the most inferior of constellations, thus implying that the unconscious (or that irrational part of man), when allowed to act on its own, as in the King's case, without the light of reason or conscious orientation, is the promulgator of savage and brutal acts. Macrobius wrote: "The realm of the perishable begins with the moon and goes downwards."[22] The King's aggressive nature both as Folial (who seeks to strangle him) and as King (who has his buffoon killed) is also expressed in the dog symbol. Dogs in the *Ynglingasaga* are warring spirits. They are Odin's companions in battle.

They went without shields, and were mad as dogs or wolves, and bit on their shields, and were as strong as bears or bulls; men they slew, and neither fire nor steel would deal with them; and theirs is what is called the fury of the berserker.[23]

Bells also play an important role in *Escurial*. Ghelderode had always been sensitive to music, and particularly to medieval and Renaissance polyphonic compositions. He wrote:

I hear an aerial music which, for me is another sign, an everlasting language which accompanies the whole of my life: I hear bells living, breathing, and rambling on. I am a bell-fancier. A strange passion isn't it. Not only religious bells, but civil bells also, those carillons that Flanders invented, both the tragic bells with bloody mouths and the triumphant with golden tongues.[24]

The collective tonalities of the bell sounds and the howling of the dogs create celestial and infernal music, a composite of conflicting emotions, rhythms, and sonorities which not only transcend the limitations of man and thus merge with the cosmic, but also add dynamism, tension, and furor to the drama itself. Bells are considered, in alchemical symbolism, as mediating forces between heaven and earth, a combination of spirit and matter. Their form represents the female, and, therefore, the emotional qualities with which she is identified. Their vaulted shape represents the head and the rationality which dominates the stage proceedings. The primordial vibrations prelude the human activities; they announce in their own language, that of subtle cosmis rhythms, the pain and anguish which will affect the human heart.

In *Escurial*, bells prolong the religious and sinister atmosphere which marked Philip II's reign. Bells are so significant in this regard that the Monk begs the King to let him sound them. "It would be an immense charity, a saintly action to let the bells ring, to lift the interdict Your Majesty has raised against bells. . . . bells annouce to Heaven terrestrial joys and pains" (p. 73). The King relents. He knows he is powerless against an implacable destiny. And just as the bells howled and wailed in medieval mystery dramas— counting the hours of Christ's agony, marking its progression—so they replicate the Queen's torment and, by extension, Folial's.

Dogs and bells are harbingers of death, which is almost personified during the stage proceedings. Death, like the medieval leader of a dance macabre, performs his gyrations in an inventive sadomasochistic round. Some in the audience are regaled by these antics, while others are terrorized; mysterious and stealthy at first, death permeates the dialogue, thoughts, and sensations on stage. "You love Death," the King tells the Monk, "its odor and its splendor!" (p. 73).

Death, for the alchemist, indicates an end to spiritual progress, a condition of degeneration and decay. Yet such separation of soul from body is a prerequisite for the healing process which puts an end to the affliction of the soul. Death means a finale to the old condition and the birth of new combinations, fresh alloys, avant-garde views.[25] Thanatos, the son of Night and the brother of Sleep, represents the King, the hardhearted one, insensitive and grim. As was the Greek god, the King is anchored in his solitude; he is caught up in his destructive ways, encapsulated in *nigredo*. Alchemical symbolism treated Thanatos or *mortificatio* as a precondition of *renovatio*, but Ghelderode's King bathes in the regressive first phase of the alchemical operation.

The number seven, as I pointed out in chapter 1, is very significant for the alchemist. In *Escurial*, it is identified with negative attributes, as is everything else in this drama. The King accuses Folial of having committed seven deadly sins and other "abominations." Never does he mention the seven virtues. The King associates his buffoon with absolute evil and with the devil. "I love you for your perfection in evil," he says (p. 77). Whereas alchemists looked upon numbers as containing both positive and negative forces, as manifestations of a totality and therefore, as archetypes, Ghelderode's King did not. He was too ego-centered and could only see the negative ideations involved, the *mortificatio* and *putrefactio* and not the *renovatio*, sin and not virtue.

To underscore the mephitic and decidedly uncomfortable condition of his protagonists and add to the play's visceral impact upon the audience, Ghelderode has recourse to images of fleas, carrion, and larvae. The Latin word "larva" means "ghost"; in Roman times, larvae were considered evil spirits that wandered about graveyards and near criminals. They grimaced and cackled as they made their way about in darkness, terrorizing young and old. Images of skulls and craniums are interwoven into the dialogue, accentuating the disgusting atmosphere. The King asks Folial whether his "cranium is filled with larvae" (p. 78), thus denigrating his thought processes. As the chief of his kingdom, the King was metaphorically the "head" of his realm. Cranium cults have existed from time immemorial and are still popular today. Skulls of ancestors and saints are worshiped throughout the world.

The crown of gold is exchanged between the King and Folial during the farce episodes. Alchemists considered both the crown and the gold from which it was made the most splendid of substances. It was God's mouthpiece and the sun's earthly counterpart. Since the crown is placed on the head, it reaches closest to heaven; in that it is made of the noblest and the purest of metals, its rays shine throughout the cosmos, shedding light. The kabbalists, when referring to the *Sephiroth*, God's Ten Emanations, considered the Crown (*Kether*) the highest expression of the absolute. The scepter also exchanged between the King and Folial is a symbol of authority, power, and justice. The transference of crown and scepter during the farce implies that the ruling authority is no longer a steady and stable force, that it dispenses neither justice nor any governing power, and that it has lost solid footing. Rulership, then, is unsteady; stability and harmony are toppling. The edifice is about to crumble.

When he plays the buffoon, the King begins to jump, laugh, grimace, whirl about, and then dance. Alchemists used to dance around their athanors. "I dance my liberation," says the King. "I dance like a widower, like a goat on a witches' sabbath, like an old satyr" (p. 82). Dancing, the most primitive of instinctual expressions, is man's way of becoming reabsorbed into the pleromatic world. The circles he weaves around the stage result in a loss of equilibrium and individual identity. Once a fixed position or view of life has been uprooted, a reblending may occur; new and fresh components may be constellated. Such is not the King's case. Siva danced the tandava, thus uniting time and space and in so doing creating the earth; the King's dance allowed him to expel his hatred, lust, and anger—but only temporarily. These emotions once again flooded his being, dimming his vision. On a stage with light only glimmering through the atmosphere, the King danced like those satyrs depicted by Goya in his drawings of the Witches' Sabbath. The stage is flooded in a libidinous atmosphere of perversion and cruelty.

"After the farce, the tragedy," the King declares at the play's finale (p. 84). Laughter is Ghelderode's mask. It is his way of deriding man's earthly condition, of expelling his own hatred, boredom, and fear of sterility, and exposing his disillusionment and bitterness. As Paul Klee wrote: "A laugh is mingled with the deep lines of pain."[26] As an alchemical drama, *Escurial* enacts an inner experience. By slaying the new and vital forces and allowing the old and decayed forces to survive, the sacrifice serves no positive purpose. Comedian and martyr are one in *Escurial*, as are mocker and moralist. Not noble metals emerge, but ignoble ones. Rather than fostering love, a spirit of hatred is engendered; rather than health, sickness; rather than the avant-garde, the retrograde. The weight of the leaden matter has crushed mercurial sprightliness; the subliminal realm has superseded consciousness. Terror, chaos, and *nigredo* reign. The *Aurora Consurgens*, allegedly written by Saint Thomas Aquinas, sums up both the alchemical and the dramatic experience. "I saw a great cloud looming black over the whole earth, which had absorbed the earth and covered my soul."[27]

Albedo

Until all be made of water,
perform no operation.
Alchemical maxim

3

Break of Noon: A Cosmic Awakening

Paul Claudel's *Break of Noon* (1905) is sensual and erotic. The protagonists of this drama, as well as those of Claudel's other theatrical works (*The Tidings Brought to Mary, The Book of Christopher Columbus, The Hostage*, and more) are earth lusting for heaven, body obsessed with spirit, and darkness longing for light. Perpetual turmoil rages in the hearts and minds of Claudel's split and chaotic souls. Each in his own way seeks to liberate himself from egotistical and arrogant tendencies, while at the same time attempting to acquire altruism, humility, and godliness. Claudel's creatures in *Break of Noon* are pagans clothed in Catholic vestments; they are hedonists rather than ascetics.

Break of Noon centers on the theme of adultery and involves a wife, a husband, and two lovers. It dramatizes, wrote Claudel, the struggle between "the religious vocation and the call of the flesh."[1] The flesh dominates. Every word in *Break of Noon* breathes and swells with Dionysian fervor and jubilation. Counterforces follow each euphoric experience, shedding feelings of shame and guilt in their wake. The intensity of these clashing emotions—exquisite sensuality in pursuit of the forbidden fruit on the one hand, and the terror engendered by belief in the damnation to follow on the other—heightens the excitement and titillates the senses. Ecstasy is reached when transcendence becomes humanized through the flesh.

Break of Noon is a giant cosmic awakening in which the four Aristotelian elements (sun, moon, water, earth) activate and energize the stage happenings. Each element, in consort with the protagonists, participates in the drama aboard a ship sailing on the Indian Ocean to China. An animistic world is therefore brought to life which allows the four characters to bathe in primitive powers and to experience viscerally the mysterious and inexorable forces that are to decide their fate.

The protagonists in *Break of Noon* are leaden in nature. They are weighted down with spiritual and psychological burdens; each longs for freedom, air, abandon. Not one is free from dross. In act 1 they are heated by the rays of the scorching August noon sun; they are calcined and brought to a state of incandescence as their ship sails on what alchemists term the *aqua permanens*, the primal waters. Act 2, which takes place on a dark April day, paves the way for the *nigredo* operation, when the protagonists return to a preformal, instinctual realm. Solids have melted; fixatives have liquefied; flaming mixtures have been transformed into charred remains. The "sin" has been accomplished; "evil" has been engendered; emotions of the most vicious type have ushered in a condition of *putrefactio*. Act 3 opens on a stage "inundated with moonlight." The chemistry of the drama has altered. The words the twelfth-century alchemist Morienus used to refer to the creation of the Philosopher's Stone are applicable to Claudel's protagonists: "Our stone is like the creation of man. For we have the union, 2, the corruption [i.e., the putrefaction of the seed], 3, the gestation, 4, the birth of the child, 5, the nutrition follows."[2]

Break of Noon is also autobiographical. Claudel wrote it when he was undergoing a severe personal crisis, a "break" between his past and his future. It was vital, he confessed, that the torment eating away at his system be expelled. Since the experience from which the play was born was so abrasive and the events so closely woven into the fabric of his emotions, Claudel had *Break of Noon* privately printed. He refused permission to have his drama produced on any stage until 1948, when Jean-Louis Barrault, working together with the author, was given this honor.

Claudel, born in 1868 in Villeneuve-sur-Fère, a small town near Rheims, moved to Paris in 1881. It was there that he came under the influence of Symbolist poets and dramatists and was also exposed to the scientific and naturalist thinkers of his day. The positivist philosophy of Auguste Burdeau, the scientific determinism of Hippolyte Taine, and the relativist historical works of Ernest Renan impressed the young writer. Claudel enrolled in the Law Faculty in 1885 in Paris, after which he studied at the École des sciences politiques.

The year 1886, however, was a momentous one for Claudel. In May he made what he considered an incredible discovery: Arthur Rimbaud's *Illuminations*. These poems were to become a "seminal" force in his life because they opened the supernatural world to him. Rimbaud the Promethean, the adolescent rebel who fought society, God, and himself, made Claudel aware of his own turmoil and dissatisfactions, of the growing chaos within his psyche. He began questioning his values and the pat answers offered him by the naturalistic, rationalistic, and scientific philosophers of his day. Rimbaud's poetry shook his circumscribed world to its very foundations. It cut, tore, bruised him. It wrenched him, Claudel wrote, out of "the hideous world of Taine, Renan and the other nineteenth-century Molochs, from the imprisonment engendered by this horrible mechanical realm governed entirely by perfectly inflexible laws."[3] But 1886 also brought Claudel the answer to his metaphysical anguish. During the Christmas mass at Notre Dame Cathedral in Paris, Claudel was so shaken by the experience of divinity that he was totally and completely converted to the faith of his fathers.

And it was at this moment that the event which dominated my whole life took place. In one instant my heart was touched and *I believed*. I believed with such adhesive force, with such powerful conviction, with such certitude, that an upheaval within my whole being occurred, and there was no place at all left for any kind of doubt.[4]

From that time on, his faith never wavered.

Claudel entered foreign service and began a brilliant governmental and literary career. He was sent as consul to the United States (1893–94) and then to China (1895–1900). His feelings of solitude during these years were expressed in his *Verses in Exile* and in *Knowing the East*. His ordeal, however, was just beginning. In 1900 he made up his mind to enter the church. He wanted to sacrifice his worldly condition to God: life for spirit, sensuality for spirituality. Claudel entered the Benedictine monasteries of Solesmes and de Ligugé. In September, 1900, he experienced a religious crisis which he expressed in "Muses," the first of his celebrated *Five Great Odes*. Some scholars have looked upon this poem as a farewell to literature. His religious rapture, however, was short-lived. His spiritual director believed the poet unsuited for monastic life. What he had looked upon as his great sacrifice was not acceptable to the church. It was, perhaps, overly filled with pride and feelings of spiritual superiority. Claudel was compelled to return to the world. His pain when faced with what he compared to Adam's fall tore him asunder. It was "a rejection pure and simple," he wrote, "a peremptory *no* and not accompanied with any explanation."[5]

Claudel felt that his rejection by the church was preordained by God. He would have to, as Adam had, experience conflict, the disorder of daily existence, and even sin. God had placed these temptations before man to test his faith. The Portuguese proverb, "God writes straight with crooked lines," would certainly apply to him.[6] Important also in Claudel's religious philosophy were Saint Augustine's words: *etiam peccata* ("even sins"). Sins also serve in man's quest for redemption. It is through the experience of sin that the believer suffers real torture, that he fights his base nature and in so doing ascends the hierarchy of spiritual values. According to Claudel's reasoning, sin becomes a virtual necessity if pardon is to be experienced. Sin is a means of strengthening one's backbone, tensing one's will, and sacrificing a life of physical pleasures for one of ascetic endurance. To bathe a metal in immaculate waters is no test of its strength.

In 1901, Claudel was sent back to China, where he remained until 1905. It was on the ship taking him to China that he met the beautiful Polish blond, Rosalie, a wife and mother. His passion for her was great and it was reciprocated. Despite the commandments of his religion and the fact that, only months prior to this traumatic love affair, he had wanted to take the vows of chastity, the man of flesh was unleashed. Claudel's liaison, which included the birth of a child, lasted for several years. No one knows the reasons for its conclusion. It has been suggested that Claudel tired of Rosalie. Others believe that he yielded to the advice of his superiors, who stated categorically that if he wanted to pursue a successful governmental career, he would have to live more conventionally. Whatever the reason for his "break up," he expressed his grief in many poems.

Claudel married Reine Sainte-Marie Perrin in 1906 and established an ultraconservative Catholic household. He again became a father. His career in government was outstanding and included ambassadorships to Japan, Belgium, and the United States. His flesh-oriented ways, however, did not change, nor did his extramarital affairs cease. Irresistibly drawn to the world of sin, he looked upon such encounters as tests of his religious fervor, temptations placed in his path which would end with confession and pardon. In "Obsession," he wrote: "What opens the wall to God is not the lance,/But the cry of an afflicted heart, because the kingdom of God is suffering violence."[7]

The world is one for Claudel the monist; the world is alive for Claudel the hylozoist; it is visceral for Claudel the animist and multiple for Claudel the pagan. When he projects his psyche and soma onto natural forces around him, nature becomes animated and he dialogues with this force as a whole in a sustained, frenetic, brutal, shocking, cruel symphony. Various levels of experience emerge as matter passes from inert to kinetic; from idea to act, unwritten to written, passive to aggressive, cacophonous to harmonious, terrestrial to spiritual. Energy is injected into each word and image. "Words have a soul," Claudel wrote. "There is a relationship between the graphic sign and the thing signified," between "the image, idea, feeling which reverberates, empowers the eyes, arouses the emotions."[8] The years Claudel spent in China and Japan gave him further insight into the semiotic importance and validity of words and images.

The title, *Break of Noon,* is in keeping with the semiotic approach to language. It implies a cleavage, schism, a severing of one life and the beginning of another. Noon, for Claudel the metaphysician and numerologist, signifies a midway mark in the sun's course through the heavens, when it has reached its zenith and is preparing for its descent. He said in *Break of Noon,* "Noon, the center of our life" (p. 35).[9] For the medieval mind, noon represented that moment when the sun is believed to be at rest, when calm has set in and man is most receptive to divine as well as to demoniacal powers, that fateful instant when the intensity of illumination may blind. For the ancient Egyptian, the sun was Ra; for the Greek, it was Apollo; for Claudel, it was God, the Trinity. Only the pure in heart could look at this body without flinching. Because of his sinful nature, Lot was unable to gaze at the noon sun; Abraham, however, whose soul was spotless, could view God face-to-face when this celestial body reached the peak of its burning force. So Claudel's protagonists would similarly attempt to gain insight into themselves by means of this solar force.

"I lost my sense of proportion," wrote Claudel; "I have maintained my balance thanks to a fragile equation."[10] Numbers, nautical and astronomical measurements, cylinders, spheres, cubes, squares, cones, circles, points, lines, and alchemical references fill *Break of Noon*. They express not only an outer orientation, but also symbolize an inner drama. Numbers have a numinous quality and frequently appear in an artist's work when he suffers from some psychological problem. They symbolize a need to compensate for a chaotic inner state.[11] Numbers are not invented by the conscious mind, but emerge from the unconscious spontaneously as archetypal images when the need arises. For Pythagoras, stars and planets, moving in perfect order in harmony with a heavenly plan, are endowed with souls and intelligences. The divine spark in the human body is part of the World Soul and therefore is eternal, mobile, and pure. Since it is imprisoned in the body, it is subject to material and sensual influences which it must fight off through ascetic practices.[12]

Noon is number twelve. When referring to the twelve months of the year, the twelve disciples, and the twelve signs of the zodiac, twelve signifies completion. The play has four protagonists, and when their number is multiplied by the three acts, or stages in their evolution, it equals twelve. The number four, the earth element for the alchemist, is associated with terrestrial existence, the square, the four seasons, and the cardinal points, and also brings to mind the faces of man, lion, ox, and eagle that Ezekiel saw around the throne of God (Rev. 4:6–8). Each animal, according to Saint Jerome, expresses a religious function: the ox symbolizes passion and sacrifice; the lion, resurrection; the eagle, ascension; man, incarnation. Each also represents one of the four Evangelists: Matthew is man; Mark, the lion; Luke, the ox; John, the eagle. Throughout *Break of Noon,* Claudel refers to these animals and others and to the Evangelists and their individual personalities. The characters' names correspond to measurements. Ysé, the name of the wife, mother, and mistress, comes from the Greek *isos,* meaning "equal," as are the two sides of an isosceles triangle. The *Y* in her name represents one form of the alchemical cross: unity which has become duality. No longer is Ysé the one woman who blends harmoniously into her surroundings, but rather one woman as opposed to three men, her antagonists. The one versus the three underscores the tension existing in life: spirit and matter, active and passive, imprisonment and freedom. The *Y* is significant in alchemical symbology in that it stands for the hermaphrodite with two heads. Ysé is psychologically bisexual: she is both man and woman, the incarnation of certain aspects of the dramatist's psyche. She is very much like Tristan's beloved Isolde, ever alluring, yet virile and powerful in her attempt to subjugate the men on shipboard. She is mystery incarnate, suggests Claudel. "She represents the possibility of something unknown. A secret being charged with significance" (p. 15).

The name of Ysé's husband—de Ciz—suggests division, friction, and tension. Associated with the words *ciseau* ("scissors"), *ciselure* ("carving"), and *ciseler* ("chiseling"), all instruments which alchemists used in their dismemberment operations. His name corresponds to his personality. De Ciz is weak, irresponsible, drawn here and there, cut off from himself and the world at large; because he is a businessman, he follows the scent of money.

The name of Mesa, the character who most closely resembles Claudel and who is Ysé's lover, comes from the Greek word *mesos* ("moderation," "balance"), but he is given to extremes. Searching for beatitude, longing to give his life to God but prevented from doing so by his superiors, he has been thrust into a world of temptation. Immoderate in his thoughts, feelings, and deeds, perpetually dissatisfied, egotistical, and inflated with feelings of spiritual superiority, he is chaos striving to become cosmos.

Amalric is Ysé's second lover. His name may be divided into three syllables, corresponding to the three stages of life, the triangle, and the Trinity. The other protagonists pronounce their names with two syllables, representing duality and unresolved conflict. Only Amalric will, therefore, emerge whole from the ordeal. The syllables *mal* ("evil") and *mâle* ("male") are included in his name. He is very masculine, driven by a love of life and a need for conquest. Strong, courageous, and expansive, Amalric resembles his namesake Arnauld Amalric, the promoter of the twelfth-century crusade against the Albigensians, who also fought the Moors in Spain. Amalric is not destroyed by events, nor is he given to bleakness of mood. He is the most sincere of all the characters; the one who accepts himself as he is and sees through the ambiguities of life most perceptively. He knows that the equilibrium which seems to exist at the outset of the play is frail and false. "Here we are engaged together in a game, like four needles; and who knows what kind of wool destiny will have the four of us weave together" (p. 39). This image may be likened to Christ's passion, since four nails were used in depicting the crucifixion in the early centuries: two piercing the hands and two the feet. Only later were three nails used; one nail pierced both feet, thereby associating the entire crucifixion with the Trinity.[13] The wool Amalric refers to corresponds to the lamb, the sacrificial animal. Amalric's statement indicates that each protagonist will experience his own passion in his own manner.

Act 1: Sun/Water Ritual—Lead Calcines

Amalric and Mesa are talking on deck. The atmosphere is still, static. Mesa sums up the feeling: "The days are so much alike they seem composed of a single great black and white day" (p. 26). The image imposes a cyclical time scheme upon the proceedings; events take on mythical dimensions. The audience is plunged into the Oriental's mythical view of time. "I love this great immobile day," Amalric comments, instilling a more powerful sense of repose into the atmosphere by contrasting it with the mobile waters that are carrying the ship to its destination. The sun pours down from an endless sky onto vast emptiness of "water behind us and more water in front of us" (p. 35). A kind of Taoist glorification of the void is implied here; a condition which enables man to experience a state of perfect availability, simplicity, and detachment.

Soon the playwright's idyllic image alters its focus: from the world at large it centers on a "black" dot, the ship—the microcosm. Heaving, tumultuous, oceanic inner forces now propel four people along their journey; these will be enlarged and dramatized. The vessel navigating through the burning/icy waters symbolizes the human being in his spiritual quest. In this sense the ship becomes a vehicle for self-discovery. An analogy may be made with Buddha, called "the Great Ferryman." He crossed to the other side of the ocean of life to experience nirvana, as the four passengers try to divest themselves of passions and acquire tranquility during their journey. The protagonists feel disoriented and dissatisfied. They are "a wandering troupe," Mesa says. "I have no place any place," Ysé confesses (p. 34). Each in his own way is cut off from purpose, from God; they are souls in exile.

The alchemical sun/water dynamism will bring about the transmutation of the metals, or, in psychological terms, the alteration of their personalities. First comes the *solutio* operation: the metals are cleansed and rid of their impurities. Later comes *separatio,* the separation of the elements, indicating a dissolution of the personality via calcination or trituration. As Arnold of Villanova wrote in the *Rosarium Philosophorum:*

The philosophical work is to dissolve and melt the stone into its mercury, so that it is reduced and brought back to its *prima materia,* i.e., original condition, purest form.[14]

Alchemists often quoted Jesus' recommendation to purify through water:

Verily, verily, I say unto them, Except a man be born of water and of the Spirit, he cannot enter into the kingdom of God.

That which is born of the flesh is flesh, that which is born of the Spirit is spirit.

(John 3:5–6).

Mesa, de Ciz, Ysé, and Amalric undergo a fire/water baptism. Jonah said to God, "Thou has cast me into the deep, in the midst of the seas; and the floods compassed me about . . . even to the soul" (Jonah 2:3); so Claudel's protagonists are cut off from the world. During this period of isolation, their energies are to be directed within, thus activating the unconscious and paving the way for a new conscious attitude.

Mesa—hard, brittle, and one-sided—had to become more malleable, flexible, and bending. Because he was unable to relate to others or give of himself, his solitary, taciturn nature needed recasting. Even Claudel described him as "very hard, dry," "antipathetical," and preoccupied with himself and his own salvation. "He had to be transformed."[15] Mesa's longing for God had become obsessive, thus creating a fixative condition. The fire/water operation would allow volatility and fusibility to be born and with them a flow of ductile sensations. To experience the tortures of the damned, as had the wicked in Job, would also be Mesa's lot: "His roots shall be dried up beneath, and above shall his branch be cut off" (Job 18:16). So Mesa would be burned, after which he would experience the chaotic, preformed, regressive condition that the Chinese alchemists termed *Wou-k'i.*

Mesa is the first to mention fire and does so when commenting on the ship's siren. "What a cry in this desert of fire!" The siren, compared to a shrill, penetrating human cry, tears him asunder, reinforcing his sense of isolation and exile. Life for him is a desert; the vast oceans and endless skies replicate the dryness of his life. The fire for God which had burned within him had consumed his serenity, dessicated his feelings, and depleted his energies. His unacceptability to God weighed him down with grief, made his outlook leaden. He would have to remain in his watery desert—as the Hebrews, escaping from Egypt, stayed in their sandy desert— facing his inner wilderness in order to discover his Promised Land. To choose the infertile land was not uncommon in ancient times. The Hebrew prophets found the desert conducive to revelation, and, in fact, monotheism has been called "the religion of the desert." It is also the land of the ascetic and of temptation. Christ was driven into the desert: "And he was there in the wilderness forty days, tempted of Satan; and was with the wild beasts; and the angels ministered unto him" (Mark 1:12–14). The ship will lead Mesa into temptation, and the sun's blinding rays will vivify his demons, which will calcinate and bruise him.

Whether fire emerges from the sun or from the alchemist's athanor, it has a dual function. It generates or consumes, fecundates or destroys, ushers in life or death. The struggle between light and darkness, good and evil, is the focal point of *Break of Noon* as well as of Manichaeanism. Saint Augustine (and Claudel was an inveterate reader of his works) had been a Manichaean. After his conversion to Christianity by Saint Ambrose in 387, he wrote voluminously about the evils of his former religion. In his *Argument Against the Manichaeans and Marcionites,* he stated that evil was nothing more than the privation of good, and therefore it could have no existence except in some good thing. Evil is thus relegated to being a defect in good things or to the Anti-Christ, suggested C. G. Jung.[16] For Claudel, however, evil is an active and powerful force which must be fought at every turn.

Fire/sun will serve to illuminate the evil in Mesa—his impure, arrogant, and egotistical ways. It will bring to the open what lies hidden and repressed within him and revivify what is dead or dormant: love, feeling, emotions for and toward others. According to certain medieval legends, the alchemist Christ and his saints succeeded in revivifying corpses by passing them through fire as a metalsmith does when refining his metals: achieving a golden state. Mesa will experience his ordeal by fire, his sacrificial ritual: that inner burning which brings knowledge to the one who seeks it, perception to the one who sheds the outer core and burrows to the heart of humankind. Fire/sun is heaven sent, Mesa believes. It originates in the celestial spheres and then descends to earth to remold man. Just as Lucifer ("light-bringer") fell from heaven into the flames of hell, so Mesa will bring illumination but be consumed in the process, perhaps to be reborn from his own ashes as the alchemical phoenix. "Heaven smiles down to Earth with ineffable love," wrote Claudel. Since this alchemical marriage, "air and water burn with a mysterious fire."[17]

De Ciz must experience the fire/water ordeal because he is weak, disoriented, and irresponsible; he is always yielding to his desire to go elsewhere, to do something new. Referred to as "thin," "with tender eyes," and with "woman's eyes," he represents for Claudel the male failure. Although Ysé does not love her husband, she is nevertheless drawn to him sexually, and when he looks at her in a certain way she feels "shame." He does not love her and she knows it. "He loves only himself," she remarks (p. 46). Amalric describes de Ciz as a "parasite," a "gluttonous creeping ivy," a "rubber plant" (p. 50). His fluidity contrasts directly to Mesa's stability. De Ciz must become fixated and coagulated; his inner flow must be reworked so that a fresh arrangement of components can take place.

Ysé, blond, beautiful, sensual, and proud, needs to be loved and longs for the affection and security denied by her husband. Only her senses have been aroused, not her soul. Her unfulfilled existence has made her consider herself "a stranger" to the world and imprisoned in superficiality. Ysé is not weak; she is strong and elegant, even virile. Amalric describes her as a "warrior," a "conqueror," and not a "coquettish" person. She must "subjugate" others, "tyrannize," or else "give herself" completely. She was made to become a "chieftain's wife," to have "great obligations" to tie her down. Amalric calls her a "high-bred mare," and he adds that it would "amuse" him "to mount her back, if he had the time. . . . She runs like a nude horse." He also sees her as a "maddened horse, breaking everything, breaking herself" (p. 30). Amalric knows her well. They are alike in many ways. He understands the power of her instincts and the lengths that they would take her if sufficiently stimulated; they would lead her to disrupt her even-tempered, conventional existence.

Claudel wrote that "the word MYSTERY is inscribed on Ysé's forehead" (p. 15); she is an autonomous person, remote, ambiguous, and chaotic. She is an archetypal figure; her power works in arcane ways. She is the sun's female counterpart, the one to light the flame of passion, the catalyst who consumes and is consumed, the one to touch off the catastrophe or transfiguration process. Like Amaterasu, the Japanese sun goddess about whom Claudel wrote a poetical essay, Ysé dazzles with her brilliance and beauty. Important too is the association made between Ysé and Amaterasu by the name of the island on which great temples to the sun goddess have been built: Isé. Its name is pronounced in French in the same way as the name of Claudel's protagonist.

Sun and water will work in concert for Ysé. The Indian Sea and her psychological submersion within its primal waters will renew and purify her in preparation for her *recoagulatio*. The alchemists called water "exalted" because they considered it "a living water that comes to moisten the earth that it may spring forth and in due season bring forth much fruit. . . . This *aqua vitae* or water of life, whitens the body and changes it into a white color."[18] As a female principle—yin as opposed to yang—water darkens and ices; it spreads lugubrious and unworldly feelings. For the alchemist it blackens, and according to the trigram *k'an,* it stands for the abyss. "There is no solidity around me," Claudel wrote in *Verses in Exile.* "I am situated in chaos, I am lost in the interior of Death." These words are applicable to Ysé.

Amalric is courageous, powerful, a conqueror. He will be the only one to pass the crucial fire/water test. He enjoys the world, feels comfortable in it, relates to people, and is ebullient and naturally joyful. He is handsome, virile, sensual. Women cannot resist him. Sincere in his outlook, he follows his penchant and travels around the globe. He is able to "see clearly, to see thoroughly/ Things as they are" (p. 37). He had met Ysé before her marriage, ten years prior to the events taking place on shipboard, and had wanted to make love to her then. Proud and independent, she resisted his advances because she felt he did not really need her.

Claudel singles out Amalric's hands for scrutiny. Amalric says: "With this hand here, with this hand you now see, and which is a large and an ugly hand. . . . When I choose, my warrior, I shall place this hand on your shoulder" (p. 55). Hands are supportive entities; they symbolize activity in the outside world. For the Romans, the hand (*manus*) corresponds to authority, the *pater familias,* the emperor. For the Buddhist, hand gestures (*mudras*) take on religious significance; they manifest both an inner spiritual situation and the exteriorization of inner energy. Hands are instruments, tools, armaments which convert passive into active. Alchemists looked upon hands as part of space symbolism, as a means of paving the way for the *dissolutio* and *coagulatio* processes, and many of their diagrams centered on designs made in space. Ysé predicts Amalric's success in life because he is "clever with his hands" (p. 34). Mesa comments on his "pleasant hands" (p. 34), which are well suited to milking a cow: they draw nourishment and are earth-oriented.

Although self-reliant and independent, Amalric is nevertheless caught in the play of light, the sizzling heat on shipboard. At first he is troubled by blindness and searing pain. "I am blinded as if by a gun shot. That isn't a sun! . . . One feels horribly visible, like a flea between two panes of glass" (p. 24). Unlike Samson, who was divested of his masculinity when Delilah lulled him to sleep and cut his hair, leading to his blinding by the Philistines (Judg. 13–16), Amalric was only momentarily blinded by Ysé's sensuality. Despite his desire, he quickly regained his composure and would not be humble or weaken before her. A man of the earth, his legs and hands were always balanced, thus giving him the equilibrium necessary to cope with the events to come.

As a solar hero, Amalric is a source of light, heat, and life. His is not a sweet, gentle, understanding illumination, but the brash and violent fire of the alchemist's dazzling red coals. Amalric is Sol Invictus, the active male, the yang principle. He is the antithesis of the solar Christ, whose daily rise and fall spelled the cycle of light and darkness, ascension and descent. Amalric will not change dramatically during the course of the play. He will remain righteous as he faces the sun, whether with exultation or with a tinge of terror. Even his passion for Ysé stimulates his lust for life. The conqueror in him vibrates at the thought of possessing her, the Eternal Feminine.

As the trip continues, the sea turns into a limitless mirror reflecting God's universe. Striking, brilliant, and perverse, the water-mirror is shot through with solar rays which magnify, and sharply delineate what had only been subsumed at the outset of the drama. The mirror holds and retains the formerly fleeting, coagulates the flowing, reveals the hidden to the all-seeing and roving eye of the Creator. It contains, absorbs, reproduces, and distorts the protagonists' feelings. As the speculum (Latin for "mirror") on a telescope or surgical instrument allows more accurate observation by enlarging the image before it, so the water-mirror reveals more minutely the passengers' needs, thus leading the audience to greater speculation about their real motivations.

Mirror and glass exteriorize what lies concealed. Glass and crystals serve many functions and alter in consistency and use according to need. The twelfth-century *Alchemista* says:

Glass is among stones as are the foolish among men for it receives all colors. It is liquefied easily by fire and quickly returns again to its stony condition. It softens and cleanses and liquefies all bodies, and is removed from them by fusion just as salt is by washing. Hence salt and glass are things in which lies the whole secret of the art nor is it possible to produce the stone [philosopher's stone] without them, particularly without salt.[19]

Plato believed that mirrors and glass empowered the soul to reveal itself; Plotinus suggested that the entire universe was an ensemble of mirrors in which the Infinite Essence contemplated itself in forever altering forms and tones. Mirrors and glass not only render the unmanifest visible, they also cut and incise. Glass was turned into instruments which alchemists used to dismember and pulverize elements; they also used glass as crucibles, alembics, and retorts. Glass and crystals have medicinal value. They were used by Roman surgeons to cauterize: when held against the sun's rays, they would burn out wounds as well as draw pus from them. So Claudel places his glass and crystal between sun and water, attempting to relieve the protagonists of their leaden ways by revealing and exposing what festers beneath. Glass and crystals have religious value. Oracles such as Saint Helen, who used "water-green" crystal, told the future by means of these shining stones.

Each protagonist reacts to the sun-water-glass-crystal complex. De Ciz sees it as clusters of infinitely replicating flashes of lightning, saying: "How small and how consumed one feels in this reverberating oven" (p. 24). His personality assumes form in this one image: lightning consumes and destroys because its energy is so powerful and concentrated that it reduces everything within its reach to cinders. The oven, of his image, like the alchemist's atha-nor, corresponds to the womb which cooks, melts, and smelts met-als. De Ciz will be annihilated during the course of his inner trajec-tory, his *regressus ad uterum.*

Mesa looks upon the sun-water-glass-crystal composite as a "hard" substance which possesses a "resplendent backbone" (p. 25), and as a "vat of dye," and a "deep pane of glass" (p. 100). Each of these images indicates durability and liquidity which will be trans-formed through the heating or calcinating process and blended and mixed when inundated by the *prima materia,* that "basic moist-ness" which contains "the seed of all things."[20]

Chemical compounds are as important as forms in Claudel's drama. Each time the waters darken or lighten, they become com-parable to sulfur or mercury. Sulfur represents earth: it is visible and solid. Since it is igneous, it corresponds to fire; because it is fluid, it possesses occult powers. Its yellow color likens it to citrini-tas, the third alchemical operation, when metals are burned and purified prior to the creation of the Philosopher's Stone. Sulfur is a celestial spirit which many alchemists considered the "Spirit of God." It may destroy or fructify. Sodom was consumed by a rain of sulfur (Gen. 19:24); the evil ones in Job were punished when the "brimstone" (sulfur) destroyed their habitation (Job 18:19). The yellow smoke emanating from sulfur destroys light: Lucifer's arro-gance, for example, transformed light into darkness (Luke 11:36). Mesa's haughtiness will lead to guilt and punishment. "Take heed therefore that the light which is in thee be not darkness" (Luke 11:35).

Mesa is sulfur. He ignites instantly. No chemical, claimed Pliny, becomes combustible more quickly than sulfur, which proves "that there is in it a great affinity for fire."[21] When Mesa meets Ysé (mercury), his entire being flares, as if in an alchemist's alem-bic when the heating operation has reached its height. Amalric is also sulfur, but not the igneous, unsettled, hyperactive Mesalike chemical; a more virile, rational quality permeates his being. Amalric burns continuously, but never loses his smoothness or power. Perhaps for this reason he despises tempests and rough seas, and speaks of the "madness of the wind" (p. 44). Claudel makes many puns and plays on words referring to the wind which arouses waves, thus revealing their crests (*crêtes*); they are associated with height, white, and the island of Crete, alluding to the myth of the Minotaur, whose mother fell in love with a bull. Amalric despises the rocking of the boat because it pushes him here and there, uncontrolled, disoriented. He prefers a guided, calm, serene journey, because he knows at the outset that "All has been *resolved* once and for all" (p. 44).

Wind synthesizes the four elements of earth, water, fire, and air. It generates, fecundates, and destroys; it gives rise to hurricanes, instability, and agitation. It unleashes, symbolically, a titanic spirit, an elementary force that may, blind with rage, annihilate everything in its path. Yet wind (Hebrew *ruh*) also means "breath," the spirit of God as it moved over primordial waters in the beginning of time and created the world (Gen. 1:2).

Amalric recalls when he met Ysé. There was "a ferocious wind" blowing; it swept over everything, bruising "like the cutting mistral" (p. 47). It brought "the moonlight, the darkest night" with it. The wind "slapped him hard," shaking him to the very foundations of his being. At the time Ysé was returning from Egypt and he from the remotest areas of the world. Their love was born as was Venus from the wind-blown waves. The day was tempestuous: Sunday, the day of the Lord, of rest, the first day of the week, the beginning of their creation from the waters. Amalric expressed his baptism into her life: "Having imbibed my first great drink of life" (p. 48). He was drenched but not drowned by the experience, not destroyed, but troubled.

They met at ten o'clock. Numbers are very important to Claudel. Numerologists consider ten the union of 1 (God) and 0 (eternity); ten was the most sacred of all numbers, a symbol of universal creation because all emerged from and returned to it. Ten also symbolizes the Ten Commandments which Mesa will break.

Ysé, on the other hand, adores the wind because it forces up the salty spray from the ocean. Salt brings excitement and causes tingling sensations all over her body. It revitalizes the pagan and "silvery" Ysé; it glazes and makes everything "embarassingly clear" (pp. 24–27); it disquiets since it unmasks the mystery of being and releases repressed and reviled instincts. Salt blends, mixes; it is a universal go-between for the alchemist. It represents quintessence, ether, a mediating force.[22] Since salt dissolves in water, tantric Buddhists liken it to the absorption of the ego into the universal Self. Paracelsus considered salt the body of man.

Know, then, that all the seven metals are born from a threefold matter, namely, Mercury, Sulphur, and Salt, but with distinct and peculiar colourings. . . . Mercury is the spirit, Sulphur is the soul, and Salt is the body. . . . the soul, which indeed is Sulphur. . . . unites these two contraries, the body and the spirit, and changes them into one essence.[23]

Salt purifies when used in baptism, spells wisdom and spiritual nourishment in purification rituals, preserves and renders food incorruptible. However, if it is placed near silver, it corrodes and destroys, creating verdigris, a green or bluish poisonous compound.

The ship lunges forth to its destiny in a world where sun-water-salt, purity-impurity, black-white battle. Satan and God vie for supremacy. Claudel believed that man had to sin if he were to earn redemption. Born from darkness and sexuality, he experiences an earthen or leaden condition during his lifetime, and he must therefore attempt to ascend the ladder from darkness to light, from earthly sulfur to spiritualized sulfuric compound, reaching as best he can his golden essence. In order to ascend, he must experience the world of instinct. Claudel underscores the elemental forces surging within man, by creating a theriomorphic universe, filled with images of cows, horses, dogs, and tigers. The animal in man is represented according to a hierarchy of values. The horse, for example, to whom Ysé is compared, is as an animal of darkness, representing unbridled instinct, night (the mare as in "nightmare"), and terror. As a nourishing force, the horse is said to be able to force water out of springs by stamping his hooves. In a medieval French epic concerning the four sons of Aymon, their famous horse Bayard did just that. In psychological terms, the horse symbolizes the unconscious world: imagination, impetuosity, desire, creative power, youth, energy, and sensuality. Amalric called Ysé "highly bred." As a mare, she incarnates the Earth Mother who energizes and revitalizes. Ysé, however, compares herself to "an old white horse who follows the hand which pulls it" (p. 48). A white horse implies majesty, as when Christ mounted one (Rev. 19:11). It brings death, however, when an overly impetuous outlook is allowed to flourish. "And I looked, and behold a pale horse: and his name that sat on him was Death, and Hell followed him" (Rev. 6:8).

The cow is also a protagonist in *Break of Noon*. Mesa compared the cow to water, to a feeding, fecundating, fertilizing force, a primal mother. Such associations are understandable, because water is linked with vital heat. The lover of Baal, the Canaanite fertility god whose worshipers indulged in human sacrifice and sexual orgies, was a cow. Mesa mentions Baal in opposition to Christ. The cow, however, has spiritual values. Brahma's female aspect was given the names "Melodious Cow" and "Cow of Abundance," underscoring the animal's positive and nourishing qualities. Thus Ysé, depending on her relationships, can be positive or negative.

The dog is an active participant in the shipboard drama. Mesa calls himself "a yellow dog," a cur. Associated with death, Anubis, Cerberus, and Garm, the dog is a complex of opposites in that it protects as the keeper of the flock and devours when provoked to anger. The alchemical dog eaten by the wolf represents the purification of gold by means of antimony. For the alchemist, the wolf stage represents the state nearest to perfection in the evolution of the soul. The most difficult stage, however, is yet to come and requires a supreme effort on the part of the hierophant: the transformation of base metal into its highest form. Mesa, then, is that terrified yellow cur whose ordeal lies ahead.

Colors also reflect man's inner climate through analogy and identification. Claudel's universe is a giant canvas of kinetic hues. Light, Claudel wrote, is "decomposed obscurity"; it produces "the seven notes, in accordance with the intensity of its work."[24] Pigments, then, are related to sound for Claudel as they were for Pythagoras and for Aristotle, who compared the seven basic colors to musical intervals in *De Coloribus*. Claudel's musical analogies transforms *Break of Noon* into a tone poem with visual as well as sonorous shadings, thus expanding and deepening its impact.

Color serves to generate excitement. It accentuates gradations of emotions and intensities of feelings. It is nature's metabolism and aids in analyses of the protagonists' spiritual and physical outlooks. In that color is endowed with emotional equivalents, it is not surprising that Claudel's colors should be violent, harsh, and powerful. Mesa speaks of greens, fire, and tobacco color "in the teeming clear chaos" (p. 36). He loves fire and white, yellow, strident, and striated hues. Green has particular significance for the alchemist. In addition to the conventional allusions to fertility and productivity, it refers to the Holy Grail, that emerald chalice which legend tells us contained the blood of Christ, and to the emerald on Lucifer's forehead, and is thus equated with both salvation and perdition, ascension and descent. When Mesa looks down at the water around him he calls it a "wine pocket," associating it with the blood of Christ and the transubstantiation ritual. The brilliant sun has become a "scarlet sun" by the end of act 1, fusing spiritual with carnal essences and affording a premonition of the blood sacrifice to follow.

Gray is also mentioned in *Break of Noon*. Ysé tells Mesa that she has "gray eyes" (p. 61). She also speaks of "gray fish" (p. 38). Gray is a halfway color, a mediating tonality between black and white. It is the color of cinders, pain, semimourning for Hebrews and Christians, and of the spirit, of nebulous, enigmatic, and unclear regions. *Griser,* the slang word for "tipsy" in French, comes from *gris* ("gray"), thus reinforcing the connection between the color and an irrational condition, the diminution of gray matter in the brain. Under such circumstances, instinct is allowed to dominate. Before Mesa met Ysé, his world was bleak and clouded. He was unable to see clearly into his own soul; his pride and egotism blinded him. He lived only in a remote and undefined region: "I have left humanity" (p. 67). Ysé extracted him from these leadened realms and forced him through the life process. She compelled him to experience the alchemical transformatory operations which would bring both turmoil and ecstasy, and eventually the hoped-for equilibrium.

Black is also included in Claudel's palette. Ysé wears a "black dress" which Amalric finds suits her well (p. 52). When Ysé wonders how Amalric recognized her after ten years, he says: "The same blackness suddenly appeared in the air" (p. 41). For the alchemist, black represented a condition of *nigredo:* the abyss, the *prima materia,* the *putrefactio* condition. Black is also the color of sublime beauty, as in the Song of Songs—the Shulamite or the beloved is black. Black is also death, Ysé informs Mesa. Love is an "operation to be undergone," in which ether will be used to bring about a loss of consciousness, a moment of exquisite passivity, a "death" (p. 59). During an instance of such nonbeing and nonfeeling, Adam and Eve conceived their firstborn. Mesa lets himself be cradled by Ysé, the black, the Great Mother, the archetypal figure. She calls herself "A mother of women and men!" (p. 60). Within her being, as in black, exists a synthesis of all colors. "All beings exist in me!" she declares. "You must yield. You must die" (p. 59).

Ysé, the catalyst, will pave the way for Mesa's death and transfiguration. Why, he asks, had she been placed in his path? Why must she "disturb" his "peace of mind"? Serenity, not battle, is what his soul seeks. But if metals are to be purified, the alchemist reasoned, they must be tormented, tortured, reduced to powder, and then reblended. Fire causes fusion. Mesa knows, however, that he will never be able to give himself completely to Ysé; he will never be one during his earthly/leaden form. "There is no way that I can give you my soul, Ysé" (p. 70). Entrenched in the world of the spirit, he does not know how to cope with the emotions which swell within him. A man seeking moderation and measure, Mesa, when aroused by Ysé, reacts like the anchorite enticed by the courtesan Thaïs.

There is a side to Mesa which longs for earthly love despite all of his statements concerning his spirituality. "I long for love: O the joy of being fully loved!" (p. 73). When he is possessed by Ysé, his world begins to fall apart. His previously fixed desire to sacrifice his earthly existence to God has become weak. He compares himself to "a broken egg" (p. 74). The analogy is well founded, since, according to Egyptian, Tibetan, Hindu, Chinese, Japanese, and Greek beliefs, the world was born from an egg. Within the egg-shell, the alchemist stated, existed all vital elements. Indeed, the alchemists' crucibles were frequently egg-shaped; the alchemists placed them on cinders or sand on top of the athanors, which they then heated on a slow fire. So in *Break of Noon*, the sea waters were transformed into "a reverberating oven" and then set aflame, paving the way for the evolution of the protagonists. Mesa's "hard" exterior is broken into components, allowing nutrients to flow inward and dormant contents to leave the protective, imprisoning sphere.

Ysé poses a terrible conflict for Mesa. She has come between him and God. His guilt does not allow him to look her in the face. As their journey continues, however, she pitilessly forces him to meet her eyes. Mesa looks away. He refuses to share his pain, nor will he open his heart to her. "This, at least belongs to me" (p. 81), he tells her. The solitude and loneliness was flowing outward, passing over his former unbending metallic covering. "It is hard to keep one's heart for oneself," he tells Ysé. "It is hard not to be loved. It is hard to be alone. It is hard to wait. And to endure, and to wait, and to always wait" (p. 80). No longer intractable, his ductile sensations flow forth. Robert Hook, the seventeenth-century physicist, wrote that when certain particles are heated and then exposed to air, they "dissolve" whatever is combustible. John Mayow, the seventeenth-century physiologist and chemist, stated in his *Tractatus Quinque Medico-Physici* that within air there existed a "vital, igneous and highly fermentative spirit."

With regard then to the aerial part of nitrous spirit, we maintain that it is nothing else than the igneo-aerial particles which are quite necessary for the production of any flame. Wherefore let me henceforth call the fiery particles which occur also in the air, nitro-aerial particles or nitro-aerial spirit. . . . As regards the sulphurous particles which are also indispensable for the production of fire, the necessity for them seems to arise merely from this, that they are naturally fit to throw nitro-aerial particles in a state of rapid and fiery commotion. Nor should it be overlooked that antimony, calcined by the solar rays, is considerably increased in weight as had been ascertained by experience.[25]

Air, water, sun, and earth will combine in act 2 to bring about the flaring ferment; producing jarring mixtures which would abrade relationships, dismember attitudes, and shear principles.

Act 2: Air/Earth Ceremony—Lead Putrefies

At the beginning of act 2, the curtain opens on a cemetery in Hong Kong. It is shaped in the form of an omega. The sun has lost its glow; the heavens have darkened. The April monsoon season is about to erupt. The leaden day and the omega-shaped cemetery are the perfect backdrops for the dismemberment ritual which is to follow. *Nigredo* ushers in *putrefactio*. As John 12:14 states most clearly: "Except a corn of wheat fall into the ground and die it abideth alone; but if it die it bringeth forth much fruit. He that loveth his life shall lose it and he that hateth his life in the world shall keep it unto life eternal." Everything must experience death and decay before it can be reborn, revitalized, and reworked into new surroundings.

The omega also represents a stage of *renovatio*. The twenty-fourth and final letter of the Greek alphabet, it corresponds to the beginning and end of a life cycle. The sixteenth-century alchemist

Basilius Valentinus wrote: "O Beginning of the first Beginning, consider the end. O End of the Last End, see to the Beginning."[26] The arms of the omega envelop and imprison as well as protect. The outcome is ominous either way.

The leaden atmosphere ushers in feelings of death, decay, and darkness. The negative atmosphere is further accentuated when Mesa labels the cemetery "A rotting place for heretics" (p. 106). Dead metal such as lead may be revivified, the alchemist reasoned, only after it had passed through the "grave" experience. Nicholas Flamel (1330–1417) in his *Auslegung* wrote: "A corruption [destruction] and putrefaction must take place before the renewal in a better form."[27] Such a transformation could be effected since lead was considered a feminine substance: the Egyptians believed all metals could emerge from lead, given the proper circumstances and time. They even called lead "the mother of metals." In the Middle Ages, the alchemists thought that lead, "in spite of its softness and ugly form, acts upon the diamond, breaking and wearing it off, just as the gnat has power over the elephant."[28] In that lead was equated with the planet Saturn, the Great Divider, the god who devoured his offspring in order to assure the continuation of his reign, time was of the essence for the alchemical operation.

Mesa "trembles" in the cemetery atmosphere to such an extent that he is overcome with "nausea" (p. 107). He looks about and says: "What a shadow on the earth! My footsteps cry. It seems to me that I am speaking in a cavern" (p. 109). Shadows and cavernous regions reflect his inner climate. The cavern, which has been equated with a womb, athanor, and alembic, represents the realm of the unconscious, where unknown forms roam about and archetypal figures rumble. Plato's cave represented an area of imprisonment, where darkness gave birth to light and possibilities could develop into positive characteristics. Yin prevails in these inner regions. Only under cave conditions can the inner world become known. As Basilius Valentinus explained, such hidden regions correspond to the alchemist's abbreviations V.I.T.R.I.O.L. ("Visita interiora terrae; rectificando invenies occultum lapidem"). Darkness or *putrefactio* had to be known before illumination could occur.[29]

De Ciz, the "watered down" husband whose furtive, fluid, and unstable nature has to take on consistency or break up completely, decides to accept Mesa's offer to send him a dangerous but potentially very lucrative mission into the heart of China. He leaves

Hong Kong despite Ysé's pleas to remain or at least to take her with him. She needs him, she confesses. She fears for her own and her children's future. "I know it, there are terrible things in store for me. I am afraid of this land which is foreign to me" (p. 115). Twice she asks him to take her with him; twice he refuses.

Mesa, corporeal sulfur, now reaches the height of his power. His energy radiates. When he meets Ysé in front of the cemetery, neither looks at the other, but suddenly Ysé raises her head and opens her arms to him. He embraces her, sobbing. "It's all over," he cries. The gray condition had encouraged light, lucidity, and rationality to vanish. Drunk with euphoria, Mesa yields to his impulses and experiences the ecstasy which comes with abandon. "O Ysé, don't let me return" (p. 133). In this sequence Claudel has created an aesthetic of unconsciousness: a sense of absence overwhelms the protagonist. What is uttered is no longer as important as what remains unsaid, unmanifest; emotion prevails rather than thought; feeling instead of the spoken word.

Mesa directs the emotions he previously devoted to the celestial spheres toward the Eternal Feminine. "I am like a starving being unable to contain his tears at the sight of food!" (p. 134). The once hard and unbending Mesa has grown malleable and tractable. "I shuddered when I recognized you, and my entire soul has yielded!" (p. 138). Ysé is as "beautiful as a young Apollo!" (p. 141), he says, as resplendent in the darkness of the day as she was in its radiance. She is "straight as a column," and as "clear as the rising sun"; her hair is comparable to strands of "gold" (p. 142). Although the instrument of perdition, the vehicle through which Mesa is to sin, Ysé is alone the means of redemption. To compare her with gold, therefore, the purest of the elements, to the rose, the medieval symbol of the Virgin Mary, to the "three," which represents the marriage between Sol and Luna, to dawn, the beginning of life, and to the "flowering acacia branch," signifying *renovatio,* not only reflects the scope of her powers, but is also an animist's way of deifying her. Ysé becomes sacred in this scene. Each of the epithets Mesa uses to describe her was also used by the alchemist, painter, architect, and mystic to reflect a stage in his work. The analogy Mesa makes between Ysé and the Bird of Paradise is of singular interest. In the *Bardo-Thödol,* this bird represents the throne of Buddha; for the Christian it stands for immortality. Its tail is the sky constellated with stars—an incorruptible soul; its hundred eyes correspond to the all-seeing Catholic church.[30] It is a premonitory image of the very much flesh-and-blood Ysé who will believe in celestial values later on.

The bridal chamber is the cemetery. It is here that sulfur and mercury will be blended; two archetypal figures will be joined and tinctures will operate. As Basilius Valentinus wrote: "For one body takes possession of the other; even if it be unlike to it, nevertheless, through the strength and potency added to it, it is compelled to be assimilated to the same, since like derives origin from like."[31]

Mesa takes possession of Ysé. The sin has been committed. Two principles are welded together: sensuality and eroticism take over. Time is abolished and the external world repudiated and made void. Mesa and Ysé bathe in universal forces; their voices acquire amplitude and depth. Onomatopoeias, metaphors, analogies, repetitions, and alliterations take on the value of objects which jar, bruise, abrade, and corrode, as do chemicals biting their way through the elements. Beauty is injured, patinas destroyed, the whole cut asunder.

Ysé understands the chemistry of their union, the goal of their lust, and the stakes for which they are playing. "But what we want is not to create, but to destroy," says Ysé. "Detestable are these clothes of flesh. . . . It is not happiness I bring you, but death, and mine with it" (p. 145). Maceration and laceration occur as their two bodies unite. Mesa's emotions are expressed in eidetic imagery: he compares "the great black flame of the soul which burns" to a "devoured city." Fire illuminates anew as elements battle each other: as chaos, combustibility, energy destroy the smooth running relationships, it kills to revivify.

Mesa and Ysé's carnal love alchemically replicates the mystical conjunction, the marriage between form and matter, sulfur and mercury, the secret fire of the sages and of the philosophers, the elemental fire. Soon after the heating process has begun, Paracelsus wrote, "in the Philosophic Egg [alembic], [the blend] becomes with wonderful appearance, blacker than the crow; afterwards, in a succession of time whiter than the swan; and at last passing through a yellow colour, it turns out more red than blood."[32]

Ysé's joy ushers in feelings of shame which are experienced like flaring sparks, knives, and needles. Rapture triturates, and her hatred for her husband mounts. She no longer knows de Ciz, she claims. Although colors are few in act 2 by comparison with act

1, they are nevertheless still potent and flammable, although hazed and muted as well. Beneath the blackness of the *nigredo* condition, the grayness of the colorless realm, unfathomable depths are reached: nonverbal dimensions contain the fulfilled experience of earthly ecstasy.

The mysterious alchemical work has been operating. Mesa has become alienated from God. He has turned toward the world and been enveloped in Ysé's all-consuming presence. He lives and breathes only her. The loss of his paradisiacal state has advanced his wholeness; it has led him to become a man of the flesh, thus continuing the congenital schism which is his lot.

Act 3: *Nox Profunda*—The Lunar Phase

The curtains open on act 3 to reveal a large room in a European-style house in a port town in southern China. Mesa's inability to give himself wholeheartedly to Ysé led her to leave him a year before the events now taking place. "I did not possess him, there was something strange about him. Impossible" (p. 183). She did not answer his letters. Amalric is now Ysé's lover and is caring for the child born to her and Mesa, but their happiness seems short-lived because of the insurrection taking place in China. Ysé and Amalric are to be killed along with the other Europeans in the town. Rather than accept capture and possible torture, however, Amalric has set up a time bomb to destroy the house. They prefer to be masters of their destiny. Amalric faces his end as he has his life, with equanimity. Ysé's response is more complex. Her thoughts focus on her past sins—her infidelities to her husband, her abandonment of her children, and her betrayal of Mesa. Death, she feels, will wash away her torment. She greets it, not with fright, but with a kind of relief. Yet she also feels trapped and anguished.

Amalric asks Ysé to make some tea. Tea has a very special significance for the Chinese. Imbibing it corresponds to a communion, an offering, an oriental agape. Alchemically, it represents a transformation rite: the somewhat bitter and uncouth leaves change color, form, and consistency when distilled and purified in the boiling water. For the Taoist and Buddhist, the tea-drinking ceremony implies the overcoming of antagonism in the earthly spheres and the emergence of a state of serenity, sobriety, and detachment. Not an escape from life, the tea ritual ushers in the creation of a more contemplative existence. The cosmic principle of sun/ocean in act 1 has now been reduced to a less potent and glowing fire; the expanse of water has also been diminished. Both are contained in the kettle: the water percolates over the flickering gas flame. Limitations, this image implies, have been imposed upon Ysé and Amalric. The world is no longer young; life is no longer ahead of them; the end is approaching.

As Ysé stands near the stove, she begins to cry, her tears repeating the image of the boiling tea on a still smaller scale. Only one cup of tea is left, and she gives it to Amalric. He can also have the little milk which remains, an intimation that the child will die. By giving the tea to Amalric, Ysé is symbolically nourishing those qualities that he represents: courage, straightforwardness, and realism. Ysé's course is different. "I hunger and thirst for death," she says (p. 176).

Ysé walks toward the mirror and peers into it. She smooths down her white woolen bathrobe and loosens her long blond hair. Flowing hair in medieval paintings symbolized penitence, a state Ysé will soon be experiencing. Amalric leaves the room. Ysé hears a noise in the stairs. The door opens. A shadow becomes visible. Mesa enters. Ysé remains motionless and speechless. He questions her. Why hadn't she answered his letters? He cannot live without her, he tells Ysé. Mesa grows irate because Ysé does not respond. He accuses her of having an "iron" heart—a metallic personality—of being unbending, unyielding, inflexible, and brittle. Ysé has branded him, fettered him. He informs her of her husband's death and that they are now free to love each other "without secret and without remorse" (p. 188). He begs her to leave with him. He will save her from death and take her children with them. Mesa informs her that he has a pass for two people which will allow them through Chinese lines. Still Ysé remains silent.

Mesa reacts violently to her ironlike exterior. His attitude ignites as does the alchemist's earthly sulfur. The air is heavy with dank fumes and smoke. He vilifies her in a passage revealing the chaos within.

> Bitch: tell me what went through your mind the first time
> You gave yourself, after having decided to do so, to
>   that stray dog,
> With another man's fruit in your body, and when the
>   first signs of my child's life

Mingled with the frenzy of a mother tingling with
   the excitement of a double adultery?
I gave you my soul and I communicated my life to
   you,
You prostituted these; and what thoughts went
   through your mind during those heavy days when my
   child was ripening in you,
And you brought it to this man, and you slept in his
   arms while my son's limbs were filling you?

(P. 191)

Mesa approaches the stonelike Ysé. He is carrying a "sepulchral"
lamp; the dark flames are reflected in Ysé's eyes and in the full-
length mirror on the side of the stage. Mesa blows out the flame
and says: "Goodbye Ysé, you never really knew me! This great
treasure that I carry within me, You could not uproot it" (p. 192).

Amalric enters. He strikes a match which lights up the room.
The men look at each other. Friction has reached incandescent
force. They are two sulfuric substances brought together. Mesa
declares his intention of taking both mother and child with him,
but Amalric will not give them up. He asks Ysé to choose between
dying with him or living elsewhere with Mesa and the child. Mesa,
who cannot stand the tension, draws a weapon from his pocket.
Amalric throws himself on him. In the mirror, Ysé watches the
struggle, an outer manifestation of an inner conflict. Muted moon
rays, replacing the burning sun tones, now penetrate the room and
encircle the struggling men.

The fight has ended. Amalric has thrown Mesa to the ground,
where he lies lifeless, broken in body and soul. His right shoulder
has been dislocated, his leg "demolished." The dismemberment ritual has begun on the physical plane with the displacement of his
limbs, which symbolizes a break with the manifest world. Mesa
will no longer be able to order or orient himself in the existential
sphere. Relationships will be severed. Amalric carries him to the
couch and removes the pass from Mesa's pocket. Ysé goes to the
next room to get the infant, remains for a time, and then returns
alone. The child is dead. Amalric extinguishes the lamp. As they
leave the room, Ysé begins laughing hysterically.

In keeping with the practice of French dramatists since the
seventeenth century of using a monologue to reveal the protagonist's inner conflict, Claude wrote "The Song of Mesa" as part of

act 3. It is also a monologue, but inspired by the biblical poetic dialogue between two lovers, the Song of Songs. Mystics consider the Song of Songs to be an allegorical representation of the relationship between God the bridegroom and Israel the bride, or of the human soul in union with the divine beloved, while Christian exegetes look upon it as the blissful encounter between Jesus the royal bridegroom and his bride the church.

Mesa's Song begins with a salute to the heavens above, the constellations, and the queen of heaven (that is, the Virgin Mary)—images which are reminiscent of Revelation 12:1: "And there appeared a great wonder in heaven; a woman clothed with the sun, and the moon under her feet, and upon her head a crown of twelve stars." Like astral influences, which alchemists believed activated the generation and growth of metals and souls, so Mesa's love for the terrestrial woman Ysé has evolved from its existential and impure condition to love for the collective image, the cosmic figure of the Virgin Mary. Rather than the iron creature of flesh and blood, Mesa now communes with the "Mother of Mothers," the resplendent moon virgin. Moon rays flood the stage in a kind of epiphany, enveloping the entire atmosphere in the glow of a religious mystery. The tea ceremony was a prelude to the events now taking place—the sublimation, decantation, and distillation of emotions.

The light filtering from heaven in variegated forms and hues transforms the dismal room into an awesome and majestic cathedral. An entire universe becomes visible from the room. Stars and planets shine; their light corresponds to illumination fighting darkness in the soul; it is spirit in conflict with matter, fragmentation versus unity. Mesa's Song, with its mysterious rhythmic and tonal patterns, takes on the power of a chant.

> And from left to right, all over, I see a forest of
>   torchlights surrounding me!
> Not illuminated wax, but powerful heavenly bodies, similar
>   to those great flamboyant virgins.
>
> (P. 203)

The entire universe responds to his offerings, as though the celestial spheres inhabited by the patriarchs, the bishops, and the entire clergy—all constellated in the stars—were reaching out to each other and to the penitent in a sublime cosmic tone poem.

Mesa asks for the remission of his sins and prays for his sanctification as the biblical David had done: "Have mercy upon me, O God,
according to thy loving kindness; according unto the multitude of
thy tender mercies blot out my transgressions" (Ps. 51).

Mesa has grown detached from terrestrial longings, from the
mortal Ysé. He is ready for the highest form of drama: the sacrifice.
No longer made of combustible sulfur, Mesa has been transformed
into the alchemist's incombustible sulfur, the antinatural element—the purest aspect of human and chemical evolution. The
Spirit has intervened. In this condition the human soul vibrates and
contemplates. *Pneuma*, the breath of divinity, has taken hold.
Mesa's heart and mind, exiled from paradise by God and then
geared to human needs, had been pulverized and mutilated by the
forces with which they collided, corroded by the powers of the metals. Like Christ, Mesa, who has known physical dismemberment
and spiritual flagellation, now longs for death. Only then will his
soul be allowed to leave what he calls his "detestable carcass"
(p. 207).

The room grows whiter; the *albedo* condition has cleansed the
darkness. Similar to the alchemist's quicksilver when sublimated,
which is described by Bernardus Trevisanus in *The Forgotten Word*
as clothed in "so pure a white, that it looked like the snow on top of
a very high mountain," so the room and all within view is ready for
sanctification.[33]

Ysé returns and walks through the room as if in a hypnotic
trance. Like an automaton or a cloud, she crosses in front of the
mirror. The whiteness of her gown and the blondness of her hair,
accentuated by the reflection of the moon rays in the mirror, concretize the sanctity of the preceding moments. Ysé goes to the room
where the dead infant lies and cries strangely. Mesa calls to her.
She returns and again passes in front of the spotless mirror in
search of something; then she pauses, inundated by the moon, as
Artemis, Isis, and the Virgin Mary had when experiencing moments of similar sublimity. Ysé's image is caught in the occult
mirror; it is flooded by the moon's spiritual essence, the alchemist's
moon dew. The soul has been purified. It has suffered enough.

To this point in the play, Ysé was a carnal female principle. As
she walks toward Mesa and sits at his feet, however, he experiences her presence as a soul force, an anima. Their love has now
been sublimed and bathes in pure visual essences. "Full of glory

and light, creatures of God," Ysé says, "I see that you did love me,
And you have been granted me, and I am with you in ineffable
tranquility" (p. 213). Similar to Goethe's Marguerite, whose past
came to her in a series of visions prior to her redemption, so Ysé
relives her sins. It was earthly love that had compelled her to act
in such a despicable manner, and which had bound, tortured, and
imprisoned her. No longer the sun-drenched Ysé of that August
day at noon, she has become the Ysé of midnight. "This is the
Break of Noon," she intones. "And I am here, ready to be liberated"
(p. 233). The cycle has been completed. The number twelve, representing the New Jerusalem in Revelation, has become actualized
for her. The Great Work has been completed. "All veils have been
dissipated," and the flesh now becomes spirit. The alchemical experiment is similarly concluded:

All flesh, born of the earth, will be destroyed and given to the earth again,
just as it has already been earth. Then the earthly salt will bring forth a
new birth by means of the breath of heavenly life. For wherever earth is
absent at the beginning, there can be no rebirth in our work. For the earth
in the balm of nature and the salt of those who seek knowledge of all
things.[34]

Dying to the world is a necessity, believes the alchemist, if the
birth of inner consciousness is to be realized. No longer expended
in fruitless outward activity, energy has been turned inward and
used to nourish the seed, the creative and spiritualized part of
man. Although both protagonists are doomed to die, it is Ysé who
emerges in her Golden Essence. Mesa's sacrifice was not authentic
and therefore did not lead to redemption. He returned to Ysé to
take her and his child away with him. After his struggle with
Amalric he was physically unable to leave; the pass had been
taken from him, and he could not escape. Ysé, on the other hand,
chose to return. Her sacrifice was profound and complete; it earned
her transfiguration and redeemed her from the weightiness of her
leaden condition.

4

The Only Jealousy of Emer: Recycling the Elements

W. B. Yeats published *The Only Jealousy of Emer* in 1919. Based on an ancient Celtic myth, it is a brief one-act play in which the characters are put through two alchemical operations. They begin as *prima materia*, in the preformal state of oneness, and move to *separatio* and *coagulatio*. The "subtle separation" which takes place within their beings is experienced via the water and fire rituals. During these transformative procedures, matter (personalities or events) is liquefied or made malleable through the alchemist's heating process. Old attitudes are thus separated, objectified, and explicated, finally to surface in a new manner. With their expanded understanding, new insights and potentials develop in the characters and then, in alchemical parlance, fixate.

A member from 1890 to 1903 of the English Rosicrucian Order of the Golden Dawn, Yeats claimed to have communicated during that time with the *Anima Mundi* or the Other World through certain psychic experiences. "The mystical life," he wrote, "is the center of all that I do and all that I think, and all that I write."[1] However, while he believed strongly in experiencing what he termed "Unity of Being" through altered states of consciousness that brought him momentary relief from divisiveness, he did not ignore the positive side of conflict. He considered discord to be an important factor in psychological and aesthetic evolution. Opposition and contradiction in the life process, though creating violent antitheses, strengthens character and firms up the artistic endeavor. The tension of conflict increases energy, engenders passion, and activates growth. It breaks up hardened and stereotyped attitudes and in so doing prepares the individual to accept new ideas and create fresh yields. Yeats was a partisan of Heraclitean thought. According to doxographic documents, Heraclitus wrote:

War is the father of all and the king of all, and some he has made gods and some men, some bound and some free. . . . The immortals are mortal, the mortals are immortal, each living in the other's death and dying in the other's life.[2]

The opposing forces of life and death, spiritual and physical, abstract and concrete, eternal and ephemeral are locked in an everlasting struggle.

The alchemist's belief in monism, cosmic unity, appealed strongly to Yeats. A man haunted throughout his life by conflict and duality, he sought to heal the breach corroding his existence by transcending the workaday world or the state of human consciousness, which he believed was composed of "a series of antinomies."[3] The *prima materia* is devoid of conflict. Only in the phenomenological world does it take on many forms, combining and recombining in a state of perpetual becoming. Nothing ends; nothing is destroyed; all is transformed in an eternal death-birth mystery. The goals of the Yeatsian hero and of the alchemist are similar. Each seeks to transcend the human condition—the differentiated, phenomenological world—by shattering the existing outlook or arrangement of chemicals. Each then examines and evaluates entities from which new blendings emerge, bringing fresh behavior patterns or alloys into existence and, with them, a *renovatio*.

Yeats wanted to create an esoteric theatre which would appeal only to a few. "I want, not a theatre, but the theatre's antiself. . . . an unpopular theatre," he wrote in *Plays and Controversies* (1923). He knew that his ritualistic and hermetic theatre, like the mysteries of old, could be experienced only by a minority and not by the masses. Thus he felt free to rid his stage language of rococo embellishments and create an atmosphere of metaphysical oneness by uniting word, dance, music, mood, and gesture. In order to suggest a sense of awe in the staging, characters and events were kept "an appropriate distance" through stylized decor, costume, gesture, and mask. Yeat's hieratic figures, stripped of specific traits and attributes, were endowed with collective natures which combined divine and earthly spheres.[4] In "The Tragic Theatre" (1911), Yeats wrote:

If the real world is not altogether rejected, it is but touched here and there, and into the places we have left empty we summon rhythm, balance pattern, images that remind us of vast passions, the vagueness of past times, all the chimeras that haunt the edge of trance; and if we are painters, we shall express personal emotion through ideal form, a symbolism handled by generations, a mask from whose eyes the disembodied looks, a style that remembers many masters that it may escape contemporary suggestion; or we shall leave out some element of reality as in Byzantine painting, where there is no mass, nothing in relief; and so it is that in the supreme moment of tragic art there comes upon that strange sensation as though the hair of one's head stood up.[5]

Cuchulain

The Goidelic mythical hero Cuchulain was eternalized in *The Tain*, an Irish epic dating from the seventh or eighth century A.D. After numerous battles and as many loves, Cuchulain loses a powerful struggle with the waves. His wife, Emer, brings his lifeless body to a fisherman's cabin. Yeats's play opens as Emer is caring for her husband. She calls for Eithne Inguba, Cuchulain's mistress, who is standing at the door of the cabin, and asks her for help.

Although Yeats's hero is sophisticated—a highly personal and poetic individual—he bears many of the ancient Goidelic hero's characteristics. The mythical figure, Yeats's Cuchulain is a man of instinct and prone to blind rages. He feels his way into events and situations. He acts and does not think. Unlike the original Cuchulain, however, Yeats's protagonist does not possess an anthropoid psyche. He is a sensitive and suffering hero whose ways and words are marked with finesse. He is a man who, while needing to be loved for his personal well-being, also uses his passion for creative purposes: to transform feeling into poetry.

According to Goidelic heliolatry, the original Cuchulain's name was Sétanta. His birth was quasi-miraculous. He was said to have been born three times. His mother Dechtirde, an Irish princess, swallowed the god Lugh in the form of a winged insect.[6] This fly remains in its nymphal state for two years, only emerging in its adult state for one day in order to mate and die. Cuchulain seems to

mirror the primitive and adolescent condition of the winged creature. It has also been said that Cuchulain could swim like a trout
and was endowed with the strength of a bull as soon as he was born.
Cuchulain's foster parents, Sencha, Fergus, and Cathbad, taught
him wisdom, warfare, and magic. His exploits were many and included the killing of the smith Culann's watchdog, a heroic feat,
after which he was called "the Hound of Culann." He was then given
the honor of guarding the kingdom of Ulster.

Hero figures throughout history have been marked with certain unusual physical traits. Cuchulain is no exception. In *The
Tain*, he is described as having seven pupils in each eye, seven
toes, and seven fingers—comparable, perhaps, to the seven alchemical operations. His cheeks were colored yellow, blue, green,
and red; each of these colors has an emotional and alchemical
value. Three colors were visible in his hair: a dark color close to
the roots, red in the middle, and a lighter red at the tip of each
strand. In battle a "spot of blood or spark of fire" was visible on
each hair. From his mouth "spurted fire," and from the top of his
head "a jet of black blood."[7]

The sensitive, suffering, and disenchanted Cuchulain of *The
Only Jealousy of Emer*, patterned after Yeats's own personality,
experiences his battle in "The Labyrinth of the Mind," in those
lunar spheres where spirit and matter blend, where the ancient
druid and the creative artist communicate, and not in the environs
of Ulster.[8] Alchemically, the original Cuchulain may be associated
with the element air, since his mother was inseminated by a
winged insect. Because this fly appears in Ireland during the
month of March, one may assume that a relationship exists between Cuchulain's birth date and the planet Mars and its corresponding metal, iron. Cuchulain's struggle with the waves (an alchemical recycling of the elements), compels him to experience a
regressus ad uterum, thus paving the way for the *separatio* and
coagulatio processes.

Cuchulain's association with air indicates that he possessed
sublimating characteristics which usually accompany "air born" or
winged creatures. Basilius Valentinus expressed the alchemist's
understanding of air:

It is the Principle to work Metals being made a spiritual Essence, which is
a meer Air, and flyeth to and fro without Wings, and is a moving Wind,
which after its expulsion out of its habitation by *Vulcan* [fire], is driven

into its *Chaos*, into which it entereth again . . . . by this Spirit of Mercury all Metals may be, if need requireth, dissolved, opened, and without any corrosive reduced or resolved into their first Matter. This Spirit reneweth both Men and Beast, like the Eagle! consumeth whatsoever is bad, and produceth a great Age to a long life.[9]

According to other alchemists, air represents breath and is an intermediary between heaven and earth; it combines spirituality and fertility. Claude de Saint-Martin believed it to be a sensible manifestation of the invisible world, a vibrating and communicating principle.

Air may also be looked upon as an eternal present, a space/time continuum, or as a transpersonal force in the shape of a mythical hero. Because it is a mysterious force, air represents a world *in potentia*—that Other World or *Anima Mundi*—as does Yeats's Cuchulain. As the alchemist Robert Boyle wrote in *Suspicions about the Hidden Realities of the Air* (1674):

I have often suspected that there may be in the air some yet more latent qualities or powers different enough from all these [from gravity, elasticity, light, refraction] and principally due to the substantial parts of ingredients, whereof it consists. . . . For this is not as many imagine a simple and elementary body, but a confused aggregate of effluviums from such differing bodies that though they all agree in constituting, by their minuteness and various notions, one great mass of fluid matter, yet there is scarce a more heterogenous body in the world.[10]

Since the Celts considered air creatures to be messengers of the gods and thus representatives of superior types of beings, so Cuchulain, the Goidelic hero, was endowed with great strength and energy. Yeats's creature was imbued with poetic insight.

The mythical Cuchulain's association with the fiery red planet Mars is another indication of his energetic, violent, and ardent temperament. Always tense and dissatisfied, he became disruptive and unpredictable as time passed. Cuchulain's desires and wants were always potent. Mars's redness found an emotional equivalent in Cuchulain's flammable traits: his petulant, fickle, childlike choleric nature. As the god of war, Mars, was known for his irascible, cruel, and inflexible nature. The Yeatsian hero possesses these qualities in a mitigated form, reflecting the psychological and aesthetic outlook of a man at odds with himself and with the creative process.

According to astrologers, iron belongs to the domain of Mars. A
metal used by the Egyptians and Babylonians as early as 2500
B.C., its characteristics are solidity and, interestingly enough, per-
ishability, since iron rusts. When attributed to the human sphere,
iron may be said to reflect pugnacity, might, and virility. Vincent
de Beauvais wrote in the thirteenth century: "Iron belongs to the
domain of Mars, its nature is warm and dry, of sour taste and of
vehement strength expelling and resisting fire. It is liquefied by
four things, namely arsenic, lead, magnesium and markasite."[11]
Because iron was used in plowing and cultivating the soil, it was
considered an earthly metal, and vulgar in the sense of being common; it was also associated with blood since instruments of war
were made from it. The druids, therefore, were not permitted to use
iron when cutting their sacred mistletoe; only sickles of gold were
allowed.

The variety of reds in the mythical Cuchulain's hair was an
accurate measure of his emotional state. In this *rubedo* condition,
according to the alchemists' color chart, Cuchulain would be capable of liquefying solids and melting iron. He thus becomes a mediating principle between forms as well as a symbol of regeneration
and action. Fire purifies, spiritualizes, and illuminates. It also destroys, consumes, engulfs, and overpowers. In *The Tain*, Cuchulain
is described as being powerful, violent, and passionate during a
battle: he is inflamed. After he was knighted he became a threat to
the community; once his fury was so great that a way to cool him
had to be found. A vat of cold water was thrown on him at the
height of one of his rages. "In the second vat the water escaped [by
boiling over]; in the third, the water was still hotter." By this time
his fury died down. The fire was subdued by the water. In the third
magical vat of water he was restored "to his natural form and
features."[12]

Since Cuchulain's flame for conquest and domination had
turned into blind violence, thereby creating an unbalanced situation within his psyche, the cold water was transformed into steam.
In this form, the solid liquid became gaseous; the combustible energy was sublimated. Alchemically, it could be said that Cuchulain
had transcended the norm, that he had opted for a superhuman
rather than a human state. The spirit of fire contains gold, and
when Cuchulian was in harmony with himself and acted in consort
with his people and community, his gold scintillae came to the fore.

That was his condition when he became the protector of Ulster, but not when Yeats eternalized him in *The Only Jealousy of Emer*. The elements of earth, water, air, and fire were not in harmony; his kinetic energy did not work positively; he was no hero, but rather was victimized by his own sensuality and frenetic drive. He had lost the freshness of inspiration and the joy of love.

A moon appeared on Cuchulain's forehead, indicating the duality of his nature. As a masculine solar hero, he symbolized strength, courage, bravery, and spirituality. His lunar female side was the powerful and unconscious force within him. This dual personality likened him to Achilles, who was also given to erratic and highly volatile behavior.

Yeats tells us in the beginning of *The Only Jealousy of Emer* that Cuchulain struggled with the "waves" and that "he fought the deathless sea" which then "washed his senseless image up" and placed it at the door of the fisherman's cabin in a state "beyond hearing or seeing" (p. 116). Throughout the play, reference is made to water in a variety of forms: stormy, troubled, dark, foamy, white. In accordance with Archimedes's principle, which Yeats mentions in the opening lines of his drama, Cuchulain was raised above the waters and brought back to land.

Water, an indifferent mass representing infinite possibilities and the unformed germ of all matter, is that force in nature which paves the way for Cuchulain's rebirth. According to Plato, water is the most powerful solvent: it can liquefy stone.

[Water] when it is compacted, we see [as we imagine] becoming earth and stones, and this same thing, when it is dissolved and dispersed, becoming wind and air; air becoming fire by being inflamed; and, by a reverse process, fire, when condensed and extinguished, returning once more to the form of air, and air coming together again and condensing as mist and cloud; and from these, as they are yet more closely compacted, flowing water; and from water once more earth and stones: and thus, as it appears, they transmit in a cycle the process of passing into one another.[13]

Like Plato, Paracelsus considered water to be a universal solvent which enabled liquefaction or a reshuffing of views to take place. Only through dissolution or a fusion of elements could the later process of filtration, distillation, and decantation occur.[14] Solids—whether metals or elements—can be dissolved by water. In psychological terms, personal and limited views may be fused into impersonal and larger frames of reference. When Cuchulain's masculine ways are immersed in the maternal waters of the unconscious (or the feminine components of the psyche), he acquires new perspectives with their reemergence. A blending of antithetical ways prepares him for a *coniunctio*. Jagged edges are rounded out; harsh corners are smoothed.

Before his immersion in the waves, Yeats's Cuchulain was one-dimensional. His attitudes and ways had become arid and ossified. He had to be dissolved in order to regenerate. Such a transformation is dangerous because loss of identity and drowning could result, yet Cuchulain had to expose himself to the water ritual. He had to allow himself to be absorbed by this solvent, inviting danger in order to return to nearly embryonic state. As Arnold of Villanova wrote: "The oftener the Medicine is dissolved, sublimated and coagulated, the more potent it becomes. . . . in each sublimation its projective virtue is multiplied by ten."[15] Only after the dissolution of the original material has taken place can the stagnant ruling authority or idea be altered. Cuchulain had reached a state in his development where his strength, candor, and creative force had ceased to be fruitful. His negative characteristics, cruelty and immorality, predominated. An inner and outer reevaluation of his being had to be undertaken if he were to evolve. His ego had hypertrophied; his arrogance and aggressive ways had become repetitive and unproductive and had to be washed away or cleansed. The *regressus ad uterum* motif into the undifferentiated primal state of oneness could pave the way for the creation of new poetic insights.

After Emer brought Cuchulain's body into the cabin, she placed it in a curtained bed. Yeats refers to the inert Cuchulain as the "Figure of Cuchulain," and he wears a heroic mask. Another Cuchulain is crouching in the corner, unseen by the protagonists. He is referred to as the "Ghost of Cuchulain." He remains in the shadows because he represents the unconscious self, the darkened and blackened being, the alchemist's *umbra solis* ("sun's shadow"). As the representative of the unregenerate aspects of the psyche, the Ghost of Cuchulain must pass through "the valley of the shadow," altering that which is defective and illuminating that which remains shrouded in darkness.

The fisherman's cabin sets the stage for the powerful transformation ritual. Fish live in the interior and subterranean realms of deep waters. They stand for the inner riches and potential forces within the psyche; they are representative of both the formal and the physical universe. They allow mankind to be nourished by them; as psychic beings, they symbolize spiritual fecundity. Christ was called "the fisher of men" since wisdom was extracted from him. Parsifal meets the Grail King as a fisherman.

Emer's fisherman's cabin is a closed and protective area which calls for introspection. It was in just such an inner sanctum that Apuleius was initiated into the rites of Isis or that Faust experienced the Realm of the Mothers. Emer will be forced to sound out her depths, to come to terms with her needs and motivations. It is in this halfway station between life and death, earth and water, that Emer's consciousness will expand.

Emer's conviction that Cuchulain is not dead, but that some cosmic force possesses his body, enables the alchemical process to pursue its course. In very powerful and moving language she tells of Cuchulain's past. She describes his feelings of guilt after having killed his son in a rage.

> And being mad with sorrow, he ran out;
> And after, to his middle in the foam,
> With shield before him and with sword in hand.
> He fought the deathless sea.

> (P. 115)

No one dared disarm Cuchulain or call him back.

> all stood wondering
> In that dumb stupor like cattle in a gale,
> Until at last, as though he had fixed his eyes
> On a new enemy, he waded out
> Until the water had swept over him;
> But the waves washed his senseless image up
> And laid it at this door.

> (P. 116)

In alchemical terms, the Figure of Cuchulain lies in a grave. In this regressive, unconscious state, he experiences the waters of forgetfulness. The undifferentiated ego has become a *massa confusa*. Yeats delineates the chaotic emotions involved in terms of antithetical eidetic images, rhythms, and tonalities. The frail seabird is opposed to the bold and aggressive eagle, and the wind which brings storms is opposed to the gentle breath of air. Verti-

cality adds to the scope and breadth of the emotions involved; the
vision of the bird spells ascension or elevation, while the mole
represents a descent into abysmal depths. A separation of earth
and heaven, higher and lower spheres, coarse and fine, light and
heavy particles or feelings, prepares for the ensuing objectification of feelings and situations, the *separatio*. Nuances of color also
activate the dichtomy implicit in the personalities: the white seabird and the dark furrows, the white color of shell, foam, and
wing are set against the blackness of the storm. Black usually
accompanies sensations of fear and tremulous excitement and
earthiness, caves, and closed, magical domains where the ancient
initiate relived his death/birth mysteries. The color white, or the
alchemist's *albedo* condition, indicates a cold, feminine world.

When Yeats refers to the white "foam of the waves," he indicates abrupt changes in the emotional reactions of his protagonists.
Waves may be looked upon as the realization of sudden disruptive
qualities emerging from the unconscious, inner forces or drives
ready to assault the spirit and overwhelm the rational function.
The "white shell" (p. 115) is reminiscent of an inner, subterranean
world where creativity occurs, as in the case of Aphrodite who was
born from the foam surrounding a shell. "White wing" suggests a
creature inhabiting the higher realms, the sky. Driven by wind or
spirit, he is seemingly disoriented. When a Yeatsian storm arises,
agitation, instability and inconstancy permeate the atmosphere:

> At daybreak after stormy night
> Between two furrows upon the ploughed land:
> A sudden storm, and it was thrown
> Between dark furrows upon the ploughed land.
>
> (P. 113)

A titanic principle is at work—blinding, passionate, and instinctual. *Pneuma*, spirit, begins to predominate. It is God's spirit which
moves about the primordial waters as it had when endowing Adam
with a soul or in sending the Great Flood. For the druids, wind was
an arcane power, a vehicle for magic, an energetic principle, a
manifestation of a hermetic light.

Emer calls to Eithne Inguba. Her position close to the door
indicates the role she plays in the drama. The door represents a
passageway between two states and two worlds: the known and the

unknown, sea and land, heat and cold, wind and calm, life and death. It was Emer, as the earthly and conventional wife, who helped Cuchulain through the early part of his ordeal. It is Eithne Inguba, symbolizing the hetaera type, the sensual and ever-alluring inspirational woman, who will take him through the *separatio*, the next step of the initiation process.

The stage is set. A fire must be lit to dry out the watery masses in the form of the two Cuchulains. Emer lights the hearth, comparable to the alchemist's athanor. Now the secret fire will burn; subterranean forces will start their work. The coals glow. The operation starts: "And throw new logs upon the earth and stir/And half-burnt logs until they break in flame" (p. 117). The alchemical waters recede, and the "dreaming foam" dries out. The *massa confusa* stills as the components separate. Analysis can now begin as anguish, pain, and guilt are expelled in dialogue form, bringing about a *purgatio/purificatio*.

Emer, the earth wife, tells Eithne Enguba to come close to Cuchulain's bed and summon his soul: "Bend over him;/Call out dear secrets till you have touched his heart" (p. 117). Only when the feeling principle is activated can blood again begin to circulate in Curchulain's heart and life's energy be restored. "We're two women struggling with the sea," Emer states (p. 117). To battle death means to transform inert into kinetic energy, to counter *stagnatio* with *circulatio*. Only by means of emotions can the double movement of life, systole and diastole, pave the way for transformation. These feelings affect will and intelligence and become activated in Yeats's drama at the very moment the fire is lit in the hearth. While Emer stirs the living coals, Eithne Inguba kindles the emotional flame. Cuchulain moves. Love has changed the rigid metal into molten mixtures. The transubstantiation begins. Eithne Inguba kisses him. The elements activate the immortal brew—the blood of life, the *aqua permanens*.

Eithne Inguba, however, starts back after her kiss, saying: "I felt some evil thing that dried my heart/When my lips touched it" (p. 118). Something has altered. She hardly recognizes her lover. The heat of passion has dried him out and he has grown remote. She comments on his withered right arm. That it is no longer able to function indicates that Cuchulain's relationship with reality is defective and that his unconscious is in full sway. The right arm usually symbolizes a rapport with the workaday world. It is also aggressive: it grabs things; it holds weapons. Cuchulain is now incapable of such activity. He has become a passive entity.

Eithne Inguba's kiss brought Cuchulain back to life, but not as the great hero previously known to his wife and mistress. He returns as Bricriu, the god of discord, to inhabit the Figure of Cuchulain. As Bricriu, the Figure of Cuchulain sits up. He is no longer wearing the heroic mask, but a "distorted" one. Yeats uses the mask as a metaphor, a theatrical convention further to suggest the divergence between conscious and unconscious attitudes. Eithne Inguba leaves, and Bricriu becomes the catalyst. He is in charge of continuing the alchemical operation. He will arouse conflict and objectify the emotional situation. As Yeats wrote: "We can only become conscious of a thing by comparing it with its opposite. The two real things we have are our natures and the circumstances that surround us. We have in both a violent antithesis."[16]

As the *separatio* process begins, the personalities are reshaped. What had been fluid is dry; what had been dark is enlightened. Bricriu, the messenger of self-knowledge, will be the separating agent and bring the light. The distorted mask he wears represents the pain involved in bringing lucidity and the split engendering illumination. He is a composite of Nietzsche's Superman and the Ugliest Man.[17] A "bridleless horse" brought Bricriu to the fisherman's cabin. As the agent which carries him from the watery depths of the unconscious to the rational sphere of the articulate being, the horse symbolizes the intense energy needed to pave the way for illumination and lucidity. Endowed with the strength to surge forth from the primal depths to the drier spheres of solid matter, Bricriu is the one who will force Emer to choose and thus mold her destiny.

Emer has a dilemma. She must either renounce Cuchulain's love forever or pursue her fruitless attempts to possess him. Another possibility is that she will lose Cuchulain to the death-dealing Fand, a new figure whom Yeats introduces. Emer refuses to sacrifice her earthly love. She claims to live for two things: the memory of her life with Cuchulain and the hope of being his once again. To warn her of the possible outcome of her indecisiveness, Bricriu touches Emer's eyes "to give them sight." That his left hand is the healthy one is significant. The left side is usually equated with the unconscious, the liquid realm; this is no longer the daylight or rational sphere, but the darkened realm of subliminal life. Both worlds will be experienced simultaneously during the play.

The Ghost of Cuchulain, as the unconscious personality, lives in a world inaccessible to mortal beings. Bricriu explains:

> He cannot hear—being shut off, a phantom
> That can neither touch, nor hear, nor see;
> The longing and the cries have drawn him hither.
> He heard no sound, heard no articulate sound;
> They could but banish rest, and make him dream,
> And in that dream, as do all dreaming shades
> Before they are accustomed to their freedom,
> He has taken his familiar form; and yet
> He crouches there not knowing where he is
> Or at whose side he is crouched.
>
> (P. 120)

As a shadow figure, the Ghost of Cuchulain symbolizes the primitive factors in the personality which until this point are in their embryonic state. Untouched by human reason, they live in darkness and operate according to their own logic. The Figure of Cuchulain, with Bricriu as its spokesman, represents the conscious outlook that is needed in the differentiated, mundane world. That Bricriu, as the Figure of Cuchulain, confronts his opposite, the Ghost of Cuchulain, indicates that a *separatio* has been accomplished. An objectification of feelings and needs is coming into being. Previously Emer had never understood Cuchulain's shadowy nature. It had either remained invisible to her or she had repressed any knowledge of it. Now that Bricriu is concretizing it before her, she begins to understand the situation and may learn to cope with it.

Yeats's drama takes on a new dimension as the *separatio* process continues to divide, cut open, and disconnect. Fand enters. She tells the Ghost of Cuchulain, who seems to be suffering from guilt and remorse, that she has come from "the Country-under-Wave" (p. 120). She promises him beatitude and forgetfulness, the obliteration of everything, including the memory of his wrongdoings.

Fand, referred to in Celtic mythology as "a Woman of the Sidhe," represents Ideal Beauty. She is cold and remote, "more idol than human being."

> [She] dreamed herself into that shape that he
> May glitter in her basket; for the Sidhe

> Are dexterous fishers and they fish for men
> With dreams upon the hook.
>
> (P. 120)

Fand, an archetypal figure, emerges from the deepest areas of the unconscious. Her function is to mesmerize and overpower man in her embrace. Her desire is to reenter the realm of the absolute. As Yeats presents her in her still partly mortal state, she longs for Cuchulain's embrace. Only after his acquiescence can she know "Unity of Being" or experience a complete separation from the existential domain. If Cuchulain gives her the kiss she seeks, he will know oblivion—which means death to individuality, activity, frustration, and, ultimately, death to life.

Emer is Fand's antagonist, a representative of the weariness of the workaday world with its struggle for survival and its frustration of activity. Emer would use any means to destroy her rival and even attempts to slay her with a knife. Bricriu warns Emer that no weapon can "wound that body of air"; no earthly force can destroy man's dream or fantasy figure—the Eternal Feminine, the ideal which the poet nourishes in his heart and mind—and bind the ethereal to the physical universe.

Fand begins her seductive gyrations, dancing around the crouching Ghost of Cuchulain. Ever-alluring, she attempts to captivate her victim and enclose him in her embrace. Her undulations grow quicker, like those of Salome. She circles about her prey, leans over him, and enshrouds him with her lustrous hair. The Three Musicians whose songs opened the play now accompany Fand's arabesques with flute, drum, and stringed instrument. The Ghost of Cuchulain moves. He begins to question Fand as she pursues her wavelike patterns in space.

> Who is it stands before me there
> Shedding such light from limb and hair
> As when the moon, complete at last
> With every labouring crescent past,
> And lonely with extreme delight,
> Flings out upon the fifteenth night?
>
> (P. 121)

He sees her as a "labouring crescent," a moon figure ready to enclose him in her world and bring his world of conflict to an end. Fand, in turn, taunts him.

What pulled your hands about your feet,
Pulled down your head upon your knees,
And hid your face?

(P. 121)

She grows more aggressive, fighting to conquer her host and bring him to her realm "beyond the human" sphere, to possess him totally and eternally. No longer is he to be loved by many earthly women, but only by the Eternal Feminine.

The Ghost of Cuchulain must chose between the atemporal realm of bliss and the temporal realm of suffering. He is no longer the youthful dreamer, the idealist, the poet. His misdeeds have wrought havoc upon his soul. His memories "Weigh down my hands, abash my eyes" (p. 122). Once he had been an "amorous" and "violent" man (p. 141): ruthless, cutting, destructive. Resembling the eagle, with whom Yeats associates him, he represents power and ability; like the mole, to which he is also compared, he burrows beneath the ground, refusing to take stock of his immoral deeds. Endowed with equine energy, Cuchulain has galloped through existence, surging forth in Dionysian frenzy from one amorous adventure to another, from one battle to the next. Fand's goal was to force him to give up this power, which had instilled in him feelings of guilt and suffering, as well as lusty joy and the satifaction of conquest. Should he succumb to Fand, Cuchulain would never know want or thirst, for his heart would be forever stilled.

The Ghost of Cuchulain turns away. He clings too desperately to life with all of its difficulties and traumas. He calls for Emer. Fand grows angry and insists upon kissing him. Tension heightens. The alchemical brew boils. Bricriu cries out to Emer, "Renounce your love," just before Cuchulain succumbs to Fand's wiles. "And cry that you renounce his love forever," he repeats (p. 123). Still Emer refuses. She has not yet understood the forces at stake. Her all too human ways indicate the limitations of her perception. Bricriu speaks:

Fool, fool!

I am Fand's enemy come to thwart her will,
And you stand gaping there. There is still time.
Hear now the horses trample on the shore,
Hear how they trample! She has mounted up.
Cuchulain's not beside her in the chariot.

> There is still a moment left; cry out, cry out!
> Renounce him, and her power is at an end.
> Cuchulain's foot is on the chariot-step.
> Cry—
>
> (P. 123)

Emer yields. She stabilizes her emotions, coagulates her spirit. The alchemist's flame of anguish, which had brought an upsurge of emotion, subsides. The emotions involved in the relationships have been disconnected, dried out, and aired. Lucidity has cut through feelings and aided her in facing her ordeal. "I renounce Cuchulain's love for ever," she cries out (p. 123).

No sooner is her decision made than the Figure of Cuchulain "sinks back upon the bed" (p. 123). He has donned the heroic mask once again. Eithne Inguba kneels in front of him.

> Come to me, my beloved, it is I.
> I, Eithne Inguba. Look! He is there.
> He has come back and moved upon the bed.
> And it is I that won him from the sea,
> That brought him back to life.
>
> (P. 124)

Vitality now predominates. Joy, lust, heroism, and suffering will invade his existence. He beckons Eithne Inguba to come closer. "Your arms, your arms! O Eithne Inguba,/I have been in some strange place and am afraid" (p. 124). With life's return the Other World, Fand, and the Ghost of Cuchulain vanish.

The battle of the elements has subsided for the moment. The solution has been found. Matter has coagulated into a new mixture, though it is perhaps no better than the first if a hierarchy of values has to be established. Emer's decision, though painful for her, allows Cuchulain to pursue his flighty loves, to know "the intricacies of blind remorse," to reenter the Wheel of Life.[18]

For Yeats, the true hero-poet, exemplified by Cuchulain, must endure suffering and guilt in order to experience life's dichotomies viscerally; he must also learn to evalute the actions and feelings which he encounters in the phenomenological world. Only then can he begin to create from his own substance, mold from his flesh and blood, and drive through the core of conventional material to reach the domain of the ideal—the created work of art.

Anima Figures

Emer, Eithne Inguba, and Fand are anima figures. Psychologically, the anima is defined as "an autonomous psychic content in the male personality which can be described as an inner woman."[19] Emer, Eithne Inguba, and Fand live inchoate within Cuchulain's psyche. Anima figures have been depicted since time immemorial in all forms, from virgin to harlot. They stand for Eros, love, and relatedness: they personify the feminine principle within man. As an Eros image, the anima figure establishes feeling relationships between protagonists which may be described in terms of taste (bitter or sweet) or of color (white, red, black, golden). When man falls in love, he projects his anima onto another person. If his ego, the center of his conscious personality, identifies with the anima figure, danger arises; he is victimized by this unconscious force and is rendered psychologically impotent. A psychologically developed man who experiences the anima figure consciously may be provided with the deepest type of human relationship.

Emer, Eithne Inguba, and Fand may be viewed as projections of Cuchulain's psyche. Once they begin functioning in the phenomenological world, each struggles in her own way to assert herself. The artist in whom these forces exist attempts to embody them in his work. Yeats described the battle to articulate feelings and visions as taking place

in the depths of the soul and one of the antagonists does not wear a shape known to the world or speak a mortal tongue. It is the struggle of the dream with the world—it is only possible when we transcend circumstances and ourself, and the greater the contest, the greater the art.[20]

Fand is the most alluring and most dangerous of the three. In Ireland, the Sidhe were associated with the moon goddess and thus with tides, water, waves, the "magic of poetry," and the mysteries of the creative spirit in man. When mesmerized by the Sidhe, the individual yields to absolute passion, the ideal; the dream world becomes his realm and not the workaday domain. Since Fand comes from that "Country-under-Wave," she represents infinite riches, the alpha and omega of existence: a world *in potentia*.[21] Yeats identifies Fand with fish. As such she becomes an active force in the drama. Rather than withdraw into some remote area of the room (or psyche), she comes forth, as does a fish when looking for food, and demands her prey; "for the Sidhe/Are dexterous fishers and they fish for men/With dreams upon the hook" (p. 120). Fand corrupts the imagination. She tries to entice Cuchulain with her sweet song and rapturous sensuality. She wants him to experience her as complete woman and no longer as a "bird of prey."

> Hold out your arms and hands again;
> You were not so dumbfounded when
> I was that bird of prey, and yet
> I am all woman now.
>
> (P. 122)

In alchemical terms, what Fand seeks is a "spagyric marriage" with Cuchulain—that is, an inner psychic union with a blending of conscious and unconscious factors. If this union is accomplished, hostility and differentiation come to an end. No opposition exists; no polarities; no differentiation; no coagulation. The preformal state returns. Fand types are present in all societies and in all epochs. Though it has various names (Lorelei, Mélusine, Siren, Bird-Woman, Fish-Woman), this kind of female force captures the unsuspecting male and then devours him in an embrace. Sometimes she entices him into the ocean, where he succumbs to the comforting waves. Ulysses filled the ears of his crew with wax and had himself tied to the mast of his ship so that he would not be tempted to yield to the Sirens' songs. Aristotle, Pliny, and Ovid wrote about Sirens, and in Christian times figures of Sirens with double tails were depicted on the chapel at Saint-Michel at d'Aiguillhe at Le Puy, while siren-birds are found at Saint-Benoit-sur-Loire.[22]

Fand is also a lunar force, and therefore silver is her color. This noble metal represents the glimmering, shining, and mysterious tones she casts on those who fall within her sphere. When associated with the moon, silver expresses the occult side of nature, the unconscious as opposed to the sun principle which relates to clarity and cerebrality. It represents volatility, multiplicity, and fragmentation. For the poet, it stands for a world of fantasy and creativity. The alchemist likens moon figures to quicksilver, to the "fluid body of Man," or to the "non-formal" dynamic aspects of the personality, because they both dissolve and coagulate.[23] Fand lives in the powerful waters of the unconscious, the collective sphere where the poet draws his inspiration and the alchemist projects his struggle upon matter. In her association with the moon and water, she represents "moon dew" or the "sap of life" as well as the "miraculous water," that force which alchemists believed "extracts the souls from the bodies or gives the bodies life and soul."[24]

The moon is cold and moist and shines only with reflected light. Plutarch looked upon the moon as a "universal receptacle" which receives and pours out. It makes its way near the sun to "extract from him, as from a fountain, universal form and natural life." The moon is both passive and active—a kind of vampire who feeds on men in order to pursue and finally complete her monthly course.[25] In its more positive aspects, the moon, equated with the unconscious, is dependent upon the sun, or consciousness. Without the unconscious, consciousness would not exist, nor could the poet create. Without consciousness—with the disappearance of the sun and the domination of the moon—an unlimited void would arise. The alchemist's silvery stage must then be watched and tended so that the illumination which radiates from this metal may bring about the *albedo* phase and operate the transformative process. Once the anima is freed from the *prima materia* and can navigate autonomously in the spheres above, she may spread her poison, ensnare, and then suffocate her victim in her embrace. It is this elemental force which becomes personified in *The Only Jealousy of Emer*.

Yeats places Fand in Phase 15 of his Great Wheel and writes: "No description except Complete Beauty." He further declares:

Thought and will are indistinguishable, effort and attainment are indistinguishable; and this is the consummation of a slow process; nothing is apparent but dreaming Will and the Image that it dreams. . . . Now contemplation and desire, united into one, inhabit a world where every beloved image has bodily form, and every bodily form is loved. This love knows nothing of desire, for desire implies effort, and though there is still separation from the loved object, love accepts the separation as necessary to its own existence. . . . As all effort has ceased, all thought has become image. . . . and every image is separate from every other, for if image were linked to image, the soul would awaken from its immovable trance.[26]

Since Fand has been incarnated, she is not absolute. Her image-making power is still a potent force. She lives as form and idea and thus as a reality and can express herself in a variety of phenomena inhabiting the physical universe. She acts as a powerful anima figure for the Ghost of Cuchulain because she is still alive. She wills; she wants. To increase her statuesque and godly nature,

Yeats associated her with gold, bronze, brass, and silver. She "seems more an idol" (p. 121) than a flesh-and-blood woman. Everything about her is metallic, including her hair. Like Salome, she surpasses the human sphere; like metal, she is unfeeling. As a moon figure, she represents the unconscious. Her blatant sensuality inspires Cuchulain and entices him, as does the hetaera woman who seeks to rid man of his responsibilities and lure him into the nondifferentiated realm of serenity.

After Fand begins her dance, she comes to life in the various tones of shining metals, as though the moon itself were revealing its subdued and glimmering hues. Like other moon figures—Ishtar, Isis, Hathor, Artemis—so Fand dominates the cycles of life. Death and rebirth practices were powerful in matriarchal societies. To underscore the collective nature of Fand's dance, Yeats links her to the Three Musicians whose songs open and close the play. Yeats, like the alchemists, saw the connection between sound, metal, and quantity. Numbers could be heard in a type of music of the spheres. Indeed, it was said that alchemists used to dance and play musical instruments during their experiments, thus according them entry into various levels of the unconscious.[27]

The lascivious spatial forms of Fand's dance produce new relationships in the created world. Each gesture and sign is an abandonment to cosmic force, a linking of time and energy in visual designs. The sounds emerging from Fand's lips as she dances in spirals and circles suggest numerical relationships in the musical scale. Nature itself, as Plato suggested, was based upon a mathematical plan. Matter was an expression of mysterious cosmic harmonies.[28] Fand's kinetic and spatial forms become relationships between sound, harmony, and rhythms, each communicating with the other in a "Unity of Being." Like the ancient Celts who played their harps in three different modes—sleep, smile, lamentation—so Fand undulated about in spellbinding configurations.

Since Fand represents perfection and ideal beauty, she is out of man's reach, always eluding him and arousing his desire. Her collective and impersonal nature can never be possessed. Man can be overwhelmed by her if he succumbs to her wiles and promises of ecstasy, but then he rejects his individuality, his human memory. Although he is released from pain, he is denied his heroism and nobility. It is the earthly aspect of Cuchulain's personality, his attachment to the lustiness of life, that saves him from Fand's grasp. He chooses life, not death; struggle, not oblivion.

Terrestrial love, incarnated in Emer, is subject to change. It stands for the soul in man, the incomplete, accessible, differentiated feelings. Yeats suggested:

All power is from the terrestrial condition, for there opposite meet and there only is the extreme of choice possible, full freedom. And there the heterogeneous is, and evil, for evil is the strain one upon another of opposites.[29]

Emer is the brutal light of reality. It is she who feels the bitterness of consciousness, the tears of sorrow, the disappointment of loss, the dread alternative belonging to the human condition. It is she, as a projection of Cuchulain's psyche, who struggles to choose the best course to follow and is made lucid by the dichotomy Bricriu makes visible to her. Emer is a transient figure. She is Cuchulain's first love, but she dries up as an anima figure and becomes routine. She no longer offers the poet the excitement he needs to create. Cuchulain will succumb to his fickle nature and seek another woman. Emer is the stable force in his life. She waits patiently and in vain for her husband's return, offering him understanding, tenderness, and comfort. She is nourished by memories and hope. Alchemically, it is she who must sip the "bitter water of reason and judgment." As is stated in *The Hermetic Museum:*

O water of bitter taste, that preservest the elements! O nature of propinquity, that dissolvest nature! O best of natures, which overcomest nature herself! . . . Thou art crowned with light and art born . . . and the quintessence ariseth from thee.[30]

This secret substance, with its moral and psychological ramifications, is known alchemically as the water of grace, understanding, and compassion, the *lumen naturae* ("light of nature").[31]

In contrast to Emer is Eithne Inguba, the passing love. She is youthful, beautiful, passionate, and joyful. Cuchulain experiences her as an escapade. His attachment is superficial. Emer is not jealous of her. On the contrary, she understands Cuchulain's need of her because he is poet in search of inspiration. It is she who excites his creative faculties until the next lover appears. Emer sees Fand as the real and only danger. Once his dream world or unconscious takes over and Fand has complete sway, the poet grows impotent; memories cease and, without these archaic feelings and sensations, creativity vanishes. When Emer observes Fand's power increasing, her fear mounts. Fand is the catalyst at this juncture, just as Bricriu had been the light-bringer. Emer is compelled to act. Her sacrifice is fruitless, however, since it requires Cuchulain to return to Eithne Inguba and to reenter the world of time. With his reentry, he is doomed to rebirth and differentiation.

Yeats's tragedy, *The Only Jealousy of Emer,* dramatized the alchemical operations which take his protagonists from a state of primal oneness to *separatio* and *coagulatio.* The alchemical dictum reads: "Take the old black spirit, and destroy therewith the bodies until they are changed."[32] The *separatio* experienced during the play broke up undifferentiated attitudes and allowed heretofore buried unconscious contents to emerge into the light of consciousness. A variety of possibilities thus came into being, and with them the power of discrimination began to develop. The alchemical experience as dramatized in *The Only Jealousy of Emer* was assimilated by the protagonists with all of its psychological and poetic ramifications. The journey once accomplished, however, did not lead to *sublimatio* or evolution into a higher sphere of existence, but rather to another *separatio,* another war and another rebirth. As Johann Glauber, the seventeenth-century chemist, wrote:

> Dissolve the Fixt, and make the Fixed fly,
> The Flying fix, and then live happily.[33]

So continues Yeats's Wheel of Life.

5

The Water Hen: The Puer Aeternus

The Water Hen (1921) is a dramatic restatement by Stanislaw Ignacy Witkiewicz, Polish writer and painter, of the *solutio* operation. This phase of the alchemical process serves to destroy an unproductive conscious orientation and initiate a new birth. Water is life-giving when it moistens and irrigates, and death-dealing when it leads to drowning.

"Until all be made of water, perform no operation," states an alchemical maxim.[1] Since the protagonists in *The Water Hen* are blocked in all directions by conventional strictures, social aphorisms, and powerful guilt feelings, they are severed from their inner worlds. A washing away of those crystalline elements which obstruct the free-flowing relationship between conscious and unconscious worlds is therefore necessary. When an unconscious content breaks through into consciousness and motivates their activities, it does so in spurts and in the rudimentary forms of intuitive formulations, principles, laws, and banalities. The protagonists float about, following their momentary needs and desires. Life for them consists of an interplay of infantile impulses and projections. Devoid of feeling and substance, the characters in *The Water Hen* experience provisional existences.

The play revolves around Edgar, the Puer Aeternus, that eternal boy who, because he is psychologically stunted, is unable to grow to maturity. Rather than achieving independence and balance by

111

forging ahead on his own, he yearns for a return to a preformal womb condition. This primal state, which exists outside linear time, constitutes the seminal stage of existence. There no demands are made of him; that he lacks the will and perseverance necessary to confront problems is meaningless. Such a condition is antithetical to life. Yet it is consistent with the Puer's negative psychological orientation. The alchemist believed that *solutio* through death (*dissolutio*) brought a solution through rebirth (*coagulatio*) into a higher and more spiritual realm, but *The Water Hen* concludes on a note of despair. Descent, not ascent, is envisaged in the play. When a return to earthly condition does occur in the stage happenings, it is marked by the individual buried within his solipsistic domain—vegetating, reminiscing, shuffling about—prolonging the agony that is his life. It is no wonder that a suicidal motif runs through *The Water Hen* and that, for all the activity within the play, it culminates in nonactivity, a static condition.

Critics have said, and perhaps rightly so, that Witkiewicz's theatre (*They,* 1920; *On a Small Estate,* 1921; *The Madman and the Nun,* 1923) reflects not only the author's disjointed psyche but also the contemporary political, economic, and spiritual fragmentation of Poland and of Europe in general. For centuries the fate of Poland had been directed by Russia, Prussia, and Austria in a succession of partitions: 1772, 1793, 1795. Throughout the nineteenth century, Poland was marked with uprisings, revolutions, and repressions. Only after World War I was it restored to the Poles, to be dismembered once again during World War II and reassembled after the Holocaust.

Added to the cultural strains on Witkiewicz were personal conflicts triggered by his domineering father, a well-known painter, cultural anthropologist, and critic. The father had adopted a Nietzschean attitude toward life: his son was to be an *Übermensch* in the field of the arts. Rejecting the prevailing artistic credos (positivism, sentimentalism, and academism) which he felt to be arid and uninteresting, the elder Witkiewicz left Warsaw with his family and moved to Zakopane in southern Poland, where he believed a more creative atmosphere prevailed. There he was in touch with peasant traditions and folklore, and he considered the atmosphere healthy and creative. He attracted some of the most distinguished men of his era to his home, including the pianist Arthur Rubinstein, the writer Sholem Asch, and the anthropologist Bronislaw Malinowski. An elitist, he inculcated his son with the idea that the world was created for superior beings. If those with great creative minds comported themselves morally and nobly, they could prepare the way for a utopia on earth. In keeping with these ideas, he had the young Witkiewicz tutored at home, believing that the standards of both public and private schools were inferior. In this controlled atmosphere, the young lad's intellectual curiosity was stimulated. He read voraciously in the works of Shakespeare, Gogol, Maeterlinck, and many others.

Witkiewicz's father's ideas concerning the *Übermensch* were out of tune with the times. Children were demanding independence from their parents and not guidance; they were leaving their homes and rejecting the cloistered environments imposed upon them by the patriarchal society in which they had been raised. Dissension between Witkiewicz and his father manifested itself when the young man decided to enroll at the Krakow Academy of Fine Arts for the academic year 1904–5. The numerous and passionate love affairs carried on by the youth during this period added fuel to the flames. These simmered, however, when the budding artist went to Paris to study the canvases of the Fauves, Cubists, and Futurists. Impressed with the works of Georges Braque, Pablo Picasso, Raoul Dufy, Maurice de Vlaminck, and André Derain and the aesthetics of Paul Gauguin, Vincent van Gogh, and Edvard Munch, the Polish visitor began painting truncated and dismembered figures and distorted landscapes. He discovered in himself a growing predilection for the unnatural—monsters, caricatures, grotesque and eerie sites— which was mirrored in the subject matter and titles of his canvases: *A Man with Dropsy Lies in Ambush for His Wife's Lover* or *The Prince of Darkness Tempts Saint Theresa with the Help of a Waiter from Budapest.*[2]

Upon his return to Poland, tension between father and son grew more pronounced, owing mainly to the young man's economic dependence. An unhappy love affair increased his grief and led to a nervous breakdown characterized by months of extreme lethargy and passivity. Freudian analysis followed, and then optimism. Witkiewicz became engaged. Shortly thereafter, however, his fiancée committed suicide in a strange manner: her body was found at the bottom of a cliff with a bouquet of flowers next to it. The shock of her death caused another breakdown. This time Witkiewicz's father arranged for him to accompany Bronislaw Malinowski, in the capacity of secretary, draftsman, and photographer, to the South Seas, Australia, India, and Ceylon.

When World War I broke out, young Witkiewicz enlisted in the Russian army. He suffered shell shock and was decorated for bravery in 1916, a year after his father's death. He spent the rest of the war in Russia, painting and studying the works of the avant-garde: Casimir Malevich, Vladimir Tatlin, Alexsandr Rodchenko, Wassily Kandinsky, and Marc Chagall. It was during this period that he began experimenting with drugs of all types, including cocaine, peyote, morphine, ether, and nicotine.[3] He returned to Poland in 1918, enriched with a wealth of new experiences, ready to concretize his own pictorial and dramatic fantasies.

Stanislaw Witkiewicz is a seminal force in modern theatre. Like Alfred Jarry (1873–1907), he rejected the framework of the so-called well-made play so popular in his day and banished sentimentality and rational coherence from his dramas. Both men possessed a corrosive way of looking at life that was somewhat mitigated by a powerful sense of humor. Not perhaps as monstrous and grotesque as Jarry's vengeful and brutal King Ubu and his cohorts, Witkiewicz's characters are equally memorable. Jarry was more shocking, however, in his use of provocative words, strange verbal associations, harsh alliterations, and unusual rhythmic patterns than was Witkiewicz, whose creatures speak in a more socially acceptable manner and bear more conventional physical traits. Both playwrights, however, succeeded in destroying all semblance of logic between character and situation—Jarry through the shock of the stage events and language and Witkiewicz through his bizarre philosophical and metaphysical arguments.

As had Antonin Artaud (1895–1948), Witkiewicz rejected a didactic and psychological theatre. Both advocated a mythically oriented drama in which spatial language (gesture, movement, lighting, stage accessories, and so forth) would create a new optic, allowing for greater dimensionality. The preeminence of the dream world or the unconscious in the drama, advocated by Artaud, was practiced by Witkiewicz; his intent was to touch and stir the spectator into a state of new awareness. Unlike Artaud, however, who considered the word as only one of many aspects included in the spectacle as a whole, Witkiewicz gave primacy to language. "The most important thing is the spoken word," he declared, "and the other elements must be adapted to it."[4]

Similarly important in the formation of Witkiewicz's theatrical aesthetic were the works of his Polish compatriots. Stanislaw Wyspianski (1869–1907), a practitioner of "total theatre," not only staged his plays, but made the costumes and properties. Banishing realistic sets, he advocated a juxtaposition of the real and supernatural worlds on stage and required a more poetic delivery on the part of his actors than the declamatory style then in vogue. In *Akropolis* (1904), he incorporated image, shape, color, and sound, thus adding to the intensity of the symbols used to dramatize the dream visions within the drama and in this way adding to its deeply moving mythical aspect. Tadeus Micinski (1873–1919) could also be counted among those who influenced Witkiewicz. Fascinated with the occult and mystical side of the dramatic ritual, Micinski suggested a return to the theatre's original function, that of enacting a religious mystery.

Surrealism was also a powerful feature of Witkiewicz's innovative dramatic technique. Every word, gesture, or happening in each of his plays has spiritual, artistic, and arcane ramifications. As André Breton, the founder of surrealism, later suggested: "The esoteric . . . offers . . . an unlimited field to man, allowing him to link the most apparently disparate objects, enabling him to discover in part the mechanics of a universal symbolism."[5] The Surrealists advocated the liberation of the unconscious through dream writing and the recording of inner visions. In his *Surrealist Manifesto* (1924), Breton defined the role of the authors. They should become "the deaf receptacles of so many echoes, modest RECORDING INSTRUMENTS of another world." Primacy was given to dreams and to "the undirected play of thought."[6] To expose the inner workings of man through the artistic medium would free him from the grasping tentacles of an overly constricting moralistic and bourgeois society as well as from the predominant literary and artistic conventions. Giorgio de Chirico, practicing what he called "Surrealist Illusionism," depicted dreamlike states in his canvases rather than conventional exteriority. In his painting *Grand Metaphysical Interior* (1917), silence, coupled with an inner light, encapsulates an atmosphere of ambiguity, mystery, and terror. *The Philosopher's Conquest* (1914), in which cannon balls are juxtaposed with artichokes, arouses disquietude and solemnity. Conventional views are completely shattered; feelings of alienation ensue. De Chirico wrote: "Art is the fatal net that catches these strange mo-

ments in flight, like mysterious butterflies, unnoticed by the innocence and distraction of ordinary man."[7]

In the true Surrealist manner, Witkiewicz's stage was peopled
with creatures in both dream and waking states; they were archetypal forces gesturing their way through the dramatic sequences and ushering in a world of mystery and magic. The techniques of dissociation, displacement, dislocation, and distortion
used by the Cubists, Futurists, and Surrealists were also adopted
by Witkiewicz, with the effect of disrupting rational coherence between the characters and the world about them. Dichotomy was
the rule rather than the exception in his theatre.

Witkiewicz described his aesthetics in the Introduction to the
Theory of Pure Form in the Theatre (1918), *Theoretical Introduction
to Tumor Brainard* (1920), and *Concepts and Principles Implied by
the Notion of Being* (1935). Plays, Witkiewicz declared in this last-
named work, must express intuitively the "absolute sovereignty
and particularity of each Particular Existence," since these are
experienced in a referential space-time continuum. Tensions must
be aroused with the purpose of inspiring a "metaphysical sense of
the strangeness of existence." Both dramatist and viewer must
come away from a performance tormented by such questions as:
Why am I me and not some other living entity? Why was I born
here and now and not elsewhere at some other time?

Witkiewicz was plagued by the philosophical and metaphysical
notion of *"Unity within Plurality."* Each individual functions as a
unit, an individual biological entity, as well as a unit within a
social organism, a plurality of biological entities. Similarly, each
human being is made up of an infinite number of particles ("mo-
nads," as he called them), forever tugging at each other within the
body (unit). These single and plural entities may be measured spa-
tially (exteriorly in the so-called real world) and also as duration
(the inner autonomous realm).[8] The tension arising from the one
and the plural creates anxiety within the feeling and thinking
being. The creative act is capable of relieving this conflict of polarities, and he therefore described painting and the theatrical spectacle as composites of "oriented tensions." Witkiewicz reasoned:

The essence of art in general is the directly given unity of personality
or what we call metaphysical feeling, expressed in the construction of
whatever the elements are, such as: colors, sounds, words, or actions.
Painting and music possess homogeneous elements. In addition to its

sound values and possibilities for evoking visual images, poetry still works with concepts, the meaning of which are in our opinion, just as good artistically as any of the pure qualities. However, the theatre has the additional element of actions, whoever the individual beings may be who act.[9]

He stresses the general absurdity of life in his theatre by deforming "the external world, by violating the logical feeling principle." Going beyond the linear time scheme, he advocates the abolition of a chronological approach. The vicissitudes experienced by his protagonists are realized as impulses and affects, brittle spasms and movements enacted in conglomerates of disconnected sequences. The goal of the theatre, he stated, "is to put the audience in an exceptional state, which cannot in its pure form very easily be attained in the course of ordinary daily life, a state where the mystery of existence can be apprehended emotionally."[10] By abolishing logic and verisimilitude, Witkiewicz allows chance to predominate. The stage becomes an acausal or non-Euclidian world: sublime and monstrous forces, tragic and humorous, sardonic and satiric, punctuate the stage happenings with their illogical interplay, veering from the most superficial and banal of ideas to the most meaningful indictments of contemporary civilization. In this manner the spectator is exposed to the "mystery of existence," both as an individual and as a polyvalent force: the contact gives birth to anxiety, which in turn triggers a metaphysical feeling. *The Water Hen* is as absurd as a world dominated by the gratuitous act, as seemingly ridiculous as the sublime and sordid beings allow: a play which explodes with candor.

Act 1: The Alchemical Cryptogram

In act 1 of *The Water Hen*, the curtains part on a web of enigmas, signs, ciphers, and acrostics reminiscent of an alchemical cryptogram with metaphysical, psychological, and dramatic ramifications. As the alchemist assigned body, soul, and spirit to his metals, thereby endowing them with personality traits, so Witkiewicz animates his decor. Each object becomes the manifestation of an inner content, an expression of a particular mystery. A series of objects comes into view as in a photomontage: an open field where "the horizon meets the edge of the sea"; yellow flowers; juniper bushes; a tall mound topped with a crimson pole to which a large octagonal lantern with green glass is attached. A very pretty, though "not at all seductive," twenty-six-year-old girl is waiting to be shot.[11]

The open field which blends into the sea instills a disquieting feeling of vastness, openness, and solitude, an extraterrestrial and unnatural spacelessness. It is a fertile field for Witkiewicz's faceless and identityless characters. Reminiscent of an Yves Tanguy landscape with its endless skies and masses of mangled objects, here too are premonitory feelings of doom.

The scattered green and yellow flowers indicate earth's fertility, on the one hand, and the proliferation of matter which may lead to destruction, on the other. In medieval times, green was associated with the Holy Ghost, that spiritual force whose function it was to inseminate a mortal, thereby linking divine and terrestrial realms. Heinrich Kunrath, the sixteenth-century alchemist, linked green with Venus. Arnold of Villanova pointed out that Aristotle wrote of

our gold, not the common gold, because the green which is in this substance signifies its total perfection, since by our magistery that green is quickly turned into truest gold.[12]

Yellow, or the *citrinitas* operation, indicates in this instance the presence of the solar or golden factor.

The crimson color of the pole represents for many an alchemist the blood of Christ, that life-giving substance powerful enough to bring dead bodies back to life. Owing to the ability of blood, both overt and covert, to alter form and consistency through the energetic process, red has been associated with the central fire or earthly man. The power of the athanor is similar; it is instrumental in altering the amalgams, consistencies, and effects of his Great Work. The redness visible within the athanor as it burns at a steady pace contains the secrets of vital heat, as does libido or psychic energy or the heart, as it warms and exudes love and understanding or generates hate and envy.

The pole may be associated with the Tree of Knowledge, the Tree of Life, and the Cosmic Tree. Each of these trees functions in its own way as a connector linking heaven to earth, spirit to matter, body to soul, *Gnosis* to *Physis*. That it rises vertically from the mound indicates iconographically its longing for eternity—that is, the spiritual way—rather than temporality. The mound itself, reminiscent of the tumulus or Buddhist stupa, encloses sparks of divinity, the potential world which lives inchoate within the *prima materia*.

The lantern comes to signify wisdom, illumination, and eternal truth, which mystics consider to be the goal of life. In connection with the Tarot card the Hermit, it brings to mind Diogenes the Cynic, who carried a lantern around with him. It was he who taught independence of spirit and condemned social conventions and traditions. The lantern lights up unconscious realms, illuminates conflict, and objectifies hidden issues. (That the lantern was green is in keeping with the dicta of Hermes Trismegistus, the alleged founder of alchemy.) It is through light that wisdom is born and vision is experienced, that differentiation and evaluation are made possible. Since the goal of alchemy was to heal the conflict between metals and chemicals, to cure physical and psychic afflictions, a dismemberment was usually in order, after which the process could continue on its efficacious course. The separation of the metals came first, the loosening of "the age-old attachment of the soul to the body," thus making conscious "the conflict between purely natural and spiritual man."[13] That the lantern was octagonal is also significant in alchemical cryptography. Eight represents an eternally spiraling movement, that of spirit, as contrasted to the square, which represents matter and earthly orientation. That two circles are represented in the shape of the number eight signifies the duality of eternal order: the finite within the infinite and their eventual harmonization into the one circle.

It is within water that the heteroclite objects comprising the decor and the cast take on meaning and texture. The alchemist looked upon water as both the preserver and destroyer of life. Since water circulates throughout nature in the forms of rain, sap, blood, milk, and other liquids, it is considered limitless and immortal. It is the *fons et origo* of existence and paves the way for growth and renewal. Because it is a formless, eternal fluid and continuously altering substance, it is claimed that soul, spirit, or psyche exists within its essence.[14] The thirteenth-century *Aurora Consurgens* reads: "Send forth thy Spirit, that is water . . . and thou wilt renew the face of the earth."[15] In *The Water Hen*, water is just that element needed to break down the complexes which have solidified within the protagonists' psyches and have transformed them into brittle, fixed, and unbending creatures. Blind to present realities, they are wedded to the timeless world of unregenerate nature.

As an anima figure, the Water Hen is soul and spirit. Like water, the Water Hen represents the nonformal, dynamic, motivating force within the protagonists' personalities. She is intuitive wisdom. She circulates throughout the play. All activity emanates from her. She generates and regenerates, and in so doing she prepares the way for the death/birth ritual. As mother, mistress, and wife to the male protagonists Edgar and Tadzio (who really are two stages in the development of the antihero Edgar), she stirs and inverts the order of things. The statement made in an ancient Egyptian alchemical text is applicable to the Water Hen: "I refresh your heart that you may be satisfied."[16]

The Water Hen is also an archetypal figure who lives both on a personal and collective level, bringing happiness to some and misery to others. In that she transcends man's understanding, she assumes the stature of a mystery woman corresponding to the sibyls of Delphi and Dodona. She functions as a psychopomp, and it is she who entices the male partners into her mysterious realm, there to prevent the youth from evolving into maturity and encouraging him to dissolve into death in her. As an anima figure connected with water, she symbolizes the Eros principle, love born from water. In that the Water Hen initiates birth, she alters consistencies and relationships, thereby indulging in the love play which increases the drama's pith and point.

The Water Hen is also "hen." Like a mother hen, she looks upon the male protagonists with compassion and affection at times; at other moments, she rejects, belittles, and despises them. It is she, however, (or that factor she represents within the male psyche) which becomes the agent of sacrifice. As long as the anima functions on an unconscious level, which is true in the cases of Edgar and Tadzio throughout the play, she takes on reality as a projection. Consequently, the male cannot be expected to grow psychologically; individuation is impossible.

The opening lines of the play usher in the sacrificial motif. The Water Hen most matter-of-factly tells Edgar that he must shoot her: "Couldn't you be a little quicker about it?" By way of encouragement, she tells him: "You'll spend more time in your own company." Edgar, however, cannot see it her way. "But I don't want to be myself." Life is "Boredom and suffering—a vicious circle, endless and self-contained and closed upon itself forever" (p. 11).

Edgar's image of the circle describes his psychological state:

the uroboric stage of development when the child still lives in a *participation mystique* with the parent; the ego is unformed and identity has not yet come into being. Self-consciousness is nonexistent. Edgar, although thirty years old, has not grown up. He is dependent upon others. Although he has had many jobs, including those of factory manager, revolutionary, and general, he can still say: "I'm a man without a profession and without a future" (p. 11). Life holds no meaning for him. His entire existence has been spent trying to please his father, who wanted him to be a great artist. Now, however, he realizes he has no talent.

Edgar's life has been built on a "sack of illusions" which he has carried around with him since birth. He is the product of his father's desire for him to become an *Übermensch*. Having failed to live up to his father's expectations, he has become despondent, unsettled, and directionless. Never having found fulfillment nor having had the energy to see things through to the end, Edgar always took the easy way out. He dissipated his energies in fruitless activity, avoiding the toil and conflict necessary for growth and independence. Edgar, therefore, lived peripherally. He floated along. Like the young flower gods Hyacinth and Narcissus, so Edgar's future may be stemmed.[17] Since Edgar's ego remains undeveloped, he has never discovered his own river bed, his reason for being, his own identity. He is a kind of ghostly figure, his father's creation. He is so identified with the persona he donned in an attempt to live up to his father's image of him that self-knowledge has become virtually impossible. Scattered, fractured, and undeveloped, his disconnected personality consists of a series of split-offs, each unrelated to the other.

Alchemically, Edgar could be described as phosphorescent, as could Tadzio, the ten-year-old boy, and his father. Phosphorus is described in *The Living Webster Dictionary* as a "low-melting distillable corrosive poisonous white or yellow soft wax crystallizable solid which glows faintly and ignites readily in warm moist air giving off dense white smoke." Phosphorus also appears as "a violet to red nonpoisonous less active powder obtained by heating white phosphorus with a catalyst (as iodine) and is used on abrasive surfaces on which safety matches are scratched." Edgar's personality traits are phosphorescent. He is multivalent: he combines and recombines with others, but never for long periods. In that he is a projection of his father's psyche and the Water Hen exists as a

projection of his own, a "corrosive poisonous" concoction is forever
exuding from him—the poison which comes from unauthentic and
deceptive relationships. Edgar is yellow phosphorus; his color is
not the yellow of the sun or of the solar hero, but the mud-yellow of
a pusillanimous youth.

The Water Hen grows impatient. She does not really dislike
life; in fact, she has grown rather fond of Edgar, who is both child
and father to her. He represents "something indefinable, something without form and without contour, filling my world with its
indeterminateness" (p. 11). He projects his formlessness onto her,
his anima. That she is his creation, a receptacle for his projection,
is evident each time he broaches his feelings of ineptitude in rela-
tion to his father, whenever he longs to wash away his guilt feelings and be baptized into a world free from torment, to reenter the
fresh, unstained realm of preformal existence in water. Tired of
standing under the pole, however, the Water Hen finally asks him
to pull the trigger, and he does muster the psychological strength
to put an end to this parasitic relationship. The Water Hen's death
means dissolution of the present condition. Edgar's weakly structured ego is now dislodged; it returns to his own *prima materia* or
unconscious, there perhaps to be nourished and be reborn. The
death ritual is now completed as it had been countless times during the Dionysian fertility mysteries—the *sparagmos*—and dismemberment begins.

Shortly after the Water Hen drops to the ground, Tadzio, a
younger version of Edgar, arrives on stage. He is walking as if in a
dream. He does not know his parents, nor does he understand why
he has been placed in this particular situation at this particular
time. When Edgar asks him where he came from, he replies: "I
don't know. I woke up when I heard the shots. And you're my
papa" (p. 12). Neither does Edgar know the answer. "Who knows?
Maybe I'm a father too." Tadzio represents nonego life; devoid of
emotional ties, he is dissociated and as passive as Edgar.

Tadzio symbolizes white phosphorus. As a child, he lives close
to nature, unsullied, unformed, and untutored. Polyvalent life still
exists within him, and therefore he shines at particular moments.
His vision becomes intuitive and flamelike and his wisdom so profound that he is capable of "poisoning" the atmosphere by asking
tormenting questions. True to the Puer type, he is usually sleepy
and periodically lapses into the dream world. He is not in touch

with the world of practical reality. Undisciplined, wandering about indiscriminately, he remains uncommitted in all senses of the word. Guided by affects, his spontaneity and naiveté allow his impulses and fantasies to dominate him. He flows along as does phosphorus when heated. Once exposed to the light of consciousness, his feelings cool and take on the consistency of a "waxy solid," characteristics still compatible with a ten-year-old boy's psyche, and not with Edgar's.

There is a sudden change of scene to the courtyard of a barracks. A patriarchal world order marked by rigidity, repression, and constriction is dominant. Associated with soldiers, war, fear, and economic and political unrest, the barracks and qualities with which it is associated may be linked to acids biting into metals. Abrasive forces emerge in this restrictive environment. They heat, like elements in crucibles and retorts, then distill and are decanted into new and more potent amalgams. Edgar and Tadzio seem victimized by their own fluctuating and directionless impulses, as life in this abysmal area, consisting of conglomerates of fluid emotions, takes on the steadiness of quicksand.

Tadzio asks what death is. It is a long sleep from which one never awakens, Edgar suggests. Tadzio asks more questions. "Never . . . Never . . . Never—I understand now, it's the same forever and ever" (p. 14).

For the protagonists, living in a cyclical time scheme, chronological time has no meaning. All occurs over and over again as if dictated by some extraterrestrial force. Like the writer's stream of consciousness technique which conveys psychic life by allowing for the presentation of thoughts, impressions, and feelings on a preverbal level, so the dialogue between Edgar and Tadzio takes on an entire chemistry of sensations—from the most acidulous to the most mellifluous, from "primitive" to "civilized" ideations. Rather than dramatizing linear events, the characters follow their unconscious yearnings and reveal their multiple points of view and their conflicts, unhampered by conventions. Time is reversible: there is no past, present, or future. Only mythical time exists, undifferentiated and eternal.

It is perfectly proper in such a time scheme for Edgar and Tadzio to regress. Edgar becomes increasingly childlike while Tadzio matures intellectually or at least gives that impression. Indeed, the boy talks about the "Infinite," "God," and claims to "understand everything" (p. 13). He is white phosphorus, exuding the purity of natural knowledge unadulterated by society's artificial views and imposed dicta. But suddenly Tadzio grows sleepy and uncertain. He wonders whether he has been dreaming these happenings. Is there a difference between illusion and reality? Reminiscent of the prisoners in Plato's allegory of the cave, who were unable to see beyond their limited domain, so Tadzio and Edgar are unclear in their outlook. Edgar declares: "I should have been somebody, but I never knew what, or rather who. I don't even know whether I actually exist, although the fact that I suffer terribly is certainly real" (p. 14).

The Lamplighter emerges. "Eight concentric rays of intense green light fill the stage." Edgar, musing about life, begins to question the work ethic. If an individual "doesn't work towards a goal, like a horse with blinders over his eyes walking around in a treadmill" (p. 15), he is looked upon by his family and society as a failure and an outcast. "The goal is in the goal itself" (p. 15), he states unequivocally, reiterating the credo of the Surrealists. He tells Tadzio that this art for art's sake aesthetic was first enunciated by his dead friend, Duke Edgar of Nevermore. The doubling of names further diorients the spectator, increases the fragmentation of the personalities, and underscores the cyclical as opposed to a linear time scheme. The linking of life and death are effected by the association with "The Raven" of Edgar Allan Poe. Timelessness, the mystic's eternal present which stays the fleeting and stems the anarchical, prevails.

Whenever Edgar has attempted to transcend his limitations, escape the dichotomy of existence in the creative work of art, he returns that much more painfully to the heaviness of his present condition. His life exists in a world where nothing alters; boredom is constant. "Nothing happens, nothing. I thought that something would happen, but there's no change" (p. 15). As are the characters in Samuel Beckett's plays and novels, so Witkiewicz's protagonists, devoid of identity and individuality, are echoes, symbols, essences, who progressively disintegrate. Without hope, each inhabits his somber universe, lost in duration. Edgar and Tadzio exist as presences and absences; they are antiheroes struggling against themselves (as the one and the multiple) as well as against the world in which they live (as individual and plural). Hounded by theological, social, and sexual problems, they are unable to emerge from their solipsistic realms. Like Narcissus, so they are forever looking at themselves through their projections in others. They never penetrate their own psyches; they never understand their own motivations. They eat up their lives and devour time. The continuity of their existence is preserved in such habitual acts as chatter, whether it focuses on painting, philosophical topics, or emotional relationships. Faceless beings whose lives are divested of meaning, each pursues his course buried in his circumscribed domain, vegetating and prolonging what should be cut short.

Disenchantment pervades the atmosphere: sardonic, cruel, and cutting. Not only are human relationships impossible, Edgar and Tadzio come to realize, but art—the great buffer against pain—has also become a superficial pastime. The canvas or the poem in which life's complexities and polarities are concealed enable its creator to overcome the fear of his world and of death, but only momentarily. As Hamlet declared the dream to be "the rub," so Tadzio fears only one thing: his dream. For him it iterates a sense of doom and oblivion.

The Father appears. He has the Water Hen's body removed. Once again he begins encouraging Edgar: "I tell you you'll be an artist" (p. 17). He repeats in different terms what the Water Hen said to Edgar before she was shot: "Remember what I told you. You must be great in one way or another" (p. 13). "Great," as defined by both the Water Hen and the Father, implies the committing of an irreversible act, such as falling in love for the first time, losing one's virginity, or dying. A great act can be accomplished only once and nevermore. Thus the individual defies eternity; man marks timelessness.

The Father, as red phosphorus, is a fire principle, a catalyst who arouses excitement and then sears and pains. He defies time by living an active, aggressive, forceful existence, by creating a goal for himself through his son. He does not waste time by indulging in passive ways. Although life is dominated by chance, the Father understands that to a limited extent he is in charge of his own destiny. Unlike Edgar, who adheres to Zeno's principle that motion and change are illusory, the Father chooses the *Übermensch* credo as his way of life. Like phosphorus, he continuously gives off sparks of light when subjected to friction or radiation and shines with his aphorisms, platitudes, and gleaming generalizations. It is never too late, he tells his son, to become an artist.

Gauguin began painting at twenty-seven; Shaw wrote at thirty. Since Edgar is incapable of living a normal life, he realizes, he must live his life "in reverse and walk backwards along wayward paths" (p. 17). Edgar meets his father halfway. He informs him that he is "beginning another life. Not a new life, but another one—do you understand, father?" (p. 17). Edgar will attempt a rebirth despite knowing that such renewed activity is useless.

Act 1 concludes with the arrival of the Duchess Alice of Nevermore, who is now Edgar's wife and the widow of Edgar Nevermore. Her dead husband, she tells everyone, was devoured by a tiger in some remote African jungle while reading Bertrand Russell and Alfred North Whitehead's *Principia Mathematica*. The humorous image is reminiscent of some canvases by Henri Rousseau, called le Douanier, with their exotic landscapes and tigers placed beside nude women, depicting in childlike reality unconscious fantasies as they roam free through the time-space continuum.

Edgar confesses to his crime. He has killed the Water Hen. The twenty-year-old Korbowski, "the Scoundrel" who "strangely" enough resembles Edgar, arrives. He too confesses—to being the duchess's lover. The protagonists do not react to either statement. Since relationships are meaningless, no disenchantment is expressed, except by Edgar who feels victimized by everyone.

It's people and circumstances that have always made me what I am. I am a mannikin, a marionette. Before I can create anything, everything happens all by itself exactly the way it always has, and not because of anything I've done.

(P. 24)

He is the antihero par excellence and indulges in self-pity because he is unable to solve any of his problems. His passivity encourages his paradoxical nature: he is both detached from and yet involved with those surrounding him. He rages, therefore, as does a child when he is unable to dominate events and people. He neither relates to himself nor sustains any kind of rapport with anyone else. Edgar is overcome with both inertia and anguish. He longs to escape into the twilight of death.

Act 2: "Without Ferment Nothing Happens"

The curtains open for act 2 on the Nevermore Palace. An atmosphere of unreality is established. Both objects and people seem alienated from their surroundings. A touch of "warm blue" and "cold grey" is visible. Red predominates in shades of strawberry, orange, and carmine, colors attributed by alchemists to blood and to the Great Whore of Babylon. Like red oxide of mercury, which when heated precipitates activity, so energy is constellated in this scene and fermentation is heightened.

The characters float around as do amnesiacs, without family, past, future, or even a present. They are unaware of themselves and of life as a whole; they resemble chemicals blending into one another, vanishing finally into oblivion. Tadzio's opening remarks to the duchess, when referring to Edgar, set the atmosphere: "Mama, I forgot why he's my papa" (p. 24). Like the student in *The Lesson* of Eugène Ionesco, who is capable of all types of complicated arithmetical sequences but cannot subtract the simplest numbers, so Tadzio knows the meaning of "Infinity" and in fact claims to know everything, yet he does not know his own father. He grows increasingly frustrated because his question about how he came to be remains unanswered.

Edgar now seems to have a new lease on life. "I'm devoting my entire life to penance" (p. 28). Similar to the martyr, the penitent, the flagellant, and the masochist, Edgar decides to pay for disappointing his father, thus relieving himself of his guilt feelings and experiencing redemption. Associating himself once again with the marionette, he claims to feel "outside of whatever happens." He experiences himself as an object moving about "on a screen" like a Chinese shadow play figure: it is a schizophrenic state. He observes his own movements but has no control over them. Now, however, he declares he will make a fresh start and create "a new skeleton inside of what already exists" (p. 32).

Edgar's constant comparison of himself to the marionette is antithetical to alchemical thought, which stresses man's ability to enhance his existence by deepening his spiritual views. Marionettes, of course, lack individuality and will; they are manipulated by some outer being. Just as the marionette is directed by the puppeteer, so man is the plaything of the gods. Rather than accepting his subservient position, however, man deceives himself and identifies with the manipulator of the dolls. His inflated opinion of himself only points more powerfully to his weaknesses when confronted with forces beyond his control. Edgar seems to be echoing Schopenhauer's formulations in *The World as Will and Idea* (1818).

Man's will over which he has so little control, the philosopher declares, is the source of his unhappiness. It is the will that forces him to strive and wish for the impossible. Only dissatisfaction, frustration, and anguish can ensue. By controlling or suppressing the will through the intellect, by overcoming or diminishing desire, Schopenhauer contends, man can experience a peaceful and pain-less state of contemplation on earth.

In that the protagonists of *The Water Hen* are dehumanized entities without individuality, they may be considered archetypal figures. Complex and ambiguous, they infuse a superhuman or extrahuman dimension into the stage happenings. Inhabitants of two worlds—the real and the unreal—they can be transformed into anything at any time: god or man, saint or sinner. They strut about like phantoms, enunciating thoughts in disconnected clus-ters and strident cacophonies. They stir, terrify, and mutilate each other, both spiritually and physically, unwittingly and wittingly, in strange ways. Like metals covered with powerful acids, they insinuate themselves into the beings of each other, corroding the very essences of their existences. Passive, remote, impersonal, and automatonlike, in part they also represent the collective existence, facelessness, and detachment of modern man.

The Water Hen suddenly appears, alive and well. It is not unusual in the theatre for characters to return to the stage after death. Hamlet's father came back as a ghost; the dead consul in August Strindberg's *Ghost Sonata* leaves the house where he had died the previous day; in Roger Vitrac's *Mysteries of Love* and Jean Cocteau's *Orpheus*, life and death are reversible. Since Witkiew-icz's characters are puppetlike and not flesh-and-blood human be-ings, they are not subject to life and death. The Water Hen speaks bluntly to Edgar. Instead of bemoaning his fate and wallowing in despair, he must face facts. "But you have no talent—not for any-thing whatever." He has come to realize this, he confesses, and that is why he has settled for managing his wife's estate and in-vesting in the "Theosophical Jam Co." He points to three men on stage who are guiding the company's affairs. Yet, he tells her de-jectedly, although he has started a new life, the results are the same. He remains a "mannikin," a puppet figure for the company's directors. "I hate reality," he shouts (p. 33).

The Water Hen tells him he has not yet suffered sufficiently. In order to reach the locus of his problem, he must undergo excoriating torture. Footmen bring in a box eight feet long with yellow wheels and cranks. Like the victim of the medieval torture wheel, Edgar is to be physically pulled apart, dismembered at the suggestion of his anima figure, the Water Hen. Torture and mutilation in alchemical parlance refer to an alteration of chemical components. Alchemists frequently explained their processes by using such words as "torturing" the metals in order to "test" them for purity, incorruptibility, and their ability to withstand "the torment of fire." [18] In a metaphysical context, the alchemist compared such conditions to Christ's dismemberment on the cross and to the Dionysian fertility rituals in which flesh was torn apart with hands and teeth. Dismemberment, psychologically, implies the sacrifice of one state for another. Edgar's dismemberment ritual brings about what alchemists term a *massa confusa*, when the heat of pain and emotional chaos pervade. In a state of ebullition, metals and emotions melt into one another, recreating a preformal state or water condition. Previously rigid and crystalline, fragments break down, thereby removing, psychologically, the blockage between conscious and unconscious spheres and paving the way for a reorientation, a new order which alchemists refer to as the birth of "the inner man." The *Turba Philosophorum*, translated from Arabic into Latin in the eleventh or twelfth century, states, "Excite the battle between them and destroy the body of the copper, till it becomes powder."[19]

The battle is on. Edgar suffers excruciating pain. He faints. The Father enters and has him withdrawn from the torture box. In a moment of compassion, Tadzio begs him not to cry. "Papa, I love you, I woke up from my dream." He lashes out at the Water Hen for having brought Edgar such misery (p. 35). The Water Hen, however, is not moved. She has not yet completed her work. Another catalytic action occurs. She tosses a package of letters written by Duchess Alice's first husband into the melee. It was she, the Water Hen, whom he had loved all the while he had been married to the duchess. She bursts into a cackle. "I don't exist at all. I live by lying" (p. 36). The Water Hen speaks the truth. She exists only as an anima figure and she therefore is dependent for her actions on those who have brought her to life. She becomes a reality for them, entangling them in her web and servicing them by giving them shape, activating inner and outer values.

All flows precipitously to the finale of act 2. Edgar begs the duchess to protect him from his father and his *Übermensch* ideas. "I hate art and I'm afraid of it." He seeks shelter from the Water Hen who destroys his morale and who keeps telling him he has not yet suffered enough. He begs the duchess to kiss him with feeling, "as though she loved him." The duchess bends over in a perfunctory manner and kisses Edgar in a cold, calculating, and brittle way. Edgar finally understands that he has no future: "Like condemned prisoners we'll drag on and on until death" (p. 38).

Act 3: *Spiritus Phantasticus*

In act 3, the same decor as in act 2 is featured. Ten years have elapsed. The predominant color is green. It is not a verdant, positive, and fruitful green, nor is it the spiritual green of the ascending soul. Rather, it is the biting, acidulous, destructive green engendered by verdigris. Formed by the action of vinegar on "burned copper," as Vitruvius wrote, or "rust of copper," verdigris may be used for medicinal as well as for murderous purposes.

The atmosphere is lugubrious, dominated by an obsessive desire to return to the womb. The suicide motif encroaches. Neither the Father, Edgar, nor Tadzio (now twenty and calling himself Tadeusz) are capable of evaluating their individual or collective situations; nor have they made headway in understanding their anima figure, the Water Hen. Rather than integrating what she represents into their psyches, their projection has grown more powerful. The Water Hen now appears as a vamp: a "very seductive" woman possessed of "sensuality." Edgar and Tadeusz unconsciously long for her embrace and seek to lose themselves in her world, where they believe all is love and pleasure.

Suicide is characteristic of the Puer. Having reached an impasse in his psychological development, he cannot but wither. The sacrifice of a happy childhood is too torturing an experience. Maturity, therefore, cannot be gained. The same fate may await the young man who does not meet his father's expectations. Edgar's sense of failure is too searing and thus "the process out of childhood" is not undertaken.[20]

Painful too is the fact that, psychologically, time has remained at a standstill. The characters have aged physically, however, particularly Tadeusz, who tells the Water Hen that she appears younger to him and more sensual. Flattered by his attention, the

Water Hen tells him he has a "beautiful soul" (p. 41) and encourages him to leave with her, to rid himself of the stultifying and stifling atmosphere imposed upon him by family relationships.

A symmetrical action now comes into view. Edgar's early relationship with the Water Hen is restated. Now, however, Edgar has become the child and accuses the Water Hen of attempting to ruin Tadeusz's life as she had his own, of wanting to "make him great the way you wanted to make me great." Not only is his father indicted, but the mother hen figure as well. Tadeusz, reacting as an adolescent might when thwarted, informs Edgar that he must be allowed to marry the Water Hen or he will leave home. He also tells Edgar that he is fully awake and no longer dreaming. Moreover, he refuses to take anyone's advice and thrashes about rejecting parental domination, which is given under the guise of affection. Locked in his own egocentric world, he muses on love, which for him means a prolongation of his own fantasies and needs, a way of finding some semblance of security in a cold, dispassionate world. The Lamplighter returns trying to shed some illumination on the situation, just as Diogenes had tried to order chaos.

The cherry-colored curtain is drawn. The crimson pole comes into view. The lantern casts its eerie green about the static objects and people, as in a shadow play. A lugubrious, fearful, dissociated, and dislocated world invades the scene. Edgar's rage grows uncontrollable. He drags the Water Hen to the stairs, raises his gun, and shoots her once again. The Oedipal rivalry between Edgar and Tadeusz demanded the death of the rival. Tadeusz declares: "Now I've finally awakened from my third dream. I know everything now" (p. 46). In true Hegelian style, the thesis enacted in the first act, the antithesis of the second, has become, as far as Tadeusz is concerned, the synthesis of the finale.

Machine gun fire is heard offstage. A revolution has broken out, which is an exterior manifestation of an inner struggle. Edgar realizes that nothing binds him to life. The destruction of his anima figure, which could have forced him to rely upon himself and discover his identity through introspection, has, quite to the contrary, cut him off still more profoundly from life. The Water Hen's departure means that he no longer has anything to bind him to life. He shoots himself as would a great actor, committing the irreversible act which both the Father and the Water Hen had declared man's way of stamping his imprint on destiny. There are

no tears and no recriminations. Like an automaton, Tadeusz, the
Father, and Edgar's friends pursue their course as disconnected
beings. Time is consumed by the performing of routine and perfunctory acts; gestures take on meaning only in the temporal world
in which they exist. Unwilling to waste a moment of the infinite
number of present moments, man creates goals for himself, making
a mockery of life in general, searching for security through illusion. Neither Tadeusz nor the Father end their lives. Youth still
believes in the future, while old age has made its peace with existence and accepts the days as they come.

The Father begins a card game with his cronies despite the
fact that they have been informed that "the world is collapsing."
Cards, and Tarot cards in particular, represent man's struggle to
bring harmony to dissension, to bind the disparate, to stay the
fleeting. Red lights invade the stage. Explosions are heard. The
card game pursues its course—that of life.

The Water Hen speaks a new theatrical language. Incoheren-
cies, recriminations, repetitions, non sequiturs, and platitudes are
offered the playgoer as substitutes for the climaxes, suspense, and
flesh-and-blood personalities of traditional theatre. The technique
of linguistic and visual dissociation, dislocation, and abstraction
allows Witkiewicz to bombard his audiences with corrosive and
sardonic attacks on art, politics, society, parents, marriage, life,
and death. The breaking up of ideations and conventions called
into play by the solutio operation, in addition to the suicidal motif
so characteristic of the Puer, brings into view a deeply disturbing
universe. The individual stands between two worlds—a past and
future—the one no longer answering his needs, the second offering
him an unending, gaping maw.

The alchemist's aqua permanens did not bring matter back to
its germinal state. It dissolved conscious orientations, washed
away the old sediment, and paved the way for fermentation, but
nothing new emerged. Witkiewicz's creatures pursued their course,
cruelly and abrasively, continuing to exist in the quagmire that
they had created for themselves. The verdigris condition which
permeated their lives ate away at their psyches, just as Cronos, the
god of time, devoured his own children. Alone, dissociated, Witkiewicz's protagonists are trapped in time, with death as the finale
to a pointless existence. Chained to their circular course, they ex-

perience life as a series of mutilations within an absurd space-time continuum.

Edgar's suicide—his one great performance—was replicated by Witkiewicz's own suicide in 1939, after Poland had been overrun by the Nazis. Both returned to the *solutio* condition. In the words of the eighteenth-century alchemist Kirchweger:

For this is certain, that all nature was in the beginning water, and through water all things were born again through water all things must be destroyed.[21]

Rubedo

And I saw the places of the luminaries
and the treasuries of the stars and of the
thunder, and in the uttermost depths,
where were a fiery bow and arrows and
their quiver, and a fiery sword and all the
lightnings. And they took me to the living
waters, and to the fire of the west, which
receives every setting of the sun. And I
came to a river of fire in which the fire
flows like water and discharges itself into
the great sea towards the west.

The Book of Enoch

6

Axël: Mercury the Mediatrix

Jean-Marie Mathias Philippe Auguste de Villiers de l'Isle-Adam's *Axël* was published posthumously in France in 1894. A strange and deeply moving work, certainly not in keeping with the prevailing *Zeitgeist*, it won neither accolades nor fine reviews from critics who barely even noticed its entry into the world. *Axël* dramatizes a transformation process: man's ascension from his leaden condition to his Golden Essence. Gold is the central motif in *Axël*. It is not the common gold of existential man, but rather the invisible and incorporeal Philosopher's Gold, a symbol for the highest spiritual values.[1]

As I have stated, alchemy is not only a science but also a metaphysics. In *Axël*, the Rosicrucian sect is singled out for particular scrutiny. Although the origin of this society is shrouded in mystery, the Rosicrucians date their order back to Hermes Trismegistus, the alleged founder of alchemy. Believers in metempsychosis and in various disciplines which enabled man to ascend the ladder from a base to a sublime spiritual condition, the Rosicrucians used the rose and the cross as symbols of their secret spiritual credo.[2] The Rosicrucians believed that they must try to elevate man's soul and mind during his worldly sojourn so that he might be reborn in a purer domain. Death did not imply an end, but a transition.

Axël is structured in four acts. Each act may be viewed as a stage in the alchemical operation: each is a step toward the regeneration of a human soul from sense immersion to the divine condition. Act 1, entitled "The Religious World," takes place in a convent (a matriarchal fold) on Christmas Eve, 1828. The first scene, entitled "And compel them to come in . . ." (Luke 14:23), sets the tone for the esoteric proceedings that follow—a dramatization of man's passage from an exterior to an interior world, from the visible to the secret domain. This movement takes the hierophant from what alchemists call *fixatio* (understood as an unproductive or stayed, metaphysical, psychological, and chemical condition) to *separatio* (the emergence of differentiation and discrimination). Act 2, "The Tragic World," parallels act 1 but is set in the castle of Axël, a German nobleman and future leader of the Rosicrucian sect. A patriarchal frame of reference is implicit. The action takes place on Easter Eve. As Christmas heralds the birth of a new life force, the separation of body and soul, so Easter announces the possibility of their resurrection in a single body in another sphere. Act 3, "The World of the Occult," dramatizes the alchemical state of *solutio*: the cleansing or liquefying of the separated but still unproductive and nonviable elements. The Master Artificer (also called the Prime Mover) who enters the proceedings in this act eventually will effect the completion of the Great Work. Act 4, "The World of Passion," brings the process to its conclusion in *sublimatio*—the distillation, evaporation, and elevation of the elements into spirit. The fourfold alchemical operation is now complete. The *summum bonum*, the supreme state of perfection, has come into being. No longer enslaved by the material corpus, the etherealized body exists in the transpersonal or divine sphere.

Axël is a metaphysical, psychological, and scientific probing which reflects Villiers de l'Isle-Adam's spiritual climate. Born at Saint-Brieuc in 1838, the son of a marquis, he claimed to be descended from Jean de Villiers de l'Isle-Adam, marshal of France under Charles VI, and of Philippe de Villiers de l'Isle-Adam, great master of the Order of Malta. When he moved to Paris in 1857, he could not adapt to the mediocrity and vulgarity of the growing industrial society. He rejected the materialism around him. His writings (*Isis*, 1862; *Elën*, 1865; *Morgane*, 1866) brought him neither fame nor money. His *Cruel Tales* (1883) and *New Cruel Tales* (1888) are symbolistic, yet marked with lucidity and great sensitivity. In all of his writings, he castigates his enemies by demolishing their belief in progress and by derogating their petty ways. A great admirer of the Symbolist poets, of Edgar Allan Poe, and of Richard Wagner, Villiers de l'Isle-Adam also sought to create something new in the arts. He did so not only with his extraordinary novel, *The Future Eve* (1886), which peers into the world to come, but with *Axël*. Written over a period of fourteen years, it mirrors Villiers de l'Isle-Adam's inner landscape, and replicates in amalgams of metallic essences the interplay of abrasive forces at work en route to a descent.

Act 1: From *Fixatio* to *Separatio*

Act 1 is set in the cloister of Saint Apollodora, a medieval Trinitarian convent located on the border of French Flanders. The dark and mysterious atmosphere of this northern climate sets a mood of introversion and fear. Alchemically, it depicts the *nigredo* phase of the alchemical operation, when the elements exist as *prima materia*. (Psychologically, Christmas may be associated with the birth of the ego from the Self.) The potential for illumination is present but has not yet become manifest. The convent atmosphere, like the world surrounding it, is icy and unbending; feelings have been congealed. A state of *fixatio* reigns, preceding the spring thaw.

The protagonist, Eve-Sara-Emmanuèle, descendant of a wealthy and noble German family, dates her lineage to the remote past, thus lending a mythical quality to her presence. Her tripartite name, Eve ("before the law"), Sara ("during the law"), and Emmanuèle (God is with her"), incorporates characteristics of the Eternal Feminine and allows her to step out of the human sphere into the collective, archetypal domain. Described as a "mysterious beauty," a "pale" and "obscure soul," she is a living mystery, an anima figure.[3] As such, she reflects the shadowy lunar landscape of her surroundings, passively at first and then actively.

As an archetypal figure, Sara is a *complexio oppositorum*: formed and formless, limited and limitless, palpable and impalpable, real and unreal, feminine and masculine. She is endowed with the male characteristics of strength and hardness and is unbending when situations demand it. The fact that she remains silent throughout act 1, except for uttering one word ("No"), indicates her control over her emotions. Her female nature is concretized in her spectacular beauty and her feeling principle. Her face, described as expressionless, is illuminated by the inner light that alchemists call scintillae (or *ignis occultus* or *ignis noster*), cosmic energy made conscious and individual.[4] Sara is spirit concealed in matter or *sapientia*. She dazzles the onlooker and injects excitement and tension throughout the proceedings.

Alchemically, Sara is a personification of mercury. Considered the individuating principle, mercury is synonymous with the force in nature that separates the fixed, liquefies the solid, and transforms the frigid into viable and malleable elements. The *Aurora Consurgens* says of mercury:

I am the mediatrix of the elements, making one to agree with another; that which is warm I make cold, and the reverse; that which is dry I make moist, and the reverse; that which is hard I soften, and the reverse. I am the end and my beloved is the beginning, I am the whole work and all science is hidden in me, I am the law in the priest and the word in the prophet and counsel in the wise. I will kill and I will make to live and there is none that can deliver out of my hand. I stretch for my mouth to my beloved and he presseth his to me; he and I are one; who shall separate us from love? None and no man, for our love is strong as death.[5]

Sara is the liaison between the disparate forces within the play, the "producer of unity," the mediatrix.

Mercury is said to attract gold and to combine and recombine with this metal. Sara's character is also a manifestation of the highest spiritual values, as attested by the seven years she has spent in the convent absorbing (unbeknownst to the other nuns and the Abbess) the forbidden Rosicrucian texts. According to Vitruvius, gold cannot be gilded properly without using quicksilver; therefore mercury is necessary for the binding operation. Discorides suggested that when quicksilver is heated it distills in drops at the top of the earthenware vessel;[6] thus it separates from the mass and rises to ethereal climes. Similarly, when Sara's passion is aroused, a concomitant elevation and sublimation of the important and unimportant, of the pure and the impure, are effected. When coldness prevails, as at the beginning of her stay in the convent, Sara's countenance is like steel; her way is rigid and unyielding. As an agent of transmutation, however, Sara causes movement and adaptation, the passage from *fixatio* to *separatio*. Prior to the opening of the play, she lived in the *nigredo* phase of her development and represented the primal darkness of unevolved nature. The seven years spent in meditation and the study of Rosicrucian arcana allowed evolution to occur. The undistilled mercury residing within her being has altered in consistency and led to the birth of vision.

The Abbess asks Sarah to sign over her wealth to the convent and take her final vows. Despite the fact that Sara acquiesces, the Abbess is concerned because she knows she is dealing with a dangerous element: mercury is also a poison. Sara is endowed with "a terrible talent, Intelligence" (p. 55), the Abbess says. Wisdom, in addition to Sara's reflective and moonlike temperament, makes a fertile field for the breeding of dissension and rebellion within the convent's ordered matriarchal sphere. For the alchemist, intelligence means flame and fire. When heated, intelligence bends metals, liquefies solids, and creates amalgams of emotions, thus altering conventional and traditional consistencies and patterns.

After Sara has assigned her fortune to the convent, the nuptial ceremony begins. That it occurs on Christmas Eve points to the birth of a new attitude; psychologically, it indicates the emergence of the ego, the center of the conscious personality. Since Sara must now face her situation, she risks the pain associated with alienation and rejection. Should she remain passive, however, she will become engulfed within the order and stagnate. The consecration ceremony compels her to decide upon a course and deal with reality.

Divinity's presence is manifested throughout the ritual and permeates the accessories used in the ceremony, thereby transforming them into hierophanies. The flowers strewn about the altar come to represent celestial forces, the virtues of the soul, but they also represent a union of fire and water, thus binding the fleeting and beautiful forms. The flickering of the lit tapers about the stage indicates their active participation in the mysterious drama to take place. In the Middle Ages the Virgin Mary was frequently represented carrying lighted tapers in her hands, which symbolized the wise virgins prepared to receive the bridegroom, as opposed to the foolish virgins who were unprepared (Matt. 25:1–3). Like the wise virgins, Sara is ready to face her ordeal. She is also prepared to fulfill her secret mission, implicit in Rosicrucian doctrine. The tapers may also be viewed as a manifestation of a transformation occurring within Sara. For example, when wax is cold, it is hard and unbending; when warmed, it becomes malleable and fluid. The flaming wick, symbolizing spirit embodied in matter, melts the wax. Emotions likewise are capable of altering moods, even those of the most cerebral and unfeeling beings, thus breaking down the rigidity implicit in some personalities. The ambivalence of Sara's nature is further underscored in the description of her as "tall and white like a paschal taper" (p. 48). In this regard, she is the beginning and end of life, the sacrificial being and the one reborn. Although fixated, she stands at the door of transformation.

Adding to the ceremony are the iridescent colors of Sara's opal necklace. Associated with Isis and the Virgin Mary, opals were also compared by the alchemists to pearls and to spirit. Like spirit, opals possess energy and fire; in that they illuminate by the scintillae they radiate, they endow those wearing them with special insight. They were also considered capable of curing weak eyes and were frequently called *ophthalmius* ("eye stone").[7]

The consecration ceremony thus begins amid a symphony of glowing tones, of light emerging from darkness. Sara kneels before the altar transfixed, "sculpted in stone" (p. 59). Her habit takes on the whiteness of dawn; her countenance is cold as mercury. Her long black hair, strewn with orange blossoms, flows freely about her dress, adding to her resplendence. Sounds of church bells enhance the kineticism inherent in the proceedings. Since bells are made of amalgams of lead, iron, gold, pewter, copper, and quicksilver, they may be looked upon as an example of man's power over nature, his ability to extract metals in their unformed condition and transform them into viable and even celestial objects. The bells' vaulted shapes represent the heavens that cover and protect man; hanging from the highest point of the convent, they stand midway between earth and heaven as a link in a monistic universe. The sound of organ music (the music of the spheres) filters into the ever-expanding proceedings. Incense is added to purify the mundane. Its aroma permeates the pleromatic spheres and is a sublimating force. Incense dulls and insensitizes, thus permitting a *participation mystique*, a dissolution of categories, a fusion with universal forces.

The Archbishop informs the postulant that "her mortal life must be crucified by joining forever in the divine sacrifice" (p. 59). First she must agree to take the marriage vows; then her hair will be shorn by Sister Aloyse, who stands ready with large scissors to perform the sacrificial act, which psychologists have likened to dismemberment. Severed from the mundane world, she will be re-born and transfigured in the divine sphere. The Archbishop, a re-gressive and materialistic Senex figure, is more interested in vul-gar gold than in the sublimated spiritualized element. He stands for the alchemist's lead, the most impure of all metals. Mephisto-phelian in nature, he tempts Sara to choose eternal salvation with *convent* or *convent*ional life. To order her course and secure her for his own ends is his goal. Mercurial in essence, however, she prefers the hazards and risks accompanying inner growth to stagnation. When the Archbishop asks, "Do you accept Light, Hope, and Life?," Sara replies, "No!" (p. 68). She is prepared to confront the forces that will seek to punish her and has the strength to carve out her own destiny, to transform *fixatio* into *separatio*. The energy needed to effect such an alteration has resulted from her inner friction when she is forced to face the Archbishop and his reality. This tension (contained in the alchemist's athanor) had been burning slowly but continuously within her for seven years in an archaic and unconscious condition. Suddenly it ignited into mercury's white heat of frenzy.

The ceremony is brought to a sudden halt. The smoothly run-ning order has been disrupted. Sara's overt act has solemnized the birth of new forces, thus underscoring the Christmas spirit. Sara is celebrating her fall into matter rather than her entry into celestial spheres as understood by the Abbess and Archbishop. For the al-chemist, such a fall does not indicate a step downward. On the contrary, it stands for an ascension. Like the Gnostics, the alche-mists believed that man's earthbound state was a necessary obsta-cle that he had to overcome in his quest for fulfillment and redemption. If Adam and Eve had remained in Eden, or, psycho-logically, in an unconscious state, they would not have been forced to live in a world of tension and differentiation. The responsibili-ties imposed upon man during his earthly state create conflict and uncertainty. As exercise strengthens the muscles, so decision mak-ing and the energy accompanying it fortify the inner being, paving the way for growth and the attainment of higher goals. Redemp-tion comes to those who have earned it.

The Archbishop intends to punish and discipline Sara. He orders her to follow him into the deepest vaults of the convent. There, amid the sepulchers, dungeons, and sculptures, she will be incarcerated in a small cell until her repentance is complete. As they make their way into these depths, Sara sees an ax hanging on a wall. She grabs it and threatens the Archbishop. Rather than cause a confrontation that might lead to bloodshed and further disruption of convent activities, he yields to Sara's demands. He enters the cell meant for her and she locks the iron door behind him. He is left there to die, to return to dust, the alchemist's *prima materia*.

Although the Archbishop is a negative Senex figure, he may be looked upon as playing a positive role in *Axël*. He is the catalyst who precipitates Sara's spiritual development. A composite of domineering and materialistic characteristics, his rigidity and unbending nature force the issue between her way and his. Because he has been overly fascinated by material gold, his energies have flowed outward, leaving his inner being empty. What had once been strong and powerful has grown dry and brittle, oxydized by the elements and calcinated by the burning fires of Sara's spiritual experience. Sara, on the other hand, had been feeding her soul on forbidden mystical tracts and has emerged strengthened from her ordeal. She has confronted and crushed those forces the Archbishop stands for in a symbolic patricide or ritual sacrifice. The gleaned blood is restored to the earth, thus renewing its fertility and by extension her own. The ax has enabled her to break away from a regressive patriarchal situation and from her identification with the church as world and spiritual parent.

Two warring principles are at stake: patriarchal and matriarchal. When Saint Paul ordered the destruction of Diana's altars at Ephesus (Acts 19:24–28), he committed symbolic matricide, thus allowing patriarchal Christianity to grow and flourish. Sara has accomplished a similar goal by destroying the patriarchal order and an unregenerate matriarchal system under its domination. As a result of her symbolic patricide, blood will now fertilize the earth. A transubstantiation is the issue here: bodily heat grown cold and unproductive is now revitalized and redirected.

However, a new ordeal awaits Sara. She will have to travel in the darkness of winter through the dense forest surrounding the convent. Energized by the light of nature ignited within her by the friction caused by her overt act, Sara leaves the convent. Now a missile of passion, her urge to live has made her a psychic transformer. The passive nun has changed into an alchemical queen ready to brave all dangers to unite with her king.

Act 2: From *Fixatio* to *Separatio*

Act 2 parallels act 1 in its alchemical motif. It takes place in Axel's castle, which is decorated with the Auërsperg coat of arms, oriental standards, astral spheres, mounted eagles, tapestries, and paintings of German barons and war heroes dating back to the medieval crusades. For the alchemist, a castle is a protective and enclosed area that houses the secrets contained in athanors, retorts, and vials. A castle symbolically permits entry into an inner domain and has been alluded to by alchemists and in legends as "the Mansion of the Beyond" and "the Castle of Light."

Axël, called the "Prince of the Royal Secret" by the Rosicrucians, is around twenty-three years old. Strong, virile, disciplined, handsome, and elegant, he represents the archetypal young man. His name is a reflection of his character. *Axe* (meaning "axis") underscores his straightforward and incisive attitude; *axer* (French for "oriented toward a goal") implies his set direction; *ax* (the weapon) reflects his cutting way, his powerful backbone; *el* ("God," in Hebrew) suggests that divinity as a living presence inhabits him. Semiotically, the letter *x* represents the four alchemical steps leading to the completion of the Great Work.

Axël is the alchemist's sulfur. He is a hot, demonic principle; he ignites and fumigates the atmosphere. He contains *sul* or *sol*, that energetic and spiritual force related to the sun. In this connection, an analogy may be drawn between the element sulfur embedded in the earth (in alchemical documents called variously "sun in the earth," "central fire," "Black Sun," or "Black Sulphur") and the sun as a solar force uniting heaven and earth. In the science of heraldry, black is labeled sand, representing its association with the earth and underscoring its yellow, ocher, or solar facets.[8] Alchemists frequently identified the *citrinitas* with the *nigredo* phase: in *nigredo* exists *citrinitas*, or the golden period preceding the completion of the Great Work. Alteration of color and consistency may occur when sulfur, a fiery content, is aroused by the alchemist's fire (or heat of tension), causing the yellow flame of sulfur to alter what is arid and fixated.

Axël has the dual aspects of sulfur: his outer garments are black; his solar elements spark within. Black, like white, may be considered an absence of color or the sum of all colors, either negation or synthesis. Therefore his actions appear ambivalent: evil cohabits with good. Like that of the Black Knight in the Grail legend, who emerged from his tomb and was considered a destructive force by those who did not understand his message, Axël's comportment may seem dubious and unfortunate. The initiated understand his way and look upon him as a symbol of the generative masculine principle.[9]

At the beginning of act 2, the pensive and mysterious Axël still has not stepped out of his castle which is surrounded by a black forest. Under the dominion of these protective and restrictive forces, he receives the Rosicrucian arcana that his mentor, Master Janus, passes on to him. "I do not instruct," Master Janus states, "I awaken" (p. 195). Axël is still a passive disciple; however, his earthly slumber will soon come to an end. Now that he has been indoctrinated into the so-called cult of the planets, his identity will be linked to cosmic forces. He will come to understand the goal of his mission as Sara does hers.

Axël's cousin, the Commander, has been visiting and is due to depart that night, Easter Eve. The Commander has just learned from Herr Zacharias, Axël's guard and a former German soldier, of the existence of a hidden treasure. During the Napoleonic invasions, the German government had asked Axël's father, Count Auërsperg, to transport the treasure from the National Bank of Frankfurt to a safer area. Shortly after the task was accomplished, those involved were killed by French soldiers. The Commander is convinced that Axël was told about the treasure by his father before he died, and he suggests that it be unearthed and given to the German nation. Axël, incensed by such earthbound views, considers the Commander's suggestion an affront.

The Commander represents a negative father image and is described as "noxious"; his color is "pallid as silver!"—not the pure and noble silver of the alchemist, but the ignoble metal of Judas. Like the Archbishop, who sought Sara's money for the convent to ensure the continuation of a stable hierarchical religious order, the Commander stands for the existential domain and the status quo. He ridicules Axël's voluntary exile, his silent abode, his self-imposed restrictions and disciplines, and his obsession with spiritual matters. He calls him the "Black Hunter," thus associating Axël with the legendary Freischütz ("Free-shooter"), who had made a pact with the devil. The Commander so taunts him that he causes Axël's sulfuric personality to take fire. When the Commander demands to know the meaning of Axël's "blind friendship" for Master Janus, the nature and goal of their work, Axël blazes. The Commander further implies a similarity between the charlatans of past ages and Axël and Master Janus.

That you play at living in the Middle Ages,—so be it! This castle is made for this kind of thing; it's innocent enough and not without some grandeur. But to carry the disguise so far as to bring about the revival of the puffers of the Great Work! . . . to dream of alloying mercury and sulfur . . . I cannot believe this.—Do you understand the meaning of potable gold which remains at the bottom of the crucible? . . . Your youth. Come on now! The devil with this dried up, defrocked vestment, which really doesn't become a gentleman! Imitate me! Grab hold of life, as it is, without illusions and without weakness.—Make your own way! . . . leave the follies to the insane.

(P. 139)

Axël's sulfuric rage flows outward in abrasive color tones. The alchemist's Black Sun cuts the atmosphere. "My path?" Axel replies. "It has been traced for centuries" (p. 151). His anterior existences, hereditary lineage, and play of destiny have all been worked out eons before. He is the guardian of the secret treasure. Like the dragon protecting the Golden Fleece, Axël is the powerful force that waits, watches, and observes, ready to destroy anything and anyone threatening the treasure's safety. To the alchemist, the dragon also symbolizes fire, the psychic energy (libido) that burns in those with sulfuric temperaments. Axël will never reveal the secret. Secrets must be hidden from the unworthy, declared the alchemist and the Rosicrucians. Only a few may peer into the dazzling depths where these arcana lie buried. Thus Axël, the one singled out to guard them, though he is honored by his mission, suffers the weight of the responsibilities involved. To be different is both a blessing and a curse.

The Commander threatens to call the entire German army to search for the treasure. Axël's castle would be destroyed by this military force. No group on earth, Axël retorts, could survive entry into the forest or the castle. Axël's forest is mined by his family's faithful soldiers, "foresters with dangerous guns," retainers who have been under hereditary orders for centuries. The great dogs of Ulm, that "great race of wild war-trained dogs" (p. 174), are there to protect the treasure. If trespassers attempted a fight, they would be chewed to pieces, nor could any force penetrate the three-hundred-year-old stone fortress with its turrets, iron gratings, and vaulted dungeons.

The forest represents a primitive state of nature. The psychologist calls it the "collective unconscious"; the alchemist calls it the *prima materia*. When associated with the Great Mother, it represents vegetal life, fertility in its uncontrolled and primeval state. Because the sun's rays cannot penetrate the thickness of its foliage, this world, clothed in darkness, inspires terror in those who do not understand its meaning; its multitude of trees confuses and disorients the uninitiated; the iciness of its atmosphere congeals the unprotected. Ascetics withdraw into the forest (Brocéliande); oracles (Dodona) inhabit it. There they may experience its nutritive forces, the treasures stored in the earth's depths and, by analogy, in the individual's.

Axël's anger explodes. He challenges the Commander to a duel and kills him. "You are falling into the depths of death, as a stone in the void—without attraction and without goal" (p. 183). The Archbishop's incarceration occurred on Christmas Eve; the Commander's death takes place on Easter Eve. A new ruling principle is ready to emerge.

Act 3: From *Separatio* to *Solutio*

In act 3, Master Janus appears on stage. He represents the helpful spiritual guide, the positive father figure. Master Janus exiled himself from the world when asked by Axël's dying father to care for his son. Detached from emotional entanglements, he accepted the responsibility and devoted his life to preparing Axël in the Rosicrucian and alchemical tradition. Axël informs his master of a conflict he is experiencing. His life of exile no longer brings him fulfillment. He wants to taste the fruits of the earth and to live. Rather than reacting in dismay, Master Janus is pleased with Axël's confession. Only when duality is present, he intimates, can inner struggle occur and an individual master his destiny. Therefore Axël is ready for the supreme ordeal, the last phase of the alchemical process.

Master Janus is the third principle in the alchemical process: salt. He is a preserver of the occult art. As a condiment, he adds spice to the proceedings, dilating the events and the personalities called into action. Because of the depth of his knowledge and the intensity of his inner light, he is comparable to the rock salt mined in the mountains, and because of the purity and prismatic nature of his vision, he resembles the crystals left after the evaporation of saline springs. He shines "as the reflection between two mirrors: one would lose oneself in infinity" (p. 92). Vincent de Beauvais describes salt and quotes from *De Aluminibus et Salibus*:

Salt ('sal') is a water which the dryness of fire has solidified and the nature of which is dry and warm. It has the property of liquefying gold and silver in the vehemency of the fire and augmenting in them their natural colors, namely in gold, red, and silver, white. It converts them from their bodily nature to a foamy nature [spumalitas], and frees them from their impurities and consumes their foulness of a sulphurous nature, when the bodies [that is, metallic] are roasted with it.[10]

As salt, Master Janus blends into Axël's life, unforeseen and mysterious.

Janus's name suggests other properties of his character. According to legend, the original Janus was the first king of Latium. Because he received Saturn graciously after the god had been expelled from heaven, Janus was given premonitory powers and became capable of entering the fourth dimension (time). Hence he was able to live in what alchemists call the "eternal present"; he could span centuries. The Romans regarded Janus as the god of doors: he opened and shut them during the winter and summer solstices. Later Janus was associated by Christians with John the Baptist and John the Evangelist. The feast day of John the Baptist, celebrated in June, coincided with the summer solstice, and the feast day of John the Evangelist in winter coincided with the winter solstice. The Baptist purified and prepared the soul for its reintegration into primitive and celestial conditions; the Evangelist announced the birth of the New Jerusalem on earth. Thus Janus incorporates two cyclical periods: both phases are implicit in the action of the play. Janus was also androgynous: one of his faces was masculine and the other was feminine. Thus Master Janus represents solar and lunar forces, and within him cohabit Axël and Sara. Master Janus awakens Axël by opening the door to a new world through Rosicrucian arcana. To achieve such an end requires a transfiguration from *solutio* to *sublimatio*. Speaking of the Rosicrucians, Master Janus says:

Transfigure yourself in their silent light: think of developing through meditation, of purifying through the ordeal of fire and of sacrifices, the

infinite influx of your will! of becoming an adept of the science of the
strong! of becoming an intelligence liberated from the wills and bonds of
the moment, in view of supereternal Law.

(P. 197)

   Learning, Master Janus contends, is a question of rediscover-
ing, of immersing oneself in the collective unconscious, the alchemist's *aqua permanens*. Master Janus rephrases Plato's theory of
recollection: "He can know nothing, who does not recognize!"
(p. 197). Each adept of the Great Work must create his own essence, make his own way into the "Impersonal World of Becoming"
(p. 197).

You will only be your creation. The world will attribute to you only the
meaning you have given to yourself. Become greater still under those
veils, by conferring upon them their sublime meaning—of being delivered
from them! Do not belittle yourself by groveling, in the sense of enslaving
yourself, to that which binds and enchains you. . . . You are a future creator. You are a god who merely pretends he's forgetting his quintessence
in order to realize its radiance. What you call universe is only the result of
this pretense, the secret of which is yours alone. Recognize yourself! Offer
yourself in Being! Extract yourself from this jail which is the world; children of prisoners. Escape from Becoming!

(P. 203)

To live in the earthly domain is to drain one's energies, to enfeeble
one's vision. "You are emerging from the Immemorial. You are
now incarnated under the veil of phenomenon in a prison of analogies" (p. 197).
   As the dissolving agent salt, Master Janus is instrumental in
altering the relationships from *separatio* to *solutio*, thereby creating a new ruling principle. The superior force of an all-inclusive
viewpoint is born as a result. Axël's conflict—the existential versus
the spiritual domain—has caused a dissolution of his once fixated
orientation. It could be said that he is in the process of drowning in
the waters of the unconscious. It is Easter Eve. Spring is upon him.
The salt has cleansed the impurities of Axël's hypertrophied view
of life and calls for its regeneration. Master Janus has understood
Axël's fears: "The river fears becoming sea—it would lose itself"
(p. 192). He encourages Axël to leap into the unknown and dissolve
there, losing his orientation and regressing in the *aqua permanens*,
where corrosion, rust, and oxidation are permissible. New riches

will penetrate his immersed being and enrich it. Like Buddha, who had to participate in life and its worldly and sensual experiences to expand his vision, Axël would have to indulge his senses to alter his focus.

Axël is ready for the *hieros gamos*, the royal marriage, the fusion of sulfur and mercury. Master Janus says: "Now is the hour.—She too will arrive, she who had renounced the divine ideal for the secret of gold, as you will renounce, later on, your sublime finalities, for this wretched secret" (p. 190). Eve-Sara-Emmanuèle has ridden through the dangerous forested regions to Axël's castle to join forces with her Black Knight. "The Veil and the Cloak, both renunciators, have crossed each other," declares Master Janus. "The Work is in the making" (p. 210).

Act 4: From *Solutio* to *Sublimatio*

At the beginning of act 4, Sara secretly enters Axël's castle and makes her way down the spiral stairs to the dungeon. Her circular descent symbolizes the progression of the alchemical work. She reaches the bottom and walks among the sepulchers, vaults, and statues of knights and chatelaines. Funeral lamps are suspended from arched ceilings and a stained glass window of a rose is visible. Suddenly Sara stops in front of a heraldic "Head of Death" and, taking a dagger from her belt, strikes a spot between its eyes. The wall opens and reveals a variety of dazzling gems. Sara turns and sees Axël, who has been watching her. With a small revolver she shoots at him twice but only grazes him. He disarms her and is struck by her beauty. "Oh beauty of a forest exposed to lightning!" (p. 225). They recognize their love and the sublimity of their embrace is unparalleled.

Until now Axël has been identified exclusively with the masculine principle. He is all brawn; the feeling side of his personality has remained undeveloped. As an anima figure, Sara represents this feeling quality. In the fairy tale, it is Prince Charming who cuts through the brambles and thorns to rescue the beautiful maiden. In *Axël*, it is Sara who makes her way through the forest of darkness and overcomes her terror in face of the unknown. It is Sara, as the embodiment of feeling, who leads Axël to the treasure by piercing the Head of Death between the eyes. Known to mystics as the "Mind's Eye" or the "Inner Eye," the area in the middle of the forehead leads to the soul. It is within the head, a spheric form likened to the universe, that man's inner riches reside. The head, the governing principle in man, in conjunction with the feeling function leads to the discovery of the treasure. The precious stones (diamonds, rubies, sapphires, and so forth) are revealed in their cut, polished, and rarefied luminosities—that is, sublimated by the soul. In alchemical terms, the treasure represents the Philosopher's Stone, the element within each individual that allows for exaltation when it is put through the rigors and disciplines of the scientific, metaphysical, and psychological process.

Drops of blood come from Axël's wounded arm. As Joseph of Arimathea had gathered Christ's blood in the chalice after his crucifixion, so Sara dips her garment into cold water and wipes the blood from Axël's wound. By this gesture, she affects another transubstantiation: she has opened him to feeling. Sara then removes the royal rose, which she had found in the forest, from under her cloak. She had plucked each of its thorns, thus removing the obstacles in her path, and breathed renewed life into it, warming and protecting it from icy elements. Sara places the rose on the cross of her dagger as a sign of recognition in accordance with Rosicrucian law.

To eternalize the ecstatic nature of this moment, Axël decides they must take the poison hidden in Sara's emerald ring. Higher spheres and an eternal life will be theirs. "My dreams know another light!" (p. 228), Axël declares. Sara still longs for earthly love, however, and is not yet ready for the final step of the alchemical operation. "Let yourself be seduced!" she begs. Axël remains adamant.

You see the outer world through your soul: it dazzles you; but it cannot give us one hour comparable to the intensity of being, one second to those we have just lived. The real, the absolute, the perfect accomplishment is that inner moment we have just experienced between us, in the funereal splendor of this vault. We have submitted to this ideal world: no matter what name you give it—it is now irrevocable!

(P. 250)

Sara removes her ring. Associated with incorruptible gold and rebirth, the emerald stone is an important alchemical symbol. It is the stone that fell from Lucifer's forehead and thus represents illumination. (Lucifer comes from the Latin *lux fiat*, "light-maker.")

As I have earlier noted, alchemists believed that Hermes Trisme-gistus left his teachings on the Emerald Table, which implies the sacred nature of this stone and the mysteries embedded therein. Because emerald green is associated with vegetation and life—the *Anima Mundi*—it has taken on the hue of the "universal color of divinity" and as such is the color of the Holy Ghost.[11]

It is dawn, Easter Day. Sara and Axël take the poison. "Man takes with him in death only that which he has renounced in life. In truth—we are leaving only an empty shell here. The value of this treasure exists within us" (p. 253).

Sara and Axël have left the earth. They have become subli-mated beings. The initiation ritual is complete; the *hieros gamos* has taken place: king and queen, mercury and sulfur are one. The golden hour, the mother of the sun, has divested itself of the cold of winter and the polluted darkness of the human mind and world. Axël and Sara have "emptied" themselves of their corporeal gar-ments according to the ancient rite of kenosis, and their spirits have reentered the earth as unmixed pneuma, there to generate new essences, fresh forms, and creative principles.

7

The Dybbuk: The Spagyric Marriage

The Dybbuk (1916), written by Shloyme Ansky (Solomon Zainwill Rapaport, 1863–1920) is a religious mystery, a drama of possession and of eternal love. For the alchemist it is the paradigm of a "spagyric marriage": an inner psychic union which takes place beyond the physical realm, in a retort, as a projection. Psychologically, such a wedding acts as an escape from life into an atemporal world.

The Dybbuk is the result of centuries of persecution of Jews throughout the world. To survive emotionally, Jews had to develop a religious view which would heal the scars left by these harrowing conditions and instill hope in those who had lost it. Hasidism answered this need in many ghetto communities in eastern Europe. Rather than focusing on earthly conditions, the Hasids emphasized a spiritual view, including belief in the transmigration of souls, joy in the service of God, and faith that a benevolent and blissful condition awaited the pure in heart and soul. The belief in transmigration of souls endowed individuals and entire communities with a sense of emotional and historical continuity, particularly when living conditions were as precarious as they were in the ghettos. The belief in the eternity of ancestral souls gave archetypal foundation to the psyche. It was a protective device against the forces of oppression: to feel the presence of loved ones hovering about helped individuals overcome the very real terror of the pogrom eras.

The Hasidic sect reached out to embrace all the suffering, from the richest to the poorest, the healthiest to the sickest. It reflected the emergence of a new period: the age of the common man. As a mystically oriented creed, it accorded greater importance to the female principle than the strictly patriarchal Talmudic orientation.

The Dybbuk is based on a Hasidic tale. *Dybbuk* means "an attachment." It represents the disembodied spirit of a dead person which has been unable to find rest. Punished for its sins (or those of the person or family it seeks out), this spirit longs for asylum in a living person and takes possession of that being. Stories of dybbukim date back to the Second Temple and to Talmudic periods, although the term itself never appears in the Old Testament; in the New Testament, it is referred to as an "unclean spirit." King Saul was possessed until the evil spirits were driven from him by David playing the harp (1 Sam. 16:14–23). The Essenes were well known for their miraculous cures of possessed persons. Christ exorcised demons (Matt. 8:16–31). Kabbalistic literature includes tales and "protocols" concerning the rituals to be followed in cases of exorcism. Today, the dybbuk would be likened to a case of schizophrenia, resulting perhaps from some unconscious psychic conflict dating back to a childhood trauma.

Although eastern European Jewry suffered from the physical hardships and emotional problems resulting from nearly constant pogroms, the nineteenth-century Hasidic movement developed a rich spiritual and cultural way of life. The facts surrounding the life of its founder, Israel Ben Eliezer (1700–1760), known as the Baal Shem Tov ("The Master of the Holy Name"), however, are shrouded in mystery. We know only that he was born in the western Ukraine, was orphaned at an early age, and spent many years in solitude and meditation near his hometown of Podolia. He studied the Talmud, the Torah, and the kabbalah. After his marriage, the couple went to live in isolation in the Carpathian mountains, where he continued his studies. He also immersed himself in nature, learning about the healing power of herbs and experiencing a veritable love for everything in God's world. Of prime import to him was the joy he knew when filled with the *Ruach Elohim* ("Spirit of God"), not the rigid theoretical laws set down by the Talmudists nor their casuistic discussions and abstract concepts. Every man could open himself up to spiritual elation, he believed, through meditation, prayer, and purity of heart. Rather than diminishing man's reasoning power, such moments of divine ecstasy would heighten them. Feelings of transcendence and of the unraveling of life's mysteries allowed the Baal Shem to see beyond the strict and immutable laws with which his contemporaries had structured their universe.[1]

The Baal Shem's teachings emphasized the heart rather than the head, emotionality rather than cerebrality.[2] Furthermore, the *numinosum*, God's luminosity, could be experienced anywhere. Prayers need not necessarily be spoken to reach God's ear; they could simply be thought. Communion with the divine could be experienced through dance, song, and meditation, as well as the study of traditional Hebrew texts: what was essential was that the hierophant's heart be filled with love of God. Since God's immanence and omniscience encompass the All, nothing in the created world may be denigrated or considered completely evil. Although evil does exist in a variety of degrees, man's function on earth is to redeem the wicked within himself and the community at large.[3]

Hasidism was a kind of revivalist movement which brought forth a new religious consciousness based on love, joy, and feelings of relatedness with God and with man. Rabbinical learning was not the main path to God; the kabbalah, the esoteric and theosophical teachings of Judaism, were equally powerful. The most influential kabbalistic work was *The Zohar (The Book of Splendor)*, comprised of mystical commentaries on parts of the Bible. These dated from the second century and were handed down in the form of discussions between Simeon bar Yohai and his followers in Palestine; also included were the writings of the thirteenth-century Castilian scholar Moses de Leon and the sixteenth-century visionary, Isaac Luria of Safed. The *Sefer Yetsirah (Book of Creation)* ascribed to first century mystics and the *Sefer-Ha-Bahir (Book of Light)*, one of the oldest hermetic documents revised and commented upon by Isaac the Blind in thirteenth-century France, were also important in the creation and formulation of hasidism. The esoteric works deal for the most part with questions of cosmology, cosmogony, transmigration of souls, angelology, and demonology. Meditation exercises such as those implicit in the systems of *gematria* (giving numerical equivalents to words and letters in the alphabet) and *notarikon* and *temura* (interchanging letters and words according to certain rules) enabled initiates to understand the mysteries hidden within the lines: meaning preceding manifestation in the visual sphere.[4]

Such religious devices stimulated new associations, fresh visions, and unheard-of spatial relationships in color, form, and sound, thereby expanding the way to divinity. A new logic was discerned in kabbalistic teachings, no longer bound by linear time schemes or three-dimensional conceptualizations, but experienced in a transcendental sphere. Various levels of consciousness were subsumed: lights could be heard, sounds seen, and the formless touched. The new values derived from these unlimited spheres served to transform worn concepts and give fresh interpretations to arid texts, new luster and dimensionality to the world at large. Disorientation frequently followed periods of expanded consciousness, but once the pleromatic sphere had become known to the mystic, an apprehension of God and his creation unknown to the intellect came into being. The Baal Shem and his followers did not allow the young, uninitiated student to delve into the holy mysteries revealed by the kabbalah. Such studies were forbidden until the age of thirty, and even then, only holy men were permitted to peer into its unlimited and dazzling heights. If a student lacked sufficient maturity, understanding, and harmony of being, the arcana embedded within the kabbalah could wreak havoc on him, disrupting his course and allowing him to misuse its mysteries.

The kabbalistic concepts of *gilgul* (transmigration of souls), *tikkun* (restoration of lights), *devekut* (mystical cleaving to God), and *kavvanah* (the intention), which were adapted and adopted by the Baal Shem, formed the core of his teachings.[5] Gilgul may be understood as part of the kabbalist's cosmology and cosmogony. God's first creation, Adam Kadman (the primordial man), was an emanation composed of divine light. This essence was kept in vessels made of lower mixtures of light, which proved to be too weak to contain the force. The vessels shattered, causing these lower mixtures to scatter throughout the universe. God's next creation, the biblical Adam, whose soul held the souls of all mankind, fell into matter, alienating not only himself from God, but also the whole of mankind thereafter. Once man populated the earth, it was incumbent upon each person to help restore the light to divinity through the tikkun process. By means of this effort, individual souls would be redeemed. The tikkun may be initiated through devekut, a strictly personal view of life which implies "intimate

communion with God." Devekut must be accompanied by kavvanah, an expression of man's sincerity (or "the soul of the deed") in
the performance of altruistic acts which may lead to his union with
the divine. If a soul is not redeemed after its first sojourn on earth,
it may transmigrate three times thereafter, giving it further
chances to fulfill God's commandment and its own salvation.

Gilgul, tikkun, devekut, and kavvanah pave the way for individual initiative, personal responsibility, sincerity, and faith in the
divine. For the Hasid, God is within all beings and may be experienced by everyone, providing the effort is sufficiently powerful and
the approach pure. To assure the Hasid of a balanced existence and
some semblance of economic security, the Baal Shem taught that
work in the existential sphere is of great importance. Families had
to be supported, careers made, and futures determined. One could
not spend one's entire life in a state of contemplation. The Baal
Shem's emphasis on both the spiritual and physical aspects of life,
and on the accessibility of God through meditation, prayer, and
acts, was indeed a comforting feeling for those whose lives had
been terrorized.

It was in Vitebsk, Russia, Ansky's birthplace, that he received
a Hasidic education. Moved by the suffering and poverty of his
people and humanity at large, he joined the Haskalah, a movement
of enlightenment among Jews of eastern Europe. Influenced by the
political and economic doctrines of the Narodniki, a popular group,
he decided to live among the Russian peasants. He worked at a
variety of jobs until, in 1892, he was forced to flee Russia because
of his political ideas. He went to Germany, Switzerland, and
France, remaining in Paris for six years as secretary for Piotr
Lavrov, a revolutionary philosopher. In 1905 he returned to Russia
and joined the Social Revolutionary party, but spent his leisure
time writing tales about the Hasid, based on legends he heard
around him. From 1911 to 1914 he traveled to numerous villages
in Volhynia and Podolia, gathering material on the Jews as a
people. It was in 1912 that he heard the tale about a young girl
and her ghostly lover from an innkeeper. He noted it and later
wrote his play. Ansky died on December 9, 1920, just a month
before the successful opening of *The Dybbuk* in Vilna.[6] His Yiddish
works, which include plays, narratives, memoirs, and folk tales,
were published posthumously (1920–25).[7]

The events in *The Dybbuk* are so powerful, the feelings evinced so universal, and the characters so authentic, that the drama achieves mythical grandeur. The action takes place in a small Hasidic ghetto community (*shtetl*). It is here one meets Channon, an ascetic student of the kabbalah. He is poor and is in love with Leah, the only daughter of Sender, the wealthiest citizen in the shtetl. Channon tries, through mystical rituals and theurgic practices, to prevent Sender from finding a suitable match for Leah. Just as he becomes convinced of his power over destiny, Sender announces that he has found a husband, Manashe, for Leah. The shock is too great for the physically and emotionally frail Channon. He dies, but returns as a dybbuk who captivates and haunts his beloved. The struggle waged by Channon's soul to possess Leah's soul is enacted on stage, as are the complex rituals involved in the exorcism procedures that lead to the play's deeply poignant conclusion. As theatre, *The Dybbuk* is unique since contrasting spheres coexist on stage: life and death; the visible and invisible; the sensual and the spiritual; beauty and ugliness; ecstasy and misery.

Act 1: "White Fire on Black Fire"

At the beginning of act 1, the stage is dark. Low chanting infiltrates the atmosphere. An ancient Hasidic song, "Mipnei Mah," is intoned.

> Why, from the highest height,
> To the deepest depth below,
> Has the soul fallen?
> Within itself, the Fall
> Contains the Resurrection.

(P. 25)

The lights brighten. The inside of an ancient synagogue comes into view. It is not only a house of worship, but a meeting place as well. The walls of the synagogue are stained, "streaked as if with the tears of centuries"; that it had originally been "built under the earth" in some remote era adds to its mystery. Miracles are associated with the synagogue: it was said that once the entire community had been destroyed by a fire and the synagogue alone was saved. When the roof caught fire, "innumerable doves came flocking down upon it and beat out the flames with their wings" (p. 53).

The table in the center of the *bima* (an elevated platform where the Torah is read) is covered with a dark cloth. On the side of the stage a wooden table is heaped high with books. Two candles are burning. A prayer cabinet near the Ark and an altar are visible. A half-dozen students are studying and chanting sections of the Talmud in low tones. At another table, the Batlonim, who spend their time praying, are in a state of near ecstasy. Channon, a young man seated directly under the Perpetual Light, is lost in meditation.

Moments elapse. The Batlonim begin talking about the wondrous tales and miraculous deeds of their rabbis. Mention is made of the "Original Serpent" Satan, "the enemy of God" (p. 31). The Messenger, a stranger to the community, is lying on a bench near the stove. He sets the tone of the play when he says, "Only the heat of a too intense desire can cause the vessel to burst when the spark breaks into a flame" (p. 33). It is the Messenger who, like the ancient Greek chorus, reveals unknown forces at work; he acquaints spectators with the reigning signs and symbols and warns of imminent danger.

Fire is that force which caused the vessels enclosing Adam Kadman to shatter. Thus did the sparks of divine light scatter throughout the world of matter and fall into the "abyss" of life, starting in this way "the great cosmological drama."[8] Since that time, everything in the manifest world has been imperfect, deficient, and unbalanced. Man's goal in life is to restore these sparks to divinity, to repair the flaw through piety, virtue, and obedience to God's commandments. When light and flame become too intense to be controllable, as they were in Adam Kadman's case, they sear, destroy, and annihilate. As a sacred force implicit in divinity, fire represents man's flaming desire or quest for spiritual and intellectual evolution, transforming itself into an instrument of regeneration and purification. For the alchemist, fire melts metals and creates new alloys: it makes the fixed fluid, boils the cold, and reddens the white. Its emotional equivalent indicates passionate need, volatility, activity, and intensity.

Channon, who has not budged until now, suddenly rises. He asks the Batlonim the whereabouts of those miracle workers whose wonders they have been relating. What are the spells they utter and the incantations they recite? The theurgic rites they practice? Where are these men who can resurrect the dead, cure the tormented, and bring joy to the disheartened? They live, Channon is told, in distant, inaccessible areas.

The audience now learns that Channon had once been a brilliant student; he was said to have a brain of steel. He knew five hundred pages of the Talmud by heart. Moreover, strange things had happened to him. After receiving his degree from the yeshiva, he vanished. Some people said he had spent a year doing the "penance of the Golos," consisting of mortification of the flesh and wandering throughout the world as a beggar, helping others to gain redemption whenever and wherever he could. Upon his return to town, he had changed completely. Absorbed in meditative practices, he spent his time fasting, performing holy ablutions, and studying the kabbalah.

Prayer, recitation, incantation, and swaying allow the mystic to experience various spheres of God's creation: different levels of his unconscious. It was believed that by concentrating on each word, the initiate opened up the way to inner light, which in turn illuminated more profound universal secrets, linking man even more strongly with the divine world. One of the main differences between Christian and Jewish meditative practices is the former's anthropomorphic visualizations. Concrete images of a suffering Christ, martyr, or saint appear during moments of divine ecstasy, whereas the kabbalist experiences his meditation in a world of abstractions—secret letters, words, and numbers. Their combinations and permutations are outer coverings for an inner awareness. It is the inwardness of the meditation which serves to attach man to God and enables him to open up to universal rhythms and become attuned with God.[9]

Exhausted from his fasts and the intensity of his prayers, Channon walks toward the Ark which houses the Torah. All "secrets and symbols" are hidden within these holy scrolls, he says. "All miracles—from the six days of creation, unto the end of all generations of men. Yet how hard it is to wrest one secret or one symbol from them—how hard!" (p. 43). Why does the number thirty-six invade his mind so constantly, he wonders. What is its essence? According to the mystical science of gematria, thirty-six stands for Leah; three times six stands for Channon. Tormented, he knows he must divine the secrets and symbols in these numbers and put them to good use.

The system of gematria is similar to meditation, incantation, and prayer in that it is a ritual designed to place the initiate in tune with universal forces and open him up to an influx of divine light. Numbers are archetypal forces; for psychologists and alchemists they are idea-forces—that is, they are outer garments containing inner meanings. For Pythagoras they were a means to order chaos, render the infinite finite, and transform the amorphous into matter. The number thirty-six, a combination of three (the triangle, trinity, a synthesis) and six (a union of two triangles, as expressed in the alchemical theories of fire and water; the six days of Creation), indicates mysterious sets of correspondences at work in the universe. Why should Leah's and Channon's name be linked? Why should there be thirty-six Lamed Vovs, those men who, according to Hebrew mystics, live painful existences hidden from the world, and who appear only in times of dire stress to reveal God's secrets to the multitudes? Perhaps Channon is a Lamed Vov?

The more Channon delves into the mystery of numbers, the more firelike his personality becomes. As archetypes, numbers are "structured contents of the collective unconscious," and therefore endowed with energy, dynamism, and the capacity to activate the minds and psyches of those who approach its mysteries.[10] When numbers detach themselves from the collective unconscious and enter into consciousness (in the manner of ideas or sensations), the image they form is imbued with a force that sheds its inner light during the course of its trajectory in the mind's eye. Like the alchemist's scintillae or his athanor, in which the coals purify the most ignoble metals and precipitate the most inert substances, so Channon's spiritual energy knows no bounds. For him the goal justifies the means. Passion continually pushes him to extract God's boundless mysteries from the universe for his own private use. Dangers await such attitudes, warns the kabbalah. Catastrophes may follow. If spirit and mind grow too powerful for the body containing them, a split may ensue, as in the case of Adam Kadman. On a human level, disharmony and discord between soma and psyche may come to pass. The word "steel," used to describe Channon's powerful brain, denotes, according to hermetic tradition, transcendent toughness of spirit. The hardness of steel, however, depends on the degree to which it is alloyed with other metals. Steel may also be malleable. So Channon, fired with desire, either might possess obdurate, stubborn, and insensible characteristics or might simply display a fundamental weakness of character. All depends on the kavvanah, the purity of his spirit and the authenticity of his love for God.

Channon, whose spiritual and biological drive are manifest in the power of his fantasies, has become driven by his desire to dominate his destiny. He has in effect rejected the world of contingencies in which man is to a great extent victimized by forces beyond his control. He is no longer the pure, steely, shining student he once was; his soul has become contaminated, tarnished. The scintillae, once focused on divinity, are now attracted elsewhere. Confusion has set in. Values have altered. Channon is unaware of the dangers awaiting the individual who misuses knowledge. The alchemist has always stressed the word "contamination," indicating that the impurities within the metal lower its efficiency and may bring about the failure of the experiment. So Channon's flaw, reminiscent of Adam Kadman's, may lead to his diffusion into space.

A young scholar who has remained in the synagogue asks Channon why he has been delving into the kabbalah when he knows its teachings have been forbidden. Only the initiated may study kabbalah, and even for them it is not recommended. The Talmud gives structure and protection, containing the mind and allowing thoughts to proceed in an orderly manner, through discernment, logic, and reason. The Talmud is "cold and dry," Channon answers. It does not activate spirit nor does it fire energy. It stands for casuistic thinking, cerebral argumentation. Although the Talmud "is deep and glorious and vast . . . it chains you to the earth—it forbids you to attempt the heights" (p. 46).

A fire principle, Channon is incapable of proceeding temperately. He has always put himself through the most excruciating mental and physical exertions to experience religious ecstasy. Under the spell of God's presence, the rational world dissolves; emotions are allowed to invade his being. Psychologically, Channon's subliminal depths hold full sway; his weakened ego (that factor within the psyche that adapts to both outer and inner worlds) falters and then stumbles, rendering his already unbalanced existence even more precarious. Channon has become a spiritual cripple, unable to distinguish reality from fantasy; he is unable to adapt to a harmonious interplay between conscious and unconscious spheres. The kabbalah, Channon explains, "tears your

soul away from earth and lifts you to the realms of the highest
heights. Spreads all the heavens out before your eyes, and leads
you directly to Pardes [paradise], reaches out in the infinite, and
raises a corner of the great curtain itself" (p. 46).

As Channon speaks of his ecstasy, he grows weak. Like the
mystic who ascends to vertiginous heights, Channon becomes
dizzy. *Sublimatio* dominates the scene. Vaporous and disembodied,
his soul has become a distilled essence; the fire which generates
and regenerates it paves the way for communion with divinity.
When the intense spiritual quest serves only the individual, however, and not humanity at large, the flame lighting the way may
blind or burn the initiate.

The scholar again warns Channon of the dangers that "ecstatic
flights into the upper regions" may provoke. It is during such moments of rapture that souls are lost, burn themselves out, and then
are hurled "into the deepest pit below." The slow and sure way of
the Talmud "raises the soul toward the heights by slow degrees,
but keeps guard over it like a faithful sentinel who neither sleeps
nor dreams"; it "clothes the soul with an armor of steel and keeps
it ever on the straight path" (p. 46). As the alchemist protects his
metals from contamination and corrosion in alembics and crucibles, so the ego, psychologically, must be restrained from powerful
eruptions from the collective unconscious.

Unless properly initiated, students of the kabbalah may be
overwhelmed by its mysteries and blinded by the divine light
streaming into the soul. Rather than purifying under these conditions, the kabbalah may pervert; instead of instilling the hierophant with humility, it may fill his heart with hubris. Revelations
which only belong to the most revered of prophets, such as Elijah,
are never divulged to the ordinary being. Frequently, however,
when inexperienced individuals arrogate unto themselves that
which belongs to the immortal realm, they may be duped into
believing that they possess powers over both material and spiritual
worlds. The practitioner of theurgy, unlike the true student of kabbalah, overreaches himself, wants too much, imagines too fer-
vently, and divines too viscerally. If passion is allowed to burn
uncontrolled, the wisdom gleaned from these sacred texts may be
misapplied and destruction may ensue.[11]

Channon's kabbalistic studies raised him to a state of grandeur. Unable to understand the power of its mysteries, he felt so

energized that he believed himself imbued with almost supernatural powers. Such feelings drew him away from the workaday world and divested him of any sense of obligation to or connection with his surroundings. As the ancient adage explains, "Whoever is full of himself has no room for God."[12] Channon refuses to listen to the scholar. "I go my own way," he states. From time immemorial holy men have waged fruitless battles against sin, Channon continues. No sooner do they cleanse one soul than others, more sinful, appear to plague the world. He seeks "to burn its sin away, as the goldsmith refines gold in his powerful flame; as the farmer winnows the grain from the chaff. So must sin be refined of its uncleanness, until only its holiness remains" (p. 48).

Channon identifies with the goldsmith, as had the alchemists of old. He sees himself as a flame burning and purifying the ignoble leaden condition until it reaches the sublime Golden State. Gold and light are synonyms for Channon. The Latin word (*aurum*) is the same as the Hebrew word (*aor*) meaning light. In his own mind, Channon has become a combination of solar light and divine intelligence and inhabits the fourth dimension. Gold, as the supreme spiritual value, is an elusive treasure and igneous force. Unlike the true alchemist, who knew that making gold required slow gestation, Channon rushes forward, unthinking, driven by the power of his inner energy. Pliny wrote that to gather gold, which is found in running streams and in grains in the earth, requires periods of sifting and purification.[13] The process of extracting the ore from the earth is arduous and long. So it is for the one seeking individuation and for the kabbalist as he wrests the mysteries from the pleromatic spheres. Only after years of study, meditation, and profound understanding can he even begin to approach his goal.

Channon tells the terrified scholar that sparks of holiness exist in sin. God created the entire cosmos. After the shattering of the vessels and the dispersion of Adam Kadman, the holy sparks were scattered throughout the universe. Just as these luminosities must be gathered and cleansed of the evil or matter with which they are encrusted, so must sinful thoughts be examined, understood, and thereby divested of their contamination; thus may evil be transformed into good. The scholar is thunderstruck. Satan created sin, he counters, not God. Channon answers by asking who created Satan. "God. Since he is the antithesis of God, he is an aspect of God, and therefore must contain also a germ of holiness" (p. 48).

Certain mystics believe that in order to rescue the divine sparks from the material world and return them to their source, a descent "through the gates of impurity" is required. Once such a task is completed, the "Kingdom of Evil" vanishes since it no longer has a reason to exist.[14] Evil exists only when good remains a dynamic factor. To descend into the domain of impurity entails great danger, however. The initiate must identify with evil, thereby justifying his perversions. He may never be able to detach himself from this leaden condition. If he succeeds in returning to the Kingdom of God, however, he has earned redemption more than the nonsinner.

Redemption through sin is Channon's way. For him it means a descent into the domain of evil followed by an elevation. In Ezekiel 33:11, evildoers are pardoned: "Say unto them, as I live, saith the Lord God, I have not pleasure in the death of the wicked; but that the wicked turn from his way and live; turn ye, turn ye from your evil ways." To prove his point, Channon says that the most powerful sin for woman is lust. Yet when this sin is cleansed in a "powerful flame," it achieves the greatest holiness of all in the Song of Songs. Channon begins chanting Solomon's love verses rapturously.

The Song of Songs occupies a very special place for kabbalists and alchemists. The former understood Solomon's verses allegorically, both as a mystical union between man's soul and God and as the community of Israel and the spirit of God. The text contained God's sublimity and mystery, and those who felt it deeply could be transformed and renewed when chanting the poem or meditating on its mystical meaning.

The Christian philosopher Origen (185–254), who taught in Alexandria and Caesarea, wrote that in Jewish circles the study of the Song of Songs was forbidden to the young. No one knows the reason for the interdict, though many suggestions have been forwarded. Some feared the student might interpret Solomon's verses as erotic love poems between bride and bridegroom and therefore concentrate on base sexuality, rather than directing their thoughts toward divine realms. Others, such as Maimonides, suggested that the anthropomorphism inherent in the *Shi'ur Komah* (*Dimensions of Stature*), a mystical work in which God's greatness was expressed by attributing to him human dimensions, was anathema to Hebrew tradition. God is beyond human comprehension and may never be reduced to form. Still others, however, defended the

Shi'ur Komah, which they compared in beauty and feeling to the Song of Songs. They were convinced that both books were allegorical interpretations of God and his "Glory," his *Shekhinah* ("the body of the Divine presence," or, according to some, the female element in God). The Song of Songs was therefore considered to express God's longing for union with his Shekhinah, referred to as the "beloved" (5:11–16); in the *Shi'ur Komah*, God's "tunic" and "garment" refer to the "garment of light" which he donned when he created the world.

The alchemist views the Song of Songs in terms of its colors: red, white, black, purple, silver, and gold. Each hue represents an alchemical operation. The beloved is "black but comely" (1:5), and is compared to both a rose and a lily. The *nigredo* and *albedo* processes are embedded in her countenance and have metaphysical and psychological analogies. Comparable to a redeeming queen figure, the beloved possesses warmth and tenderness, understanding and love. She spreads joy and a passion for life. The shadow, her other side, however, which is associated with the dark moist moon forces, ushers in warlike, chthonic qualities which spread madness among her followers. The beloved then becomes a poisoner when she emerges from darkness and extracts man's soul; she is an unredeemed force of nature which sets the alchemist on the wrong track. In the Song of Songs, she has both positive and negative aspects as sister, bride, mother, and spouse, and she may therefore bring him renewal, regenerating in this manner the alchemical process, or death. As the force of *renovatio*, she becomes the archetype of life itself.[15]

Unaware of the immensity of his undertaking, Channon interprets the riches hidden in the kabbalistic works in general and in the Song of Songs in particular, on a personal, not a transcendental, level. Events in the outer world are viewed as a confirmation of his power over destiny. The fact that Sender is unable to find a suitable husband for Leah is positive proof, he believes, of his feelings. One day, he is certain, she will be his.

The congregation returns. Leah, a young and gentle girl, enters. She is accompanied by her grandmother. She walks over to the Holy Ark. Channon cannot take his eyes off her: "He alternately gazes at her thus, and closes his eyes in ecstasy." Leah sees him and "lowers her eyes in embarrassment" (p. 51). Leah, the "beloved" for Channon, is an anima figure. She personifies the feminine principle in Channon, unconscious qualities embedded within his own soul which he transfers to her. It is she (through projection) who has altered his character and aroused powerful reactions. Channon has become so dominated by his soul/image Leah that he cannot adapt to real life. He lives inwardly. His libido is repressed. Every now and then it explodes in the form of affects—as an ecstatic prayer or a power drive. She has no real relationship to Channon; she is not the product of a harmonious union between soma and psyche, or spirit and soul. Dissociated, Channon can find some semblance of solace from an abrasive world of reality only through the projection of this archaic identity with the soul object.

Leah looks at the "tear-stained walls" of the synagogue. Why are they "so sorrowful, and so wrapped in dreams . . . so silent and so sad. I wish . . . I don't know what I wish. . . . But my heart is filled with tenderness and pity" (p. 53). Leah wonders why Channon is so pale and sad. She looks at his "wonderful eyes" (p. 55). They are like diffused luminosities, flowing streams of light, nonmaterial scintillae emerging from some etheric realm. He is fire. She senses his power. Feelings of uneasiness invade her being. She kisses the Torah and is told not to kiss it too long because it is "written in black fire upon white fire" (p. 56).

The Torah is a living organism for the Jew. It preexisted creation in the form of "black fire on white fire." In this nonmaterial condition it burned before God. The commentary on *The Book of Bahir*, written by Isaac the Blind, states:

The form of the written Torah is that of the colors of white fire, and the form of the oral Torah has colored forms as of black fire. And all these engravings and the not yet unfolded Torah existed potentially, perceptible neither to a spiritual nor a sensory eye, until the will [of God] inspired the idea of activating them by means of primordial wisdom and hidden knowledge.[16]

The written Torah could become manifest only through the power of the oral Torah, since "the white fire is the written Torah, in which the form of the letters is not yet explicit." The letters on the scrolls are merely limited material manifestations of the primordial, amorphous, and unlimited word of God. Its meaning, therefore, is no longer concealed in the white and black light, but is structured and limited, its essence remaining inaccessible to man.[17]

For Leah to allow her kisses to remain too long on the Torah would be as dangerous to her well-being and equilibrium as is the study of esoteric literature to the uninitiated. She might intuit the "inwardness" of each letter; its spiritual message would therefore invade her being like lightning, energizing and stimulating her adolescent orientation.

After Leah's departure, Channon, as though intoning to himself, concentrates all of his energies on the pronunciation of certain words. He seems to be growing desperate. "I wish to attain possession of a clear and sparkling diamond, and melt it down in tears and inhale it into my soul. I want to attain the rays of the third plane of beauty. I want . . ." (p. 57). The "third plane of beauty" is to be found, according to mystics and alchemists, in Solomon's writings: the Song of Songs represents the sphere of beauty; Ecclesiastes represents that of Judgment; and Proverbs represents that of Loving-Kindness.[18] Only after he has experienced the three may the "diamond" appear for the mystic, the Philosopher's Stone come into being for the alchemist, and the individuation process pursue its course in the psychological domain.

That Channon seeks "to attain possession of a clear and sparkling diamond" indicates his longing to enter the domain of the absolute, to be bound to Leah. As an anima figure, she is, as far as he is concerned, the essence of pure divine light. In Sanskrit the word *dyu* ("diamond") also means "luminous being," "light," and "brilliance" and is connected with the Greek word *adamas* ("unconquerable"). The mystic and alchemist both seek the diamond or the treasure hard to attain, that irradiant center from which moral, spiritual, and intellectual values emerge. To possess the diamond or to create it—or to realize it in one's own being—is an extremely difficult task. The diamond, like man's moral attributes, ranges from the most impure to the purest of states. A naturally crystallized diamond is one of the hardest substances known, but in its uncrystallized form it is opaque and frangible. To seek out the diamond requires excavation; arduous polishing is necessary to perfect it and bring out its hidden light and luster. So the alchemist must likewise indwell, discover the diamond existing within, force it out of its darkened recesses, and then perfect it through the various stages of the evolutionary process until it emerges shining in its sovereignty and incorruptibility.

Channon's renegade tendencies do not allow him sufficient

time to divine the mysteries of matter or to understand the human experience. As a fire principle, he plunges into the pleromatic sphere, into his unconscious, and there escapes from the difficulties involved in dealing with reality. In so doing, he rids himself temporarily of his feelings of inadequacy. Although a fire principle, he is not a solar hero whose courage knows no bounds and whose heroism can move mountains. Channon works in darkness, in unconscious and instinctive areas. His ego is never perceptible; on the contrary, it is underfed, limp, and dwindles progressively in strength, eventually removing him completely from any sense of responsibility. His longing to reach out and possess his beloved Leah inspires him to forge ahead in his mystical quests. His connection with her, however, exists only in his mind. As his fantasy gains power over him, he withdraws still further from the workaday domain. Filled with poetic rapture, which he mistakenly interprets as an influx of divine energy, Channon believes that Leah's love for him has made him whole again: she has given him the warmth and tenderness he had never known in life. By submitting to such an obsession, however, Channon has severed relations with society. His life, therefore, cannot be renewed or nourished through positive contact with his instinctive depths, since these are now in full sway. Dangers encroach. Conscious values have been lost and his individuality drowned within the limitless sphere of the collective unconscious. Only alienation can ensue.[19]

Channon grows desperate. Nothing seems to be working; not his fasts, his ablutions, nor his spells. Perhaps "the Secret of the Double Name" can come to his aid, he thinks. Mystics believe that initiates may divine the original texture of God's name, "by which heaven and earth were created," according to certain permutations and combinations of letters and formulas. But the pronunciation of the four sacred letters YHWH (the Tetragrammaton) is no longer known to man.[20] Channon's inflated ego allows him to believe that meditation, concentration, and prayer will enable him to discover them. But as is stated in Job 28:13: "Man knoweth not the price thereof; neither is it found in the land of the living." No one may discover what preexisted the world; no one may understand "the secret life of God." As the thirteenth-century Spanish kabbalist Joseph Gikatila explained: "Know that the entire Torah is, as it were, an explication of, and commentary on, the Tetragrammaton YHWH." Woven into the very fabric of the Torah is the secret leading to the understanding of the oral and written Torah, "black fire on white fire." Only Moses understood its "hidden and invisible form in white light."[21]

By studying the kabbalah obsessively and without proper instruction and preparation to receive its mysteries, Channon became convinced that Leah was his predestined bride and that the events occurring in the outside world were a confirmation of his feelings. The more prolonged his speculations in meditation, numerology, and gematria, the greater his inwardness and the more pronounced his solitude became. When Leah's father, Sender, enters the synagogue and announces that a marriage contract has been signed and that Leah will soon be wed to Menashe, Channon falls to the ground. The Messenger, who speaks at various times in riddles, allegories, and aphorisms, now intimates that a marriage may not necessarily take place even though a contract has been signed. Sender pays no heed to these mysterious prognostications. He calls for everyone to dance. When they try to awaken Channon from what they believe to be a sleep, they realize he is dead.

Act 2: The Autonomous Couple

Act 2 opens on a square in Branitz. To the left is the synagogue. Sender's house, among others, a cemetery, bridge, river, and forest are also visible. Sender is giving a feast for the poor, crippled, and old. Baskets of food are brought out and their contents devoured. The community at large is celebrating Leah's nuptials. In front and slightly to the left of the synagogue is a gravestone inscribed "Here lie a pure and holy bridegroom and bride murdered" (p. 70) during a pogrom as they were being led to their wedding. Not only had they been slaughtered, but half of the town's population with them. The memory of this harrowing act is still powerful within the community. After marriage ceremonies, it has been claimed, rabbis can hear sighs emanating from the grave, and so it has become the custom for all those leaving the synagogue after a wedding to dance on the tombstone in order to bring cheer to the dead couple.

Death and dance set the tone for the scene. No line is drawn between the dead buried under the earth and the living above ground: each sphere may at any moment communicate with the other. By descending into the depths of one's own being, wandering "throughout the dimensions" of this unlimited sphere, psyche and soma are one, and the limits of the phenomenological world may be transcended. Traveling through the endless stages of the psyche, and in so doing examining the various soul states experienced, leads to a deepening understanding of oneself in the process of life. The mystical experience understood in this manner becomes an "instrument of self analysis, of self knowledge."[22]

Dancing on the couple's tombstone and dancing with the community at large, which is expected of Leah, is also significant. As the chosen one—the bride celebrating her nuptials—Leah has taken on the stature of an archetype. She stands for youth, happiness, beauty, and spirituality (purity incarnate); she is the future bearer of children. For those whose lives are marked with despair and suffering, she radiates the positive and fruitful side of existence. Leah, the archetypal virgin, has donned her white dress and dances with the ugliest and most wretched women of the community, thereby expressing her bond with womanhood as a whole. No matter how grotesque they may be, how sordid, sullied, and repugnant their ways, each female member may dance with her youthful, harmonious soul. As they swing her round and round, touch her beautiful gown, and encircle her pliant body, polarities are unified on the earthly level.

Leah's grandmother sees that she has grown tired and tells her to stop. Leah persists, dancing with anyone and everyone who desires her. The ugliness of some of the women inspires chilled terror in her grandmother's heart. They are similar to allegorical figures representing all sorts of earthly evils. A particularly offensive creature grabs Leah and begins dancing round and round. She refuses to loosen her iron grasp, and as she twirls faster and faster, she grows hysterical. Leah turns white. Later she describes this woman's "cold, withered hands" and then faints. When consciousness returns she feels different; something seems to have happened to her. "Someone came and lifted me from the ground and carried me far away, very far away," she informs her grandmother (p. 76).

The grandmother thinks Leah is talking about "spirits" and asks her not to mention such forces. They lurk "in every tiny hole and corner and crevice" (p. 76), and Leah must be careful. Her spirits are not harmful nor evil, she counters. On the contrary, "it isn't evil spirits that surround us, but souls of those who died before their time, and come back again to see all that we do and hear all that we say" (p. 77).

Just as prayer, incantation, and meditation are ways of expressing the joys of religious ecstasy, so dance is a path leading to this transcendent sphere. It is a rhythmic and ordered way of releasing emotion and bringing new space-time relationships into being which fuse with the world at large. It represents energy in an perpetual state of transformation: as captured or incorporated into an image; as an evolutive, active, dynamic concentration of forces. Every dance is a pantomime, a paradigm, a theurgic act. Plato considered the dance to be of divine origin: before becoming movement, it was sign. In biblical times, Miriam and the other Hebrew women danced to express their joy after safely crossing the Red Sea; David leaped with happiness when the Ark was brought to Jerusalem. In Talmudic times, rabbis danced at weddings; in Temple times, maidens danced in the vineyards on special feast days. Hasids still express their religious enthusiasm through the dance, sometimes holding the Torah in their arms. As Leah danced, she became the incarnation of the living spirit of God which nourishes, sustains, and energizes an entire community. The dance not only put Leah in contact with the world at large, but also allowed her to become emotionally attuned to the universe, and thus to participate in its very fabric. It encouraged her to release her fears, pain, and joy. Through it she created patterns in space, enacted desires and needs, and penetrated the eternal sphere, thereby divesting herself of her mortality. Leah experienced inner and outer worlds simultaneously: the light and the dark, life and death.

The circularity of her patterns made her grow dizzy and intoxicated her very being. Like the dervishes, Leah knew a kind of ecstasy. The circularity and speed of her dance allowed the rational sphere to lower its barriers and permit contents from the collective unconscious to become constellated and animated. Leah grew faint because the archetypal material within her had become so powerful that an eclipse of her conscious orientation ensued. That something foreign had entered her ordered workaday world which left her ill at ease and disturbed is not surprising. Just as the volume of water increases during a spring thaw, so Leah's circular and rotating movements released those powers (instincts) which had been building within her and had previously been held in check. The dance had created a physical and psychological condition which failed to contain her archaic world. Conflicts surfaced, and with them consciousness was overwhelmed.[23]

The image of the circle or mandala which characterizes Leah's dance is an iconographic representation of the ultimate state of oneness for both psychologist and alchemist. It is a synthesis of the four elements, a synthesis which alchemists consider the most perfect of forms; the "sun point" or the "light" and "fire" of deity. The circle symbolizes a reconciliation of opposites, as in the alchemist's hermetic vessel; the circle is the cooking pot, the womb, the chalice, the cauldron. It stands for that essential force which may eventually lead to the creation of the Philosopher's Stone or to mystical union with the All. The circle also stands for the psyche, the complete entity, including the suprapersonal values which in Leah's case have at least momentarily invaded and drowned her ego.[24]

Dazzled and dazed by the circularity of her dance, she experiences in this vertiginous condition a release from the world of conflict (reality) and feels inundated with sensations of love and beatitude. A new soul invades her being. She explains the difference between evil spirits and souls who die before their lives are over to her grandmother, saying that young souls who have not been allowed to fulfill their destinies do not disappear. She wonders where Channon's soul is.

What becomes of the life he has not lived, do you think? What becomes of his joys and sorrows, and all the thoughts he had no time to think and all the things he hadn't time to do?

(P. 78)

No human life goes to waste. If one of us dies before his time, his soul returns to the world to complete its span, to do the things left undone and experience the happiness and griefs he would have known.

(P. 79)

In a state of elation now, Leah will go to the cemetery and ask her mother (who died when she was still a child) to join her under the wedding canopy.

She will be with me there, and after the ceremony we shall dance together. It is the same with all the souls who leave the world before their time. They are here in our midst, unheard and invisible. Only if your desire is strong enough, you can see them, and hear their voices and learn their thoughts.

(P. 79)

Leah tells her grandmother that the bride and groom buried in front of the synagogue have communicated with her in both dreams and waking states. She identifies with them, experiencing them both inwardly and outwardly, as psychic and material entities. There is no separation for her between the world of the living and that of the dead.

Music is heard. Menashe is approaching the square. The Messenger explains the mysterious events about to occur.

The souls of the dead *do* return to earth, but not as disembodied spirits. Some must pass through many forms before they achieve purification. . . . The souls of the wicked return in the form of beasts, or birds, or fish. . . . They have to wait for the coming of some righteous sage to purge them of their sins and set them free. Others enter the bodies of the newly born, and cleanse themselves by well-doing.

(P. 81)

There are vagrant souls which, finding neither rest nor harbor, pass into the bodies of the living, in the form of a Dybbuk, until they have attained purity.

(P. 82)

Sender encourages Leah to go to the graveyard and invite her mother to the wedding.

Ask her to be with you, so that we may lead our only daughter under the canopy together. Say that I have fulfilled her dying wishes to devote my life to you and bring you up to be a true and virtuous daughter of Israel.

(P. 83)

Leah asks the Grandmother if she can invite friends to her wedding, but she is told only relatives are acceptable. When she nevertheless insists on inviting Channon, the Grandmother warns that because of his "unnatural death," fearsome consequences may be in the offing. He has come to her in a dream, Leah confesses. "He told me his trouble and begged me to invite him to the wedding" (p. 85).

The Grandmother reveals that Leah, when communicating with the dead souls, had fainted; afterwards she is a changed person. As Menashe and his family are about to come on stage, Leah suddenly tears off the veil which hides her face and screams out: "No! You are not my bridegroom!" (p. 92) She runs to the grave where the holy bride and groom are buried and asks them for protection. She "looks wildly about" and in a masculine voice shouts: "Ah! Ah! You have buried me. But I have come back—to my destined bride. I will leave her no more!" (p. 92) The Messenger speaks: "Into the bride has entered a Dybbuk" (p. 93).

She is no longer the Leah she was. A new being has taken possession of her. Psychologically, she is split. As long as she had been able to remain the virgin girl, the adolescent answerable only to her father and to the community at large, equilibrium was maintained within her psyche. In the way that Channon represented the fire principle, Leah symbolized air. She functioned well in the dreamy atmosphere of one who looks forward to marriage and motherhood at some remote time. As long as she could circulate as lightly as air, her spirit found release and contentment in her imaginary lover. No demands were made upon her on a personal level. Once responsibilities were imposed, her balance shattered. Her spirit became compressed and heat and fire mounted, burning their way through her already enfeebled ego. With the breakdown of relationships between fantasy and reality, a redistribution of values came into being with which she could not cope. The world of fantasy took over.

That Leah maintained such a close relationship with her dead mother's soul, as well as with the souls of the deceased couple, indicates that she had no individuality, no reality of her own, and that she lived a sublimated existence as an airborne principle. She took on stature only as a collective object: as her father's daughter, Channon's soul image, and the community's symbol of purity and beauty. In her white wedding dress, her amorphous personality reflected the innocence, spontaneity, and openness of one with singleness of vision. Leah could be called a medial woman. She stands at the threshold of two worlds: a bridge between the living and the dead, the real and the unreal. She reflects both the moods of the community and those of the protagonists. She thus is a moon image, unable to generate energy but reflecting it. An agent, vessel, and intermediary, she is a conveyor of feeling and remains, therefore, embedded in the psychic atmosphere of her environment. As a carrier of the positive side of the community's psyche, she is joy, luster, balance, and health incarnate. When representing the community's shadow, she becomes a negative force, the carrier of death and destruction. Since she has no perception or objectivity of her own, she lacks the power to discriminate and is overwhelmed by the community as well as by her own collective unconscious. Leah's case is tragic because she is undeveloped and emerges from her ordeal victimized by the very forces she had hoped to serve.

While Channon's protracted experiences in religious ecstasy destroyed whatever rational attitudes he had possessed, the dance, with its circular and swirling movements and ensuing vertigo, diminished Leah's conscious orientation. Once the barriers protecting her feeble ego weakened, the collective forces within her psyche flowed forth. The cemetery sequence, when Leah lost consciousness for the second time, encouraged her further to fall under the spell of nonpersonal powers or the plurality of autonomous complexes within her psyche.[25]

There is a "rite de Leah" in kabbalah which is performed by the devout at midnight. This rite symbolizes God uniting with his formerly exiled Shekhinah.[26] It is a powerfully solemn and moving celebration of mystical nuptials which enriches the believer and fills him with harmony and divine benevolence. It is an outward manifestation of an inner fusion in the psyche. Such a union was described by alchemists as a marriage of king and queen, a harmonious blending of metals in their purest Golden State. Mystical hymns drawn from the Song of Songs were frequently intoned by the alchemist during these sacred moments, adding to the beauty and intensity of the emotions evoked.

Leah's inner marriage, however, was not an expression of harmony. On the contrary, it symbolized destruction: the end of any hope that she could return to the real world as a functioning being. The progressive invasion of collective forces allowed Channon, an animus image (her unconscious vision of her soul mate) to reign over every area of her existence. He had absorbed her airborne nature. Darkness invaded her world, not light; idea had become form; the image of Channon, far more powerful than an abstract concept, imposed its own logic and dimensionality onto her world. It could no longer be dissolved; it had hardened like steel. The diamond Channon had so desperately wished to create had now come into being in the birth of a new soul, a divine child fashioned out of air and fire and removed from the earthly sphere.

Channon, the fire principle, had succeeded in luring Leah away from the world of reality into his own sphere of disembodied souls. Although he possessed no objective reality, he lived on in her as a most powerful force which fascinated and mesmerized her.

Leah found solace only in her subjective domain, absorbed by the fantasy figure which she found more pleasing than the patriarchal society of which she was a product. In her new land of quietude she no longer had to envisage marriage with someone she did not know. Her passion for Channon encouraged her to fall under the magic of his feeling world. Each time he calls to her, therefore, she yields to his embrace.

Act 3: Exorcism—The Transformation Ritual

Act 3 begins with the aged Rabbi Azrael Miropol, dressed in a white caftan and high fur cap, seated in his home deep in thought. Pain marks his features. He begins speaking of the Holy Land, the seventy nations, the seventy tongues referred to in the Bible, and the transmigration of souls.

> But it happens sometimes that a soul which has attained to the final state of purification suddenly becomes the prey of evil forces which cause it to slip and fall. And the higher it has soared, the deeper it falls. And with the fall of such a soul as this, a world plunges to ruin. And darkness overwhelms the spheres. The ten spheres bewail the world that it lost.
>
> (P. 101)

Leah's father has asked Rabbi Azrael to exorcise the dybbuk which has lodged in his daughter. He assures the rabbi that she is sinless and gentle; "She has never disobeyed," he adds (p. 105).

The rabbi is plagued by doubt. Is he really capable of performing an exorcism? Is he God's deputy on earth? He longs to experience the nearness of the Almighty; his being yearns for solitude and rest. Yet, despite his age, people keep coming from far and near to his door, begging for comfort and spiritual healing. Their words pierce his flesh because he feels inadequate to the task.

There are moments when he thinks back upon his forebears, great rabbis who had helped the ill; such thoughts strengthen him. His grandfather, for example, could drive out dybbuks through spells or incantations and with only a single word of command. Each time the rabbi talks about these men, he is infused with energy. He feels his continuity with the past. The generations of archetypal powers represented by these souls arouse energetic factors within him. Under such circumstances, time has become reversible. Like chemical substances, so powers condense, integrate, and fixate. Prayers, meditation, and his deep faith have put him in touch and in harmony with his inner world—his past—which lives within him in both a personal and collective state.[27]

A drastic personality change has come about in Leah. Her psyche has literally fallen apart and reorganized under two distinct, autonomous complexes. Schizophrenics have frequently alluded to voices they hear when the ego is no longer the center of consciousness. In Leah's case, the ego has been displaced by the collective unconscious. The passivity which had marked Leah's life did not permit her to act overtly once her father had prepared for her nuptials, yet she also could not pursue a course inimicable to her feelings. The only solution to the impasse was severing the link with her conscious life. Since she could not discharge strong emotion in the workaday world, she yielded to that other personality within her. The dybbuk took dominion. "I am one of those who sought other paths," Leah tells the rabbi in Channon's voice; it was not the straight Talmudic way, but the evil path of magic, theurgy, Satan.

The rabbi commands the dybbuk to leave the world of the living. He refuses.

I have nowhere to go. Every world is barred against me and every gate is locked. On every side, the forces of evil lie in wait to seize me. And now that my soul has found refuge from the bitterness and terror of pursuit, you wish to drive me away. Have mercy! Do not send me away—don't force me to go!

(P. 111)

Although the rabbi pities Channon's wandering soul, he again orders him to depart. Still the dybbuk refuses. The rabbi will now have to resort to "malediction and anathema" (p. 111). He asks for white shrouds, seven rams' horns, seven black candles, and seven holy scrolls. He requests that the city rabbi be called to participate in the proceedings and that Menashe, who had gone to his family in the next town, should return for the wedding ceremony.

The number seven, a mystic force for both kabbalists and alchemists, is archetypal and as such is endowed with energy. For the mystic whose visions of the divine realm are to be found in Ezekiel 1:26, seven created a link between man and divinity, thus healing the schism which came into being with the Creation and later the Fall. The love principle is also inherent in the number seven, which prompted the allusion to the seven petals of a rose in the Song of Songs. A complete cycle is represented by seven: the marriage of four (earthly realm, the world of matter, the square) with three (the pyramid, the triangle)—that is, the welding of the complete with the incomplete, the unconscious with consciousness, gold with lead. According to the Bible, there were seven priests who blew on seven rams' horns during the battle of Jericho. The struggle resulted in victory: the known over the unknown.

Rabbi Samson from the next village arrives. He tells Rabbi Azrael of a dream he had had the previous night: Nissin ben Rifke, a young Hasid who used to come to town twenty years ago, appeared to him three times and demanded that Leah's father be summoned before the rabbinical court, the highest religious tribunal. Rabbi Samson's dream was revelatory. Such dreams occur when the dreamer experiences a feeling of oneness with the universe. He no longer feels like a separate being, but rather as if he belongs to a fourth dimension, where past, present, and future no longer exist in a linear time scheme, but reveal themselves under certain circumstances in forms and images. The fourth dimension may be regarded as Janus-faced, "pointing back to a preconscious prehistoric world of instincts," while at the same time it "potentially anticipates a future."[28] Because Rabbi Samson's ego is so well grounded, his three visions, rather than overwhelming him, enlarge his frame of reference, activate his will, and integrate his thoughts, enabling him to deal most effectively with the problem confronting him. His dream indicated that some important act of deception, which had led to a crucial misunderstanding, had to be brought out into the open. Although stunned by Rabbi Samson's revelations, Sender agrees to be called before the court.

Act 4: The Spagyric Marriage

In act 4, the rabbinical court comes into session and the interrogation begins. Rabbi Azrael calls Nissin ben Rifke to be present at the trial. He then draws a circle counterclockwise, beyond which the dead soul may not pass. He asks Michael, the attendant, to take his staff and go to the cemetery. He must knock three times on the first grave and then ask (three times) for the dead to forgive him for disturbing their peace. He must further request that Nissin ben Rifke be present at the trial. When returning, he must never once look back, no matter how painful the cries or shrieks he may hear. To do so is to invite dire consequences.

In mystical and theurgic practices, the circle represents a protected area where evil may never enter. The same precautions doctors take against the spread of infection are taken by exorcists when driving out tainted or contaminated souls. Under such conditions, rituals are of the utmost importance. For the mystic, evil is purified; for the psychologist, the ego remains clear and cleansed.[29]

The circle or mandala isolates the personal from the collective psyche. Foreign influences or disparate psychic elements under the domination of other centers are replaced when encircled by the partial rulership of the ego, thereby giving weight and balance to the entire psyche. Since circles protect and delimit, it is believed that alien spirits are unable to cross the line; psychologically, this belief implies that when an individual is concerned with unknown factors, whether these be spiritual, scientific, or psychological, danger always lies in wait. What remains within the circle, alchemically, are all those elements connected with the actual experiments. They are contained within the hermetic vessel as if within the womb; they are protected and encouraged to grow. It is within the circle that fundamental transformation occurs: an idea cooks and foments; feelings incubate; metals alter; and insolubles become soluble. Alchemists go through seven processes which are repeated many times before the final phase of their Great Work comes into being. That the circle is drawn from left to right indicates that the left, associated with the unconscious, that darkened, sinister realm where heart and emotions prevail, will be contained within boundaries; but they will be given the freedom to exert their influence in the rational (right) or daylight sphere.

That Michael must not look back symbolizes man submitting to law, to God, to a moral consciousness that deepens through restraint. Containment is of prime importance. If allowed to circulate freely, energy may be dispersed and the strength needed to persevere in the sacred ritual of exorcism would vanish. Interdicts have both positive and negative values: they add structure to the will; they also repress, firing those contents within it and thereby increasing their power for good or for evil. The staff or stock which Michael must take with him represents the world or celestial axis. It is comparable to the various steps in a process: it guides, points the way, and is at the same time a sign of authority and sovereignty. Staff symbolism plays a large role in mystical literature and myths in general. It is a means of connecting the material and nonmaterial worlds. The magic staff of the pilgrim or warrior represents authority and sovereignty. Moses's stick, when used to prove God's immanence and omniscience, was transformed into a serpent (Exod. 7:8–12). Alchemists look upon the stick as a means of altering consistencies and stages in their experiments, thereby bringing man's soul into the manifest world.

Before the trial commences, a sheet is drawn across the left-hand corner of the stage. The soul of Nissin ben Rifke will remain in front of it during the proceedings. As the circle represents a screen or partition separating the living from the dead, so the sheet enables the two worlds to communicate and yet remain protected from each other. Rabbi Samson will hear and translate Nissin ben Rifke's solemn statements. Alchemists frequently used metals as media through and by which they conducted their experiments. Rabbi Samson is also a medium. Mercury was the "medium of conjunction" and was regarded by alchemists as a kind of soul figure, a link between body and spirit.[30]

Rabbi Samson explains the background: when Nissin ben Rifke and Sender were young they had been best friends. They married on the same day and made a solemn vow that if one should father a boy and the other a girl, the two children would marry. Nissin ben Rifke had a son, Channon, who was "blest with a noble and lofty soul, and was progressing upwards from plane to plane" (p. 126). Shortly after Nissin ben Rifke's death, his son began to wander in search of "the soul to which his soul had been predestined." Finally he came to this city and while studying at the yeshiva was invited to eat his meals at Sender's table. It was there that he saw Leah and knew she was his predestined soul mate. Sender, however, was rich, and he was poor. He understood that a marriage between the two was unthinkable since Sender was looking for a wealthy husband for his daughter. Channon grew desperate and this time, rather than taking to the provinces, he strayed spiritually from the straight paths into forbidden and "New Paths." When Nissin ben Rifke realized the dangers awaiting his son, he was struck with terror. He feared those "dark powers" and their hold upon his son's soul. His fears were justified. When his son died his soul was "severed" from "both worlds."

Since neither heir nor friend remained on earth to pray or hide his soul, he was left without name or memorial. "His light has been extinguished forever" (p. 127).

Sender listens to the testimony and sobs. He begs forgiveness for his sin, which was committed without malice. He was unaware that the lad boarding at his home was Nissin ben Rifke's son. He should have asked his name, the court replied. Never was a question put to Channon by any member of the family. The guilt of pride, of material acquisitiveness, must be punished. The court orders Sender to give half of his fortune to the poor each year for the remainder of his days and to light a memorial candle for Nissin ben Rifke and his son and pray for their souls. It also asks Nissin ben Rifke to forgive Sender and ask the dybbuk to leave Leah's body. Both men seemingly acquiesce. Nissin ben Rifke's soul is asked to return to its resting place and in so doing not to harm any living being. The sheet is withdrawn. Rabbi Azrael traces another circle in the same area, but this time from right to left, allowing the real world to prevail instead of the unconscious or spiritual sphere. All those who participated in the calling back of a dead soul must be cleansed and purified, both physically and spiritually, and basins of water are brought in for all to wash their hands.

Despite the precautions, fear invades the atmosphere. Nissin ben Rifke has not forgiven Sender. Leah is asked to enter. She is wearing her white wedding dress and a black cloak. Rabbi Azrael commands the dybbuk to leave Leah's body. He refuses. The rabbi resorts to anathema. The seven scrolls are brought out; seven rams' horns are blown, sounding *Tekiah! Shevarim! Teruah!* The ram's horn (shofar) is traditionally sounded on ceremonial occasions, usually at the close of the Day of Atonement (Num. 29:1). Since the notes are to be played in broken sounds, they resemble sobbing (*shevarim*) and wailing (*teruah*); on the other hand, *tekiah*, sounded in long unbroken tonalities, proclaims God's sovereignty and the return of all exiles to Israel. Important too is the symbol of the ram's horn: it denotes the sacrifice of Isaac, when God took mercy on Abraham's son and substituted a ram for him.

During the proceedings Leah struggles violently in her seat, as though she were being assailed by unknown and terrifying forces. The dybbuk's voice emerges from her again.

The powers of all the world are arrayed against me. Spirits of terror wrench me and tear me without mercy—the soul of the great and righ-

teous too have arisen against me. The soul of my own father is with them—commanding me to go— But until the last spark of strength has gone from me, so long shall I withstand them and remain where I am.
(P. 135)

Rabbi Azrael asks that a black curtain be hung over the altar, that black candles be lit following the anathema, and that "these words rend asunder every cord that binds you to the world of the living creatures and to the body and soul of the maiden, Leah" (p. 135).

Black and white are both positive and negative colors; each is either a composite of all colors or divested of all color. They represent duality, opposition, conflict: black magic striking out at white magic, evil against good. Similar to the *nigredo* condition, which represents the germinal stage of the alchemical process, so blackness symbolizes the shadow, those negative and unredeemed forces at work within the personality; unknown and uncontrollable, they inspire fear and trembling. Connected with primal forms, the unregenerate instincts working in darkness, like carbon prior to its crystallization in the diamond or dark earth in which the seed is implanted, represent all that is unclean, nocturnal, unworldly; all that which has not as yet or cannot become consciously known. White, on the other hand, stands for illumination and purification of spirit, the *albedo* condition; it symbolizes the celestial spheres where air circulates freely and the privileged forces reside. Yet, white, like lunar light, absorbs other luminescent forces and thus leads to absence and isolation. Similar to the color of dawn, white inspires a sense of futurity and may be looked upon as a new beginning, rich in potential, able to act on the soul in a clear and ordered manner, as does the day or the light of consciousness.

The Messenger announces the success of the exorcism ritual. "The last spark has been swallowed up in the flame" and Channon's voice is no longer to be heard. His soul has receded; Leah's consciousness is reborn. The alchemical process has been completed; the soul has been gathered into its rightful place. The athanor, once heated, has been cooled, and the chemicals reduced to their proper proportions; the condition has been corrected.

Now that the dybbuk has departed, Rabbi Azrael lifts the ban of anathema on Channon. The black curtains and other objects used in the ritual are removed. A prayer for the dead is intoned. Everyone will leave to greet Menashe and his family, who are waiting in town. Before departing, Rabbi Azrael traces a circle around Leah, from left to right. She is not to cross the line, he warns. She still needs protection from outer forces. Leah and the Grandmother remain alone.

Exhausted after her ordeal, Leah drops onto the sofa. She feels strange, a bit fearful. The Grandmother assures her that no power can hurt her if she stays within the circle. If the magic circle is broken, however, spirits from the outer world may intrude, and because Leah is unprepared to deal with them, they could possess her once again. The Grandmother falls asleep. Leah sighs deeply and closes her eyes. She awakens with a start. She hears Channon's voice but cannot see him. Enthralled by its tenderness, musicality, and hypnotic qualities, she tells him, "Your voice is as sweet as the lament of violins in the quiet night" (p. 141). She describes the beauty of her love in an emotional and lyrical passage.

I remember—your hair, so soft and damp as if with tears—your sad and gentle eyes—your hands with the thin tapering fingers. Waking and sleeping I had no thought but of you. You went away and darkness fell upon me—my soul withered in loneliness like the soul of a widow left desolate—the stranger came—and then—then you returned, and the dead heart wakened to life again, and out of sorrow joy blossomed like a flower. . . . Why have you once again forsaken me?

(P. 142)

Resplendent in her wedding dress, Leah speaks in a half-waking, half-sleeping state, as though experiencing a hypnagogic dream. Frequently such emanations emerge in mentally disturbed people when excitation or inner contents erupt into the conscious mind. The divided psyche acts as two independent forces, unconscious and autonomous. Leah views Channon as a projection; for her this psychic reality is true reality. She once again becomes the victim of an illusion. Only in such a condition could she speak words of love in such an uninhibited lyrical flow.

Channon replies.

I broke down the barriers between us—I crossed the plain of death—I defied every law of past and present time and all the ages. I strove against those who know no mercy. And as my last spark of strength left me, I left your body to return to your soul.

(P. 143)

Leah longs for union with Channon, her soul image, for the *coniunctio* which will restore her to wholeness again.

Come back to me, my bridegroom—my husband—I will carry you, dead, in my heart—and in our dreams at night we shall rock to sleep our little children who will never be born.

(P. 143)

The tones of the wedding march are heard. For Leah to marry anyone but Channon is now impossible. Leah entreats her true bridegroom to come to her, to make himself visible. Channon appears against the wall, wearing white robes. Although the exorcism has forced him to leave her body, he now lives more powerfully in her soul. With joy in her heart, Leah slips out of the magic circle, lured into her lover's world beyond physical reality, there to be bound to her fantasy forever.[31] The two blend into one. "A great light flows about me," she says lovingly; "predestined bridegroom, I am united to you forever" (p. 143).

The rabbi returns with the congregation and the bridegroom, but it is too late. The stage grows dark; voices intone the same verses heard at the beginning of the drama.

Leah and Channon, the autonomous couple, live in a celestial *coniunctio*; they have undergone a spagyric marriage, a union of opposites. For the kabbalist, such a union represents superior love—a spiritual rather than a temporal relationship. For the psychologist, it is tantamount to a rejection of life or a living death. Whatever the interpretation, Leah and Channon exist in a sphere where a different modality reigns. Their psychic suffering and passion have led to a transfiguration, a kind of apotheosis. Moreover, their spagyric marriage has produced a new psychological or spiritual orientation. No longer hidden in darkness, but recognized in the world of reality, the loss which their passing represented to the community gave birth to a new principle. Leah, in the form of an anima figure, was brought into light—that is, into consciousness—and was able to assume her rightful place beside her husband. The new unity is not the product of a one-sided patriarchal society; the marriage of alchemical king and queen placed male and female on equal footing.

Channon and Leah are carriers of a mystery. Both, therefore, are relegated to the land of the deceased, the world of shades or ashes. For the alchemist the latter is the purest of all essences. Once the residue of life has burned away, there remains only the immaculate force—the perfect diamond—which links man and woman in prismatic and flowing light.

Spiritus Mundi/ Anima Mundi

And I took it and drank; and when I had drunk
My heart poured forth understanding,
   wisdom grew in my breast,
   and my spirit retained its memory.
      4 Ezra 14:40–41, *The Pseudepigra-
         pha of the Old Testament*

8

Matsukaze: "The Moon Above Is One"

Japan is the land of the symbol and the mask. Behind each object, image, line, color, and tonality, whether these be used in the performing or pictorial arts, there lies a hidden realm, tingling with excitement and ever-alluring, which holds the onlooker enthralled. The unexpressed is more important than the expressed in Japanese art forms, which prefer silence to the spoken word, emptiness to the filled, formlessness to the formed. Noh drama, a composite art, includes dance, song, and poetic recitation as well as a feast of color combinations. Because of its ambiguous nature, its mystical qualities, Noh drama creates a very special world which viewers apprehend and penetrate intuitively.

Noh drama is religiously oriented. Taoism, Shintoism, and Buddhism are basic to its nature. According to the tenets of these sects, the transcendental and not the individual sphere must be experienced, the eternal and not the mortal, the life force (cosmic energy or breath) and not the concrete deity. Noh plays, for the most part, do not bathe in linear time, but in cyclical schemes. Since most of them have been rewritten countless times throughout the centuries, they lack the stamp of individuality which marks occidental endeavors but which is so foreign to Buddhist and Taoist doctrines. Archetypal in nature, Noh participates in a mythical world beyond the space/time continuum: only the month of the year or the season is mentioned. Decors and accessories are likewise vague. They are never representational; they do not mirror the exterior world, but symbolize an inner spiritual and emotional climate.

Matsukaze ("Wind in the Pines") takes place in autumn. It tells the simple story of an itinerant Buddhist priest who arrives at Suma Bay. He has a vision of two very poor and sad girls who had once loved and been loved by an exiled poet-aristocrat. He died prematurely. Memories are evoked by the sisters, litanies are chanted, and the poetry of their love is murmured. When dawn appears, the two girls have vanished. The priest finds himself alone once again and hears only the murmur of "the wind in the pines."[1] The imagery reflects a mood of sadness. Nature is preparing to face the difficult winter ahead. A distant past comes into view on stage; a remote era of still powerful emotions is reawakened; tension arises, controlled yet burning inwardly, altering emotions as well as that life force, that energetic cosmic principle, so important to oriental metaphysicians, alchemists, and poets.

Alchemically, *Matsukaze* dramatizes the *solutio* and *sublimatio* conditions, when metals and elements are cleansed of their impurities. Symbolically, the soul is purified; psychologically, the personality is divested of painful problems which stifle its growth.[2] In the transformation process, the concrete world of multiplicity vanishes and a formless condition of oneness comes into being. The liquidity has blended the formerly irreconcilable elements. The now distilled or sublimated experience is recollected by Matsukaze, the protagonist of the play and she after whom it is named.

The past no longer exists except as a memory. Matsukaze sings of a remote era and her individuality vanishes: form vaporizes. In this sublimated condition, polarities vanish; an ambiguous climate comes into being: costume, mask, and gesture become both weighty and weightless, active and inactive, formed yet formless. As alchemists burn their metals and elements, altering their condition to prepare for the birth of the Philosopher's Stone, so tension and pain grip Matsukaze at the height of her song and dance. During both the dramatic performance and the alchemical operation, insights are released; enlightenment is experienced; the mystery of matter becomes discernible, not perhaps in the phenomenological world, but in the deeply spiritual universe of the Japanese soul.

Unlike western alchemists, who tried to control and dominate the chemicals and metals used in their experiments, Chinese and Japanese alchemists observed the processes and attempted to learn how to act in harmony with them. The oriental alchemist focused his efforts on finding an elixir of long life. He felt that by speeding up the course of nature through experimentation, he would succeed in slowing down her "time scales" with the help of the "time-controlling substances" which he would discover. Newtonian physics with its concept of causality is the guiding force of occidental alchemists, but oriental experimenters believed in "simultaneous resonance" between linked physical forces—that is, in a correspondence between nature, body, and emotion, resulting in a harmonious interchange. Important too is the fact that exoteric alchemy (*wai-tan*), which uses tangible ingredients such as mercury, lead, cinnabar, and jade, is less important than esoteric (*nei-tan*) alchemy, which works on the "souls" of these elements.[3] According to the Taoist view, as expressed by the seventh-century alchemist-physician Sun Ssu-mo in the *Tan Ching Yao Chüeh* (a collection of formulas for the preparation of elixirs of immortality), the metaphysical experience gained during the course of the operations was of prime importance. These insights allow the practitioner to deepen his understanding of the cosmic role he is to play in an unfolding and expanding universe.

My sole regret was that the divine Way is so remote, the pathway through clouds so inaccessible. I gazed in vain at azure heaven, not knowing how to ascend it. I began to practice techniques of preparing elixirs by cyclical transformation and of fixing substances in the fire, and the formulas for making potable jade and liquid gold. But they are obscure and difficult to fathom, abstruse and unpredictable. How can one without occult virtue comprehend them?

Now, man's aspiration being what it is, he values above all else his physical existence. . . . But it is evanescent as the dew of spring, perishing easily as the forest of autumn. It seems that everything passes in the flicker of an eye. Magnificence and penury truly are not enduring, melancholy and jubilation never last. How saddening to speak of these things![4]

The alchemical experience viewed metaphysically gives reality to *Matsukaze*; its essence, mood, and meaning acquire form and power and penetrate deeply into the fiber of the onlooker.

Noh: A Religiously Oriented Theatre

Noh theatre is an expression of a people's cultural and religious beliefs embedded in an art form. Implicit in its aesthetic and philosophical outlook are the principles of Taoism, Zen Buddhism, and Shintoism.

Tao ("the Way") is "the unchanging unity underlying a shifting plurality," that energetic force which creates all forms of life and motion.[5] Taoism is a religious philosophy based on the teachings of the Chinese sage Lao-tzu (sixth century B.C.), to whom the *Tao-Tê-Ching* ("Book of Tao") is attributed, and those of Chuang-tzu (369–286 B.C.), who expounded and spread his master's doctrine. Taoism preaches silence, meditation, and inwardness. According to its doctrines, the individual is not apart from nature, but implicit in it even after oneness has been divided into yin and yang. The *Tao-Tê-Ching* says:

> Before the Heaven and Earth existed
> There was something nebulous:
>   Silent, isolated,
>   Standing alone, changing not,
>   Eternally revolving without fail,
>   Worthy to be the Mother of all Things.
> I do not know its name
>   And address it as Tao.
> If forced to give it a name, I shall call it "Great."
> Being great implies reaching out in space,
> Far-reaching implies reversion to the original point.[6]

Taoism banishes fear. It imposes calmness on the individual practicing contemplation. Tao implies the "immanent Order of Nature, a mystical acceptance of and incorporation in Nature." Whatever the individual's attitude or goal, life must be lived in harmony with nature; no action must go contrary to nature.[7] Tao also contains the wisdom which enables man to transform himself. Contemplation allows the psyche to unfold and become integrated with the cosmos. The liberation of the ego's spiritual component from its physical limitations is the Taoist's goal: longevity may be known, or even perhaps immortality.[8]

Unlike the Buddhist, the Taoist does not believe that the phenomenological world is illusory or that life is a vale of suffering caused by desires and passions. Life is good and is to be lived fully, and lived contemplatively. The inner path allows activity to take place in an inner domain where truth may be apprehended, not through fruitless exterior action, but through depth perception. Three currents exist in man, according to Chinese physiology and psychology—the seed (*ching*), the breath (*chi'i*), and the spirit (*shên*). The physical soul dominates seed and breath and attempts to attract the conscious soul to its way. The meditative process allows the seed to become transformed into breath, which is purified until it becomes spirit; free from constraints, it is able to rise to higher spheres.[9]

Buddhism, founded by the Indian S'akyamuni Guatama (566–485 B.C.), preached the doctrine of Buddha, the Enlightened One. Happiness and salvation are the product of inwardness and not dependent upon transitory exterior phenomena; life on earth is the product of imperfection and sorrow; the annihilation of desire leads to salvation and "perpetual enlightenment" (nirvana).[10] After Buddhism was introduced into Japan in the sixth century A.D., it was modified by the Japanese and divested of most of its theology. It became a philosophy. Zen Buddhism, which follows the teachings of the monk Eisai and became popular in the twelfth century, was one of several Buddhist sects flourishing in Japan. Zen Buddhism, according to the twentieth-century monk Suzuki, is the result of the Chinese mind coming into contact with Indian philosophy. It incorporated much of Taoist belief into Buddhist metaphysics.

Zen Buddhism seeks to transmit the Buddha Essence or Buddha Mind to humankind through silent meditation and abstract contemplation. If these are properly experienced, enlightenment may result, the aesthetic perception of reality through flashes of intuition which reveal the truth about the universe. During such moments the acolyte may transcend his individuality (his self-consciousness, his personal ego) and know oneness with the universe. Unity of existence underlies all meditative practices: the mind becomes vacant and detached from worldly problems, while at the same time the individual is slowly absorbing the universe into himself. The hierophant is no longer disturbed by the vicissitudes of daily life; he remains serene when faced with adversity.

There is no God in Zen any more than there is in Tao; nor is there a denial of God, for to deny the notion of divinity would be to acknowledge its existence. Zen rejects conceptualizations. It is against verbalization. It seeks to arouse the student's mind so that it may be conditioned to experience enlightenment (*satori*), a state which C. G. Jung labels a *mysterium ineffable*, when the ego is released into the Self. Rational and syllogistic reasoning is banished by the Zen Buddhist. A device known as the *koan* replaces logic. The koan allows the individual mind to intuit. Flashes of consciousness reveal undreamed truths, lead to a sudden awakening, to "a mental upheaval," a kind of "mental catastrophe," which paves the way for satori.[11]

Zen is an intuitive experience. It cannot be taught. It is not intellectual. It is not an accomplishment. It is a way of life: the world of particulars is experienced and daily activities are attended to normally, but at the same time the individual participates in the "original mind" or cosmic consciousness. Such an interchange between the personal and the collective strengthens the mind so that it cannot be destroyed by outside events nor be disconcerted by the effects which plague most individuals. Suzuki describes the Zen Buddhist mind:

It is always flowing, it never halts, nor does it turn into a solid. As it has no discrimination to make, no affective preference to follow, it fills the whole body, pervading every part of the body, and nowhere standing still. It is never like a stone or a piece of wood. . . . If it should find a resting place anywhere, it is not a mind of no-mind. A no-mind keeps nothing in it. . . . the mind moves from one object to another, flowing like a stream of water, filling every possible corner. For this reason the mind fulfills every function required of it.[12]

Japanese art, as expressed in Noh theatre, painting, sculpture, and poetry, has been influenced by Zen Buddhism. It allows the individual to transcend the multiple world and experience timelessness and inwardness; it encourages him to express his feelings in a compressed manner, through symbols: a word, a brush stroke, an arch of the finger, an image, color, mood, or impulse. Just as Zen Buddhism rejects the logical intellectual sphere, so Japanese art also abandons balance and symmetry for the "one-corner" style.[13] Asymmetry allows viewers to abstract themselves from conventional, geometrical, causal, and rational regularity. In Noh theatre the stage is laid out asymmetrically; in Japanese garden arrangements the stepping-stones are irregularly placed. In both cases, the image created may inspire a variety of views; nothing is "complete" or "fixed" and there is always "more to be seen."[14] The notion of a dimensionless universe is also implicit in the concept of asymmetry: the space between the stones in a Japanese garden or the unfulfilled area on stage is as important as occupied space, or perhaps even more important, since the void implies a world of perpetual becoming.

The Zen artist, as Suzuki points out, seeks to observe and to relate to "individual beings" which are "perfect in themselves and at the same time" embody "the nature of totality which belongs to the One." Although a sense of incompleteness is implicit in Noh drama and Zen garden and flower arrangements, tea ceremonies and paintings, the feeling of belonging to a whole is also present. What is visible in an incomplete and imperfect state is only an aspect of the life process; an example of an object in a state of repose. Rather than expressing the outer world in detail, the artist focuses on the inner domain: emotions are awakened by the vast emptiness of the landscape. Zen poetry, known for its sparseness, has been called "poor" poetry. A word stands alone, divested of adjectives and adverbs, an entity unto itself: "the One in the Many and the Many in the One," as Suzuki states, "the One remaining as One in the Many individually and collectively."[15]

For the Zen Buddhist and the Taoist, nature is not to be conquered nor dominated nor used exclusively for man's benefit. It is to be experienced as a friend, an entity through which an individual may experience Buddhahood or Tao. As viewed in Noh drama, art, poetry, and alchemy, nature is not crushed or violated. One relates to it and experiences it as part of a whole. It is loved and appreciated spiritually, aesthetically, and physically. To truly understand nature, Suzuki suggested, "one must learn to look at a flower" and to "grasp its spirit," that "superworldly" aspect of its being which transcends the logical world of man. It must be understood in its beauty, its mobile attitudes, pulsations, emptiness, and solitude. The same may be said of Noh drama; it must be apprehended intuitively; it must be sensed metaphysically. One of the most important differences, Suzuki stated, between Zen Buddhism's and Christianity's attitude toward life can be seen in the contrast between Buddha's death and that of Jesus. Buddha departed from the earth in quietude surrounded by his equally serene disciples; Jesus suffered an excruciating crucifixion.

[Consider] the crucifixion of Christ, with blood oozing from the head and side. He is stretched upright against the cross, with an expression of the utmost pain and suffering, whereas the Buddha looks as if contentedly asleep on the couch, with no signs of distress. The vertical Christ represents an intense spirit of flight, but the horizontal Buddha is peaceful. When we look at the latter, everything that goes against the spirit of contentment is excluded from our consciousness.[16]

Zen Buddhism and Taoism produced the inwardness, the symbolical rather than representational focus, asymmetry, and sense of emptiness in Noh theatre. Shinto ("the Way of the Gods") is also an important influence on Noh drama. A religion with no official scriptures, it teaches that a life force exists in all things, whether these be animate or inanimate. Everything in the phenomenological world has a soul or spirit within it; each entity is in a state of becoming. Shinto deities (kami) are many. They include spirits of trees, mountains, flowers, deified ancestors, heroes, and emperors, and of the sun, moon, and more. Man approaches the kami without fear and in friendship.[17] Before doing so, however, he must purify himself by washing and taking part in devotions, such as standing within a sacred enclosure or in a certain area on a mountain. Shinto shrines are usually very simple. They include a symbolic representation of a kami or a substitute spirit in the form of a stone or a mirror. No image exists in ancient Shinto ritual. The Shinto attitude toward nature as a dynamic force endows the Noh spectacle with a live, incredible energy, all the more powerful and vital because it is always controlled and nuanced.

Noh Theatrical Conventions

An art which is defined as "poetic dance-monodrama," Noh theatre rests on very specific conventions. Like the theatre in general, Noh is religious in origin. It was born from a conflict between the gods. Amaterasu the sun goddess was terrified by her brother's unpleasant pranks and withdrew into a cave in heaven, placing a boulder in front of it. As a result, the world was deprived of sunlight. To try to entice her out of her isolation, the gods met in front of her cave. Heavenly-Alarming-Female decided to perform a dance, and when in a state of ecstasy she removed her clothes, the gods were so amused that they burst out laughing. Intent upon discovering the source of this merriment, the sun goddess left her cave and light was returned to the world.[18] Theatre began as an earthly replica of a divine adventure.

Noh was influenced by Shinto dances, by warrior court dances, and by Buddhist sacred pantomine. In addition to the songs and dances enacted at religious and festive occasions, a more rustic type of entertainment was influential in the creation of Noh drama. During the spring planting and autumn harvesting of rice, clowning, gymnastic contests, and amusing songs and dances were performed in order to entertain the peasants at work. Farces were also introduced, and with them the grotesque. By the twelfth century, the rustic and the sacred were unified, and actors began training in structured troupes. By the fourteenth century, dialogue had been added to both comic and tragic routines, creating a true theatrical form.[19]

Conventions regulated by tradition are at the heart of Noh. Like Zen Buddhism and Taoism, Noh is meditative, introspective, spiritual, slow-paced, subtle, and suggestive. Its meanings may be apprehended intuitively in sudden flashes of illumination. Noh plays do not have a real plot, and a westerner may need patience to understand the series of complex images which make up its song and dance sequences and the tonalities and inflections of its choral and orchestral accompaniments. Noh dramas, with an introduction, development, and finale, usually have two acts and take about one and one-half hours to perform. There are five categories of Noh plays: God, warrior, woman, realistic (or mad), and demon. *Matsukaze* is a woman play. Of import are the sensations evoked during a performance; the tension aroused by the images, gestures, and pace (that is, the timing between a knock on the door and the discovery of the person on the other side), the manner in which the lines are sung or spoken (muffled and almost incomprehensible frequently, but this is unimportant since most audiences know the plays by heart). All aspects of a Noh play are stylized and predetermined: the symbols, the spatial patterns, the actor's interpretation, his poses; each, in its own way, adds to the fascination of the theatrical experience.

Noh theatre requires a special stage built on a level with the audience. Asymmetry reigns in the construction of the stage in conformity with Zen Buddhism's rejection of logic and causality. The roof built over the stage gives the impression of being outdoors, which is reminiscent of the fourteenth-century production of Noh drama in Edo Castle. White gravel is spread in front of the stage to separate audience and actor as in ancient times and also acts as a natural reflection for stage lights or sunlight. The stage floor is made of unfinished but highly polished Japanese cypress wood, which enables the actor easily to slide, shuffle, or glide. In the old days, large earthenware jars were buried under the stage so that when the actor stamped his foot during certain dances, the echoes he caused would add to the general tension. The spatial arrangement of these jars, always mathematically determined, was so important that it was a closely guarded secret. Only Noh carpenters knew exactly where the jars were located. Since World War II, however, concrete cones filled with varying amounts of sand allow for a variety of resonances. On the left of the stage, under a porchlike protrusion, a chorus consisting of six to ten people sits in two rows. The chorus may speak for the main character in the first person or dialogue with him, giving the impression, however, of one harmonious voice. Musicians, seated to the right upstage, play percussion and woodwind instruments, thus amplifying and shading the sound made by the actor in his song or dance.[20]

There are no curtains in front of the stage as in conventional western theatre. A curtain at the end of the stage is used to separate the "mirror room," where the actor dons his mask before coming on stage, from the rest of the acting area. This curtain is a work of art in itself: it is brilliantly colored with a purple horizontal band and vertical stripes of green, yellow, orange, and white. As the actor steps onto the stage, this curtain is lifted slowly and ritualistically, projecting a specific mood onto the spectacle as a whole.[21] The scenery consists only of a painted pine tree on the wall behind the stage (the "mirror" or "resounding board") and bamboo designs on either side of the wall. A railing is built across the back of a slightly raised stage where three small pine trees are planted in pots and spaced at specific intervals marking the positions of the actors and their entrances and exits. Stage properties include fans, swords, drums, and a bell made of cloth with a bamboo frame which is weighed down at the bottom. Most of these properties are extremely simple and are made for specific productions. (The hut used in *Matsukaze*, for example, consists of four bamboo poles and a roof.) They are not realistic but symbolic, thereby stimulating the imagination rather than limiting it. Stage assistants move the properties on and off the stage when the action calls for it; they also help the actor change his costume right on stage and must be well trained as actors in order to maintain the desired mood.[22]

Costumes are extraordinary, both in form and in color. The lavish combinations of colors contrast sharply with the simplicity and austerity of the undecorated stage. Every detail of a costume—its cut, pattern, and the way in which it is worn by the actor—is extremely important. A sleeve raised above the head means one thing, but another when it is tossed back.[23] The actor's body is completely covered. First he dons white tabi socks and white underwear, and then a silk garment. Next a collar is placed on his neck to represent, according to its color, the character's social rank. The actor then chooses a brocaded kimono: it may be green, red, purple, yellow, white, vermillion, blue, gold, silver, or other colors. Kimonos are frequently of such dazzling beauty and such works of art that they are preserved by families and handed down from one generation to another. A sash harmonizing with the rest of the attire is added, and then wide trousers. The actor will also choose a wig and headdress if his role requires them.[24]

The most important actors in a Noh play are the *shite* (main actor), the *waki* (secondary actor), the *tsure* (who may accompany the shite or waki and is usually a shadow figure), and the *kyōgen* (who plays a comic or menial role). All female roles are acted by men.

The shite is either an old man, a god, a warrior, a woman, a ghost, or an animal. He wears a mask when playing a nonhuman or female character, or if he has some special characteristic, such as being very thin, very old, blind, or dejected in some way. When the shite plays a normal middle-aged male, his face is not made up, but it remains expressionless, as do his eyes. In this case his face takes the place of the mask, and because of its immobility is in sharp contrast with his bodily movements and vocalisms. The tsure accompanies him at times and also maintains an expressionless visage, as do the members of the chorus, the orchestra, and the stage assistants.

The mask is one of the most important features of Noh drama. It severs the actor from the outer world; it encourages him to look inwardly. Usually made of cypress wood covered with many layers of paint, masks are also works of art and are frequently passed down from one actor to another. They are endowed with life, it is believed, when worn by a great thespian. Once an actor is completely dressed he goes to the room behind the stage, looks at himself in the mirror, lifts up the mask he has chosen for the performance, bows to it in greeting, and then places it on his face. Until this moment the actor is still himself. Once he has donned the mask, however, he has been transformed and becomes the character he is to portray. The mask symbolizes the body and soul of the new being he is to interpret. It is not "the person wearing the mask but the mask itself" that sees and comes to life on stage.[25] The mask, however, imposes limitations on the shite. It determines his interpretation and the mood he seeks to create. The "intermediate expression" on the mask, however, allows the actor to add the "emotional coloring" to his part. He does so by a variety of poses of the head and neck, by downward or upward glances, gestures, and so forth. A Noh actor may spend days studying and absorbing the meaning and personality of the mask he seeks to use for the performance. The ensemble of all the accessories integrates the once disparate elements into a new unity, thus making for a total effect: the individual character as he embodies cosmic drama.[26]

The waki usually establishes the scene, the situation, and the shite's identity. He is unmasked and is most frequently "the intermediate between spirit and reality."[27] It is he who reveals how souls may be saved, he who makes serenity and repose possible. As he wanders about in temporal and atemporal realms, in landscapes which seem limitless, dimensions are altered as is the course of the situations evoked. The waki, who frequently portrays an itinerant Zen Buddhist priest, represents eternal becoming: he resurrects a historical period or a mythical past. The emptiness of the stage, the stillness of the waki's countenance, and the concentration expended as he sings his song and conjures a world of mystery create an invisible domain where the unspoken mounts in importance and the unseen triggers tensions. The waki's costume identifies his role; his face is unmasked, without makeup, and expressionless. His essence emerges through his gestures, vocal intonations, and inflections. The waki's journey into a dimensionless area in time and space is accomplished by means of two or three steps on stage. As he takes these steps he describes his travels in a few words and gestures, after which he returns to his original place, thus indicating he has reached his destination. Then he withdraws to the corner of the stage and allows the audience to focus its attention on the shite.[28]

The kyōgen is an anonymous being who narrates the shite's part when he is not speaking. The kyōgen fills a transition or an interval between the first and second part of Noh drama, which are determined by the shite's appearance and disappearance. His function is to keep tension at a peak by explaining the stage happenings in simple and less poetic language. Sometimes he converses with the waki; at other moments he is alone. The kyōgen occasionally provides comic relief, relates vignettes, or portrays unusual incidents.

In contrast to western theatre, in which actors attempt to create roles with individual personalities, the Noh actor focuses on the creation of emotions in order to go beyond the individual character. The facts of the situation to be enacted are stated at the outset of the drama; the atmosphere, mood, and poetry of the role, rather than a personality, must be created during the course of the spectacle. For a westerner, Noh drama lacks action and conflict. For the oriental, tension is "concentrated" and "distilled" in the image, atmosphere, mood, poetry, and gesture. The "plastic form" which moves about on stage arouses the spectator's emotions; the spatial compositions create the mood. The development and pursuit of but a single emotion and the revelation of its implicit truth and beauty is the goal of Noh dramaturgy.[29]

The Alchemical Operations in *Matsukaze*

Matsukaze, written by Kan'ami (1333–84) but reinterpreted by Zeami (1363–1443), takes place at Suma Bay, an area just outside of the modern city of Kobe. A wandering Buddhist priest (waki) stops in front of a pine tree. A poem slips from its branches. The Priest reads it, and then questions a villager (kyōgen) who happens to be passing by about the meaning of the poem. The Villager informs him that it refers to two sisters long since dead: Matsukaze (shite), whose name means "Wind in the Pines," and Murasame (tsure), whose name may be translated as "Autumn Rain." The two girls suddenly appear. They are gathering salt, their means of livelihood. The sisters sing and dance their memories: they had been loved by and had loved Yukihira, an exiled poet, scholar, and courtier. Dawn emerges. The image vanishes. The Priest hears only the wind in the pine trees.

Alchemically, *Matsukaze* combines *solutio* and *sublimatio* operations. Water is the prevailing image. Since water is associated with yin, the feminine symbol, audiences know that the woman's world is to come into focus. A *sublimatio* condition is evoked as the blending and cleansing of past experiences is pursued in a present reality through the spiritual encounters between the sisters, the Priest, and their beloved Yukihira. The residue of an earthly relationship has been purified; its essence emerges in the stage proceedings; heated and distilled, the water has been transformed into vapor, into a memory, leaving the Priest alone in the phenomenological realm, ready to pursue his wanderings but enriched by the beauty of the vision he has just experienced.

Japanese alchemy, derived from Chinese alchemy, focuses on the problem of discovering an elixir of long life and not necessarily on the creation of gold. In ancient days Japan possessed numerous gold deposits and also imported gold from Siberia. To create it artificially, therefore, was not of prime importance to the Japanese alchemist. What he sought were potions which would cure diseases and allow him to live forever. (Like the Taoists, the Japanese believed in the existence of mysterious mountain abodes where the immortals lived, and where man could transcend his mortal condition.) Japanese alchemists also practiced dietetic, gymnastic, respiratory, shamanistic, magical, ecstatic, and meditative techniques; they directed their efforts to the creation of a new, imperishable body which could be nurtured like an embryo by means of yogic disciplines. According to Li Chao Kuin, a Chinese alchemist living in the Han dynasty, everything in nature may be resurrected, recreated, and altered.

Sacrifice to the furnace [*tsao*] and you will be able to summon [supernatural] beings; when you have called forth these beings, the powder of cinnabar can be transformed into yellow gold; when the yellow gold is produced you will be able to make of it utensils for drinking and eating and in so doing you will have a prolonged longevity. When your longevity is prolonged you will be able to see the blessed [*hsien*] of the island of P'eng Lai which is in the midst of the seas. When you have seen them and have made the *feng* and *chan* sacrifices, then you will not die.[30]

Matsukaze, explained alchemically, dramatizes a symbolic correlation between the individual and nature: the correspondence which exists between the cosmic domain (macrocosm) and its effect upon the individual in the phenomenological world (microcosm).

The cosmic and phenomenological realms (really one) interact, inspiring resonances and infinite patterns and distillations of sensations, moods, and feelings. The same relationship and transmutations exist in the alchemical domain. Although lead is whitish, it can be reddened to take on the appearance of cinnabar; cinnabar may be whitened to look like lead. The Japanese scientist believed that supernatural beings exist in metals and chemicals; it was, therefore, important to work in harmony with these forces, thus gaining important knowledge about nature. Life-giving substances, suggested the alchemist Chang Tao-ling in the second century A.D., exist in cinnabar, jade, pearls and other entities. To become one with nature is to have succeeded in becoming integrated with the Cosmic Whole and is a sign of moral perfection.[31] Alchemists, in their attempt to discover a harmony between metals, elements, and humankind that will result in a welding of opposites into a balanced whole, experience tension and crises which produce pain or joy, depending upon the outcome of their labors. The changes resulting from their various experiments mirror emotional alterations within their psyches: both the alchemist and his metals are manifestations of nature's various moods in its eternal state of becoming.

Belief in the alchemist's ability to alter matter (the formless becoming formed or vice versa) is implicit in Chinese and Japanese alchemical ideology and philosophy. It is not surprising then that Matsukaze should evince a variety of forms on stage, that appearance and disappearance become credible to her, and that ghosts are believed to exist. For the Priest, who experiences Matsukaze as a reality, anything and everything may emerge into actuality: Shinto gods live everywhere; nature is a breathing and dynamic force with which each individual must work in friendship. Every force in nature is forever taking on the shape most appropriate to its essence at that particular instant. When, therefore, Matsukaze and her sister are resurrected on stage, nothing is strange about their entrance into the phenomenological world. For the Japanese alchemist, imbued with Taoism, Shintoism, and Zen Buddhism, each created form works with nature and according to nature's time periods. As minerals and metals evolve slowly within the earth, so the Noh actor paces his activity in reduced time-controlled sequences.[32]

The alchemical notion of fluidity, of eternal becoming and timelessness, implicit in the *solutio* and *sublimatio* operations has ramifications in the mystically oriented *Matsukaze*. The characters, for example, live in both three- and four-dimensional spheres. They experience these worlds interchangeably. In the phenomenological world, matter and spirit only seem to operate antithetically; in reality, they are manifestations of yin and yang, that is, one central universal force. Since matter and spirit are one, so death and life coincide, as do image and reality, fiction and fact. Fluidity, a concept also basic to Noh theatre, allows the space/time continuum viewed on stage to be experienced in a timeless universe. *Matsukaze* takes place in autumn, in the ninth month of the year. Although the information given is specific, it takes on universality and timelessness because it could be any autumn or any year. Autumn thus becomes a symbol of eternal return and mirrors the notion of perpetual death and renewal. Changeless unity in the world of infinite variety becomes the focal point of the drama. The stillness of silence can be heard by the viewer as the Priest makes his way on stage; the "mind within the mind," which is the source of all energy, life, and breath, takes hold.[33]

The Priest, who has been making one pilgrimage after another, symbolizes the soul roaming throughout the universe, struggling to purify its essence by ridding itself of earthly encumbrances. A mood of aloneness prevails: the trees are bare; the mountain in the distance is austere; the water in Suma Bay is transparent. For the Chinese or Japanese alchemist there is no such thing as an individual indissoluble soul. Two souls exist within man—the *hun* soul, which comes from the upper air and returns to it after death, and the *pho* soul, which is created by the earth and returns to it after death. This double view of life is in keeping with the yin-yang antithesis. These two forces are also implicit in the alchemical process: the *t'ai-chi* or *prima materia* is developed according to yin and yang. The pho brings inner light to humankind, brightening the inner realm; hun rids man of his "evil" ways.[34]

The Priest is endowed with pho and hun, which will become manifest in the course of the play. He pauses during his wanderings at Suma Bay. Although the collective domain takes precedence, specific place names are used in *Matsukaze* and other Noh plays in order to instill an emotional climate. They arouse sensations and, in so doing, fuse time and nontime. Lin Yutang quotes the following saying in his *Wisdom of China and India*:

The Nameless is the origin of Heaven and Earth;
The Names is the Mother of All things.[35]

The alchemical process also stirs feelings through association and projects the scientist's inner world onto his chemicals and metals. The priest's wanderings, like the alchemist's experimentations, are to be looked upon as initiatory procedures, temporal disciplines imposed upon those seeking to penetrate the atemporal domain and experience nothingness, cosmic consciousness.

After the Villager tells him about Matsukaze and Murasame, their unhappiness in love and their poverty, the Priest says a prayer before proceeding on his journey.

It is sad! Though their bodies are buried in the ground, their names linger on. This lonely pine tree lingers on also, ever green and untouched by autumn, their only memorial. Ah! While I have been chanting sutras and invoking Amida Buddha for their repose, the sun, as always on autumn days, has quickly set. That village at the foot of the mountain is a long way. Perhaps I can spend the night in the fisherman's salt shed.

(P. 22)

In few words, the Priest gives the impression of infinite distances, continuity of movement, parallel rhythms, and the ever-changing density of existence. Audiences are projected into a fourth dimension where time cannot be taken into account without referring to space, as in Einstein's theory of relativity. The Priest experiences the Buddha Breath and the concomitant vibrations or music of the spheres in a timeless and spaceless dimension, in fluid (*solutio*) terms, as an active purification ritual.

The solitary pine tree to which the poem referring to the two sisters was attached is inhabited by a kami. It is immortal and timeless, since it is ever green. The older the tree, the more experience it has had in the phenomenological world and the greater is its universal knowledge. Its agelessness suggests feelings of antiquity as well as wisdom. It stirs pity and longing for bygone days, when life was young and hopes ran high. The Japanese pine tree (*matsu*) is very special because its branches are not regular and its trunk is gnarled. Asymmetry and the curves of its trunk set the mood for the events to come. As this force of nature stands strong and proud, it mirrors through contrast the solitude of man and the desolation of autumn. To the Japanese, the pine tree represents energy since its needles are always green. Unlike the rest of nature, which dies and is reborn yearly, the pine tree remains a perpetually consoling force, always ready to befriend those in need. When drenched in the misty and rainy atmosphere of Suma Bay, it evokes a mood of melancholy; its watery or *solutio* surroundings are reminiscent of tears, while the salt spray with which it is permeated purifies feelings and cleanses sensations.

The green of the pine tree is reminiscent of jade, considered by the oriental alchemists to possess very special virtues and mystical powers. Pine flowers, alchemists say, are as pure as jade. The tree with its branches reaching toward the heavens is filled with yang, that is, cosmic energy; it is strong, indestructible, and regal. Because Chinese and Japanese alchemists believed that the pine possessed fibers able to make man immortal, they ate its seeds, needles, and resin. They also believed that the sap which trickles down the tree trunk into the earth forms a mushroomlike substance capable of endowing the one who eats it with immortality. In Japan, pine trees are endowed with such magical and mystical powers that their wood is used frequently in the construction of Buddhist and Shinto temples as well as in the making of ritual instruments. The Priest stops before the pine tree at the outset and conclusion of the drama, after which he will set out on another divine pilgrimage.

The Priest mentions a mountain at the beginning of *Matsukaze*. A vaporous quality invades the scene immediately afterwards: form vanishes; the concrete disperses into its component parts. Mountains, seemingly unshakable and immovable, are in fact an accumulation of infinitesimal particles which reach into the clouds, blending with the universe in slow but forceful stages. Zen priests frequently ascend mountains (Fuji in particular) for purification purposes. On their heights man rids himself of dross and experiences the purity of the *sublimatio* condition. Many Zen monasteries are located in mountains, allowing the initiate to commune with nature in its pristine purity and encouraging the acolyte to intuit its beauties. According to the alchemist Ko Hung (254–334), the author of the *Nei P'ien*:

All mountains, whether large or small contain gods and powers, and the strength of these divinities is directly proportional to the size of the mountain. To enter the mountains without the proper recipe is to be certain of anxiety or harm. In some cases people fall ill, are wounded, or become stricken with fear. In other cases, lights and shadows are seen, strange sounds are heard. Lack of the proper recipe can make a large tree fall when there is no sound; or a high rock fall for no apparent reason, striking and killing people. . . . Mountains are not to be entered lightly.[36]

Mountains are never to be climbed with the idea of conquering their heights, any more than nature is to be dominated in the alchemical process and used for personal advantage. Mountains allow one to get in touch with nature and, by extension, one's inner world. They infuse energy into the initiate who is intent upon working in harmony with their mysteries.

The Priest, who sees the mountain in the distance and the city lying at its foot, knows that he is not yet prepared to experience this transcendental force. Like the alchemist who must not pursue his experiments unless he is knowledgeable in both spiritual and physical domains, he understands that purification is necessary before one ascends such a mountain. Otherwise, tragedy may strike. Evil spirits in the mountain may turn the acolyte away from his goal, ensnare him, and then destroy him. The water image, associated with yin, takes precedence at this juncture (as a prelude to the sisters' entrance) over the yang force implicit in the mountain reference. The Priest kneels down, indicating his withdrawal from the action. The stage grows darker as the feminine element takes over: the woman's world, the dream, the unknown, the land of mystery comes into view.

Dusk pervades; a somber note ushers in melancholy. Dreams take on form; fantasies are promoted; the unconscious dominates in preparation for the dream sequence to follow. The stage assistant places a pail of brine on a cart. Murasame enters wearing the tsure mask. Matsukaze walks down the bridgeway, having donned her mask. Although ghosts, both sisters are very real for the Japanese audience, as fantasy and shadow figures were equally real to the alchemist. The oriental does not believe that the soul migrates or survives in some heavenly sphere after death. Immortality implies materiality, a survival within the phenomenological world but in an altered state. The body has been compared by oriental alchemists to the thread of a necklace on which souls have been strung. To die, accordingly, is to go on a celestial journey and to experience oneness with Tao, that is, with the All; serenity, therefore, is to be found in emptiness and silence. A Taoist alchemist-poet wrote symbolically of death:

Spring and autumn hurried by, never delaying;
How could I always stay in my old home?[37]

Matsukaze and Murasame pull the brine cart along the beach. The salt-saturated water of oceans and tears suggests the emotions associated with vast expanses of it—sorrow, loneliness, and pain. Water has three main functions: it is the source of life; it paves the way for rebirth; and it is essential to purification rituals. Because of the great use made of water in purification rituals, Zen Buddhists and Taoists have been called "masters of consecrated waters." For Lao-tzu, water was the emblem of supreme virtue; it spelled wisdom since it was free and unattached; it could flow according to the lay of the land, with nature and not against it. Water is linked with fire, which is also a means of purifying the sullied and destroying dross. To bathe in water or in the alchemist's ignacious water, mercury, is to rid oneself of earthly impurities.

In that water is an undifferentiated mass, it represents virtuality, a world of possibilities which dissolves conflict, immerses differences, and solves problems. Because it is fluid, it is the sine qua non of alchemical *solutio* or *dissolutio* conditions; because it is cohesive and homogenous, it symbolizes *coagulatio* or fixative elements. Water exists in everything because everything can be reduced to a watery state. Wei-Po Yang, the father of Chinese alchemy, wrote about water in connection with the five elements recognized by oriental alchemists (water, earth, metal, wood, fire): "The yellow Earth [element] is the father of the [element] Metal and mercury [*liu chu*] is the mother of the [element] Water."[38] Earth, then, is the creator of metal, which then brings forth water.

Despite the apparent homogeneity and fluidity of water, it has been considered by alchemists to be double and therefore in keeping with the universal forces of yin and yang. Water may be divided into superior (rain) and inferior (earth) principles. The waters mentioned in *Matsukaze* emanate from both areas: from the heavens in the form of mist and rain and from the terrestrial regions in the form of Suma Bay, dew, and the vaporous haze on the pine tree.

Salt from the brine from which the two sisters eke out their meager living is a condiment, a preservative which symbolizes immortality. Rock salt is mined from mountains in blocks and therefore has been associated with strength and power and with the purity and clarity of crystal. Salt is left after brine evaporates; thus purified, it is sublimated. The characteristics attributed to salt are inherent in the personalities of the two sisters: courage, strength, purity, and sensitivity. Just as grains of salt dissolve in water, so the individual ego becomes absorbed into the Self, the person into the universe, the sisters into the collective. Salt purifies and protects, according to Shinto ritual. Salt plays such an important role in Japan that small piles of salt are placed at entrances to houses to protect their inhabitants. It is also scattered in areas where fighting may take place and where funerals or ceremonial functions are held, with the hope of aiding the forces of good and tranquility.

Salt is also instrumental in prolonging life. Nathan Sivin observes that it is mentioned in the *Tan Ching Yao Chueh* in a formula used to create the drug of immortality—"Grand Unity Jade Powder Elixir"—which was to be taken orally by the acolyte. A recipe for the "Golden Petal Elixir" also requires the use of "heavy salt," which must be poured into boiling water.

The salt dissolves to a metallic color like that of copper. Let the amount of solution diminish considerably by boiling. When you wish to make use of the elixir, take the salt mix, and heat for half a day. When you take it out it will be red. Cyclically transform it as before for seven cycles.[39]

For Matsukaze and Murasame, whose lives revolve around water, salt is a lifesaving force, not only because it allows them to eat, but also because of its potential for *purificatio* and *sublimatio.*

The moonlight, mentioned along with the water images, plays an important role in *Matsukaze* as well as in the world of the alchemist. Murasame says:

> The waves shatter at our feet
> And even the moonlight wets our sleeves
> With its tears of loneliness.

> (P. 22)

The moon, symbol of transformation, represents biological rhythms and other cyclical states. Its association with tides, water, and rain makes the moon important in vegetation and fertility rituals. An image so frequently evoked by poets, it represents indirect rather than direct experience and knowledge, passivity, receptivity, and the dream. As it makes its way in the night world or the poet's unconscious, it conjures up spirits and images of bygone days. For the sisters, the moon evokes the past, those moments of joy now reintegrated into the present. A constant and lonely traveler through the heavens, the moon is a visual replica of their own feelings of isolation and exile. When Matsukaze delivers her soliloquy she looks upon the moon, as its rays are reflected in the water before her, as a companion.

> The autumn winds are sad . . .
> Salt winds blowing from the mountain pass . . .
> On the beach, night after night,
> Waves thunder at our door;
> And our long walks to the village
> We've no companion but the moon.
>
> (P. 22)

Like the moon receiving the sun's rays, the sisters passively accept their lot.

The Japanese have always been "moon lovers."[40] The mysterious light with which this body shines suggests a dim, insinuating, shaded world, one never brilliant or filled with glaring lights, but rather remote and already lived. Objects lit by moonlight are not individualized, but blend into the environment, hazy, and essentially obscure. As the moon, poetized by the Noh dramatist, casts its rays through the branches of the pine tree, feelings are stirred; its soft light falls lovingly on the complex forms which inhabit the stage. For Matsukaze, moonlight encourages a shadowy world to come into being; ghostly forces—and she is one of them—make their presence known. The alchemist associates the moon with water because it is frequently encircled by vapor, particularly just before and after a rainfall. In the Nei P'ien, Ho Kung stated: "I have frequently seen people obtain water from the moon at night by means of a speculum, and fire from the sun in the morning by use of a burning-mirror."[41]

Matsukaze tells the audience that no boat can take her across the sea, nor can a dream alter her circumstances. Both she and her sister are compelled to toil alone and in poverty, to weep always "from our hearts' unanswered longing." As she speaks, the members of the chorus echo her pain and reflect her "shame" of poverty. In so doing, they look down "as if catching a glimpse of their reflections in the water" (p. 22). Unity of theme, gesture, and mood prevails. Reinforcing the atmosphere of melancholy and dishonor are words such as "shrink," "timorous," "withdrawn," "vanish," "stranded," "discarded," "useless," "withered," and "rotting." The chorus repeats "Like our trailing sleeves" (p. 23) as if chanting a litany, thus indicating the disdain they feel for themselves. They are pariahs, isolated in their sorrow. The chorus chants the complaint in musical overtones; then each member of it hides his face in shame.

> The fishermen call out in muffled voices;
> At sea, the small boats loom dimly.
> Across the faintly glowing face of the moon
> Flights of wild geese streak,
> And plovers flock below along the shore.
> Fall gales and stiff sea winds:
> These are things, in such a place,
> That truly belong to autumn.
> But oh, the terrible, lonely nights!
>
> (P. 24)

Images of water, night, autumn, and wind underscore the coldness and bleakness of the scene. Nature is divested of its color, warmth, and life. Yet Matsukaze's abject poverty and solitude are desirable states, according to Zen Buddhist and esoteric alchemy. To be homeless and poor is to enter into timelessness, where subject and object become one and dichotomies present in the manifest world are wedded—good and evil, body and soul, spirit and matter, mortal and immortal. Despite Matsukaze's intense pain, a sense of belonging to nature and of participating in its cosmic flow imbue her with quietude and a sense of belonging. In contrast to such sensations of metaphysical serenity is the turmoil she describes: the sea washes onto the shore, the winds howl, the trees blow their anguish.

Wind, which represents the breath of the universe or Buddha Breath, is important to the alchemist: it is transparent, vaporous, and blends with chemicals and metals. Wind stands for the world of intuition, immediacy, and communication. It transcends the world of the senses and enters into the timeless domain of eternity. In contrast to the howling wind, however, is the stillness of the clouds, endowing the scene with a far more frightening and sinister character. Wind arouses tension because of its sound; as the water splashes up against the shore, the tree branches crack. Wind is also a creative force; it deposits fresh attitudes and alters nature's seeming stability, spreading vapor and water spray and dispersing clouds, mist, and matter. It is a powerful instrument, a spiritual agency which points to a world embedded in mystery. As the wind forces the water to wash against the bank, it suggests a purification ritual. The moisture of the air, the previously subdued and delicate atmosphere, is now endowed with power and dynamism; images of softness and tenderness have disappeared as mounting anguish takes hold in cyclical rotations, spreading rain water about in an incessant flow, immersing Matsukaze and her sister in a passionate climate.

The world of mass, solidity, and tangibility is unleashed; concreteness grows soluble. Water and wind pound away as they invade the poetic world of Noh: so nature's waters, in the form of human tears, dissolve problems and compel them to disappear, like salt crystals which vanish in water. A blending into a larger frame of reference arouses fresh views, more comprehensive attitudes, and a certain detachment. The ego no longer dominates the scene; the Self takes over, the specific moment.

Matsukaze's mind has been cleansed of pain and freed from the defilement of the senses. The chorus intones a description of wild geese streaking across "the faintly glowing face of the moon" (p. 24). The geese represent those who are forced to leave their homes, the exiled who weep when departing into lands unknown. In their flight they mourn their past, their land, and the warmth and security of their home life. The shadows of the geese in flight in the waters below prepare for the evocation of memories and dreams.

> While the rough breakers surge and fall,
> And cranes among the reeds
> Fly up with sharp cries.
> The four winds add their wailing.
> How shall we pass the cold night?
>
> (P. 24)

The wailing of the cranes adds to the sharp and piercing overtones of the scene. The night is cold, the moon's rays subdued, the atmosphere remote and mysterious.

Nature becomes a giant symphony of howling wind, pounding

rain, and the shrill tones of the birds in flight. Even greater desolation, solemnity, and reverence pervade the scene. Matsukaze, who lives in the world of particulars and knows anguish, is encouraged, as she reiterates references to water, wind, and salt, to experience transcendental values as she passes through the *solutio* operations. Her world of pain evaporates before the dazzling universe of sounds and reflected lights. The waters of Suma Bay replicate a heart throbbing with pain as it beats against the rocklike harshness of an immutable situation. Primal relationships exist in the collective domain in which Matsukaze has now immersed herself: the world of irreconcilable opposites present in the existential domain diminishes in importance.

Fire, the yang force, enters the scene. "The smoke from the salt fires," the chorus says, activates emotions still further. According to Japanese alchemists, fire and water do not fight each other. Although they seem antithetical, each possesses its own sphere of energy and activates rather than subdues the other. Fire, in its redness harmonizing with the moon's rays, symbolizes passion, love, anger, and anguish. Fire is spirit which burns with intuitive knowledge; it is part of the divine Buddha Essence. Fire, for the Shintoist, expresses the spirit of renewal, rebirth, and purification. Taoist alchemists enter the fire operation to rid themselves of their human condition: they use it for purification purposes, to perform ablutions. Man is fire: enlightenment. Fire, as used in the alchemist's athanor, heats, cooks, transforms, and purifies the elements, and while so doing regenerates them.

Wood also participates in Matsukaze's drama: "Humble folk hauled wood for salt fires" (p. 25). Burning wood dries out the waters and prepares for further cleaning and whitening, encouraging spirit to reign supreme, unsullied in its crystal clarity. Wood emerges from the earth and in this condition is yin; when it grows into a tree, its branches reach out toward the heavens. In this position, it takes on the yang qualities of ascending and sublimating. Matsukaze mentions "pine groves" (p. 25); these "stand hazy" and "cut off the moonlight," thus disrupting the smoothness of the vision and adding a note of frustration to the beauty of the scene.

The mood alters once again and "rushing seas" take over; passion swells; a limitless expanse pervades. Matsukaze's lonely cry of anguish cuts the atmosphere. Then she adds, "I have the moon in my pail!" Once a solitary force in an empty sky, the moon has now touched below surfaces, partakes of earthly waters, and becomes contained in a pail. The sense of infinity which had prevailed moments earlier now gives way to emotions of constriction and worldly existence. "The moon above is one; / Below it has two, no, three reflections" (p. 25). A union of heaven (one) and earth (two) occurs. For the alchemist, Tao produces one and one gives birth to two, which produces three. According to the *Tao te Ching,* three is the perfect number: it expresses totality and achievement; it is a manifestation of man, the son of heaven and of earth—the great triad.

The pail is placed on the cart and rides along the road of life: "And on our cart we load the moon!" (p. 25). Like the traveler who wanders during his earthly existence, so the moon traverses the heavens in reflected grandeur, in a pail filled with brine. Yet Matsukaze realizes that life is not all misery as she sits on a low stool while Murasame kneels beside her. This pose represents two women seated in a hut, or a withdrawal into an inner realm, removed from the external world as is the moon now circumscribed by the pail.

The Priest comes forward. He sees the sisters and asks them for a night's lodging. Although Matsukaze is humiliated because she considers the hut too wretched to house any stranger, the priest understands her shame but states that "poverty makes no difference" to him (p. 26). For the Zen Buddhist, to be poor indicates the experiencing of inner riches and higher values, an aloofness amidst a world of multiplicities. He must accept little in life: a hut and a tatami, the sparsest of goods. The Priest is such a being. He lives life in primitive spiritual and physical simplicity. Only in this state can he reenter nature, experiencing its pulsations, breath, and cosmic rhythms. Artifice is nonexistent in this realm.

Matsukaze invites him to enter:

> I see in the moonlight
> One who has renounced the world.
> He will not mind a fisherman's hut,
> With its rough pine pillars and bamboo fence.
>
> (P. 26)

The Priest comes in and warms himself next to the "sad fire of rushes" (p. 26). He tells of his encounter with the Villager and the story he heard about the "solitary pine on the beach" associated with the two sisters. At the mention of their names, "Matsukaze and Murasame weep" (p. 27). The Priest is perplexed. The sisters explain that his reference to them

> Filled us with memories which are far too fond.
> Tears of attachment to the world
> Wet our sleeves once again.
>
> (P. 27)

The Priest wonders about what he has just heard and seen. They speak, he says, as though they were no longer alive. Together they chant their story and tell him that they have long been dead but yearn to reenter the world of the living. They feel "the sting of regret" (p. 27) for the joy they had once known.

Matsukaze and Murasame relate the story of their beloved Yukihira, who had chosen them above all others to receive his favors. During his three-year stay at Suma Bay, the sisters no longer wore the poor clothes of the salt-maker, but damask robes; no longer did they smell from brine, water, and earth, but from perfumes. Shortly after Yukihira's departure, the two sisters learned of his death. Their world was shattered. He was so young, they chant.

> Pine Wind and Autumn Rain
> Both drenched their sleeves with the tears
> Of hopeless love beyond their station. . . .
> Our love grew rank as wild grasses;
> Tears and love ran wild.
> It was madness that touched us.
> Despite the spring purification,
> Performed in our old robes,
> Despite prayers inscribed on paper streamers,
> The gods refused us their help.
> We were left to melt away
> Like foam on the waves,
> And, in misery, we died.
>
> (P. 28)

The hunting cloak and court hat which Yukihira had left the two sisters as a remembrance of his love are concrete objects which recall the past, never allowing the sisters to forget their beloved. They have become objects of worship. The hat, representing the head, spirit, and wisdom—the ultimate goals in the initiatory and alchemical quest—radiates life, thought, ideas, and memories. When donned by Matsukaze, the cloak hides the inner being, covers emotion, acts as a screen which cuts off the outer world, masks poverty and pain, and instills sensations of dignity, wealth, and power. As Matsukaze holds the keepsakes, however, her pain deepens. She stands as still as if she were in a trance and then cradles the cloak in her arms, holding it tightly. Wherever she turns, she weeps her agony.

The stage assistant removes her robe and places the cloak and hat on her. Endowed with a new identity, she is overcome with joy. She stares at the pine tree. From its branches she hears her beloved call to her and she goes to him. Murasame tries to break her fantasy by instilling the harsh note of reality. Matsukaze has gone mad. It is not Yukihira who is calling to her but a pine tree, she tells her sister. Yukihira will never return. As Matsukaze nevertheless continues her reverie, Murasame weeps, kneeling before the flute player. Her sobs are echoed in the soft tones of the instrument. Matsukaze walks toward the first pine tree on the bridgeway, then returns to the center of the stage and begins her dance. She speaks to the pine tree, to the mountain, to the distant lands; she talks of the "curving Suma shore" where her "dear prince" had once lived. Tenderly, she tells of her love and "circles the tree" as she expresses her sorrow.

> Through the frenzied night
> We have come to you
> In a dream of deluded passion.
>
> (P. 32)

Matsukaze "presses her palms together in supplication" and retreats from the stage as the waves recede from the bank and the wind blows offshore.

> Your dream is over. Day has come.
> Last night you heard the autumn rain;
> This morning all that is left
> Is the wind in the pines,
> The wind in the pines.
>
> (P. 32)

The beauty of the concluding image remains ever alive within the viewer's mind and psyche. The *solutio* operation, which included the washing away of pain through the reenactment of an awakening and burgeoning love, glows in its *sublimatio* condition at the end of the play: the recollection of a great passion has now distilled and crystallized, experienced in harmony with a pulsating universe.

Noh drama, a product of the Japanese culture, is both a spiritual and alchemical encounter. It reflects the Taoist's and Zen Buddhist's calmness of mind and oneness with nature; it is a manifestation of the Shintoist's beliefs which endow inanimate objects with life, thereby enlarging the scope and depth of the dramatic spectacle. Noh theatre is unique. It differs from all other forms of performing arts, yet it includes them all. It is the intensity of sustained emotion which moves audiences to tears and not the realistic portrayal of horror scenes; it is the sublimated passion, with its exquisitely nuanced poetry and its cosmic purpose and design, which impresses the viewer. Divested of personal elements, the collective spheres of love, rage, and jealousy, as integrated into the universal scheme of things, are instrumental in the creation of this dazzlingly rich, yet refined and ceremonious art form, which reflects the earlier religious and scientific thoughts of the Japanese.

9

Shakuntala: The Adamantine Essence

Kalidasa's *Shakuntala* is a dramatic ritual which draws its viewers into a love sequence experienced first on an earthly plane and concluding in the supernal realm of blissful understanding and detachment. Kalidasa is one of the outstanding poets and dramatists of Brahman culture, but scholars know little about him, suggesting birthdates for him that range from 100 B.C. to 100 A.D. In *Shakuntala* he depicts the idealism and sentimentality involved in a couple's attempt to transform, in religious and alchemical terms, the body of the flesh into the diamond body or adamantine essence. The deeply moving scenes depicting the union, separation, dissolution, and purification of the protagonists are dramatized; they are also designed to bring on a numinous experience with profound alchemical significance.

Drawn from the first section of the Sanskrit religious epic the *Mahabaharata* (c. 200 B.C.), *Shakuntala* combines liturgical drama with the elegance and sensitivity of Sanskrit theatre. Skilled in the use of metaphor, eidetic verbal descriptions, and delicate poetic harmonies, Kalidasa brings into being both the protagonists' inner landscape and the manner in which this mysterious and tremulous realm is reflected in their natural surroundings.[1] Nature is not simply background, nor is it designed to fill empty stage space. It is implicit in the play's very organism: it is an important means of expressing the intensity, pitch, and timbre of the seemingly infinite range of emotions inherent in Sanskrit drama. The Hindu scriptures teach that plants are dormant or exist in a state of latent consciousness; they are capable of both pleasure and pain.[2] In like manner, animals have feelings which, if not as well developed as those of humankind, are at least as powerful and to be considered reverently. Frequently animals are seen as holy and sacred entities.

Kalidasa's characterizations are in keeping with Sanskrit dramatic theory, and therefore differ from those typical of occidental theatre. Kalidasa did not consider the pain and distress suffered by his protagonists to be the result of some moral or psychological defect inherent in their personalities, nor was the anguish they felt tragic. Unlike western drama based on Aristotle's *Poetics,* which states that the hero's undoing is caused by a flaw in his character or some error in judgment or the like, Kalidasa believed that life's experiences were manifestations of *karma* or "cosmic justice": fate. Aristotle's theory of *catharsis,* purification through purgation, has no place in *Shakuntala,* nor does the concept of tragedy with its accompanying notions of pity and terror. Theatre, for the Sanskrit dramatist, was to be a dispassionate enactment of pleasurable experiences, during the course of which audiences would view impersonal sentiments on stage interwoven in a harmonious spectacle. To Kalidasa, moods are more important than actual events. Feelings, sensations, and optical experiences stir the Indian playgoer. Images, symbols, and signs in *Shakuntala* are designed to lead to both the protagonists' and the audience's progressive illumination and spiritual growth.

A religiously oriented play, *Shakuntala* may be considered a theatrical rendering of the Indian's four aims in life, each of which has an alchemical equivalent.[3]

Artha is the phase of material well-being, in which worldly possessions and the acquisition of a reputation seem to be life's goal. Extroversion is the rule, a seeking "out" for fulfillment and spiritual development. The alchemical equivalent is the *solutio* operation, the period of search, when flowing forward in life is a virtual necessity, fluidity marks one's views, and emotional malleability furthers the growth process. The opening scene of *Shakuntala* is a forest: the *prima materia* or the Hindu's *prakriti*—the undifferentiated world of phenomena.

Kama is the period dominated by the pleasure principle. Kama, the Indian equivalent of the Roman god Cupid, strikes the unsuspecting protagonist with feelings of joy, love, sensuality, and attachment. A virtual art of loving is lived out in this sequence, but it is always delineated with the utmost delicacy and tenderness. The alchemical parallel is *coagulatio*: a fixing of emotions, the pinpointing of energies and desires onto one person. The dramatic action—a progressive interiorization—takes place in the sacred domain of the ashram (religious retreat).

Dharma is the time when religious and moral obligations must be fused. Order and structure come into being on both the terrestrial and the cosmic planes. The tension between society's religious dictates and the individual's instincts and passions burns the protagonists, bringing pain and suffering. This phase is similar to the heating process of *calcinatio,* which destroys all peripheral sensations and emotions that might lead the protagonists away from the strict code of ethics imposed upon them by society. The palace or worldly order, with all of its constrictions and injunctions, is the scene of this sequence.

Moksa is the phase of eventual salvation, redemption, or liberation from the phenomenological condition which besets man in his earthly goals. A higher sphere is brought into play which ushers in the *coniunctio* operation. The protagonists are no longer viewed in terms of their fleshly bodies, but as purified adamantine beings, incorruptible forces. The celestial sphere is depicted in this scene—a fitting background for the *sublimatio* stage.

Shakuntala opens as King Dushyanta, ruler of India, is hunting in a forest. Just as he is about to wound a stag, he comes upon a hermit who tells him that this animal is sacred. The King is given hospitality in the neighboring ashram. Its beautiful flowering plants and trees and its tamed animals set the tone for Shakuntala's entrance. It is through her, the daughter of a nymph and a mortal, and through the forces she represents, that the King will be able to fulfill his karma and experience heightened consciousness. The events which follow their meeting bring pain to both protagonists, but pain is considered necessary for the spiritual ascesis leading to moksa.

The alchemist works on his metals and minerals in order to purify them, and in so doing he experiences a concomitant cleansing of his own psyche and soul, thus enabling him to communicate more freely with divine spheres. The Indian ascetic uses his body as his laboratory. Through special disciplines (breathing, fasting, and so forth), he learns how to free it from its physical dependencies and encourage a condition of immutable wisdom and multidimensional consciousness. In hatha and tantric yoga, as well as in Buddhist and Tibetan disciplines in general, an occult correspondence exists between matter and man's "physio-psychic body."[4] Each in its own way attempts to find the elixir leading to spiritual and physical immortality. The practitioners of religious rituals seek to create a "body of diamond"—that is, "incorruptible" and strong enough to be able to experience its last transmutation into immortality; they seek the Transcendent Principle, the Self which is eternal, immutable, and surpasses the world of causality and linear time to become the "adamantine Self."[5]

Shakuntala is not only a drama, but also a spiritual and alchemical ascesis: each dramatic sequence relates the growth of the protagonists; they are progressively extracted from the *prima materia,* or what is considered bondage to the phenomenological world. An interplay between material and cosmic spheres, personal and impersonal domains, is inherent in *Shakuntala.* The performers, whether animate or inanimate, visible or invisible, influence one another. God and man act in consort with the mineral and vegetable world, each an element in a giant symphony of varying dimensions and multiple tonalities. The entire spectacle—a microcosm of the macrocosm—may be understood as a manifestation of Absolute Reality or Universal Oneness, of the unknowable, ineluctable sphere which man apprehends only through signs and feelings during an endless "sea of change" (*samsara*) or "the vicious circle of existences."[6]

The Principles of Sanskrit Drama

Hindu scriptures declare that Brahma—who was called "the Breath" or "Master of the Word"—revealed the mysteries and delights of theatre to Bharata, one of the earliest theoreticians of Sanskrit drama (first century B.C.). These revelations known as the *Natyasastra* ("Canons of the Dance and Drama") were handed down orally from generation to generation before their recording in the fourth century A.D. Siva, "the Master of the Dance," taught Bharata that all theatre was part of a cosmic process. All matter, visible and invisible, moved about in a dance pattern in eternally transforming particles. Everything that is created, even that which does not enter the manifest world, is subject to destruction; nothing is permanent except the All called Absolute Reality or the original Brahman which is the "source, sustenance, and end of the universe" and "partakes of every phase of existence."[7] Siva also made it known that his wife Sakti (a projection of his own feminine nature into the manifest world) represented the energetic force within the universe, thus acting as the catalyst. It was she who, like Agni, the god of fire, consumes (as do passions), titillates, and illuminates. Together with Sakti, Siva is eternal motion, solar activity, the process of fusion and dissolution. The Rig-Veda describes the King of the Cosmic Dance as white, red, and black flames, the same colors which represent the three stages of the alchemical process. Symbolizing the union of time and space, color and the absence of it, matter and nonmatter, Siva incarnates the universe's creative principle, that force which enables man to transform himself into God and God into man.

For the Hindu, the theatre is a rite of passage, taking him from one state of being to another. The spectacle, therefore, is not to be considered merely as a work of art, entertainment, or an object to be admired for its fine craftsmanship and expert character delineations, but rather as an experience to be absorbed and assimilated. It gives its participants spiritual nourishment. Through the multiplicity of theatrical conventions—that is, created forms—the participants in the theatrical spectacle become integrated as individuals into a collective sphere of complex forces implicit in the cosmic plan.

A double movement arises from this conjunction of forces during a theatrical performance: the voluntary destruction of the primal state of unity which exists prior to the enactment of the theatrical spectacle and the birth of multiple forces on stage (decor, actors, lights, sound, and so forth), each struggling with the other to find expression within the framework of the performance. The experience dramatized during the course of the play, with its vicissitudes and complex series of identifications, concludes with the annihilation of the personal ego—or individual—and its assimilation into cosmic being (Brahman), Absolute Reality, Universal Oneness. The movement on stage then ranges from monism to plurality back to monism: in other words, from construction through dissolution and reconstruction.[8]

This fluidity in the stage happenings parallels the alchemical operation. In both cases a process is occurring; matter is continuously altering in form and consistency. According to Hindu alchemists, atoms, as single units, live on eternally; as aggregates or compounds, however, they change perpetually in form, potency, and consistency. When grouped together as elements on stage, they become part of the phenomenological world and are subject to birth and decay. Each dramatic production is viewed by the Hindu as a combining and recombining of elements or atoms, a reworking of these tangible and intangible forces in single or aggregate forms.[9] When a numinous experience is undergone, when feelings condense, distill, and crystallize, such activity is not to be considered as an isolated expression of man's inner world of passions, but as an expression of nature's eternal flux, of its manifestation in man's limited sphere of being and its disappearance from view in the universe. Buddha understood the duality involved in what is called the instability of the phenomenological world, as well as the "non-changefulness" (*nirvana*) of the eternal condition. That notion is expressed as Brahman in the Upanishads; Brahman is transcendent or Absolute Reality.

He wakes with the waking man, dreams with the dreamer, and sleeps the deep sleep of the dreamless sleeper; but he transcends these three states to become himself. His true nature is pure consciousness. . . .

The Self being unknown, all three states of the soul are but dreaming—waking, dreaming, and dreamless sleep. In each of these dwells the Self: the eye is his dwelling place while we wake, the mind is his dwelling place while we dream, the lotus of the heart is his dwelling place while we sleep the dreamless sleep. . . .

O thou self-luminous Brahman, remove the veil of ignorance before me, that I may behold thy light.[10]

Words, gestures, sounds, and lighting in the theatrical world are viewed, as is Brahman, as both changeable and immutable, continuously evolving and dissolving; building situations, conjuring moods, and impregnating the listless particles with kinetic impulses and cognitive abstractions. The dynamism triggered by this multidimensional language, consisting of visualizations and sonorities, provokes the affective systems of both protagonists and viewers, enabling them to absorb and assimilate the mixtures and blendings occurring on stage. It is not the one but the many that is significant; not merely the plot, characterizations, dance, and other theatrical conventions, but also the complex interplay of these factors. According to René Daumal, the Surrealist writer who learned Sanskrit in order to translate mystical writings in that language into French, spectators "taste" feelings in Hindu drama but do not "submit" to them. They remain aloof in their own way and may, therefore, view the stage proceedings in a more advanced state of consciousness, thereby transcending the particular and experiencing the whole.[11]

Shakuntala is an initiation ritual by means of which the protagonists, although given human form, become part of a transcosmic sphere; they are incarnations of superhuman or subhuman forms which touch, irritate, and terrify those with whom they come into contact. Initiations in general require prior spiritual preparation, and, in the case of the Hindu procedures, "inner recitation of the Vedas" is necessary. These recitations must be accompanied by very scientific mental and physical gymnastics, operations which require a disassociation between the text and the actor, the event and the atmosphere, the mortal and immortal elements. Once a deepening understanding of the stage ritual has been experienced, certain sonorities (*mantra*), gestures (*mudra*), visual configurations (*yantra, mandala*) enable protagonists and audience alike to pierce the veil of illusion (*maya*) which binds them to the limited phenomenological world and perceive the realm beyond and its infinite scale of meanings. Such activity, accompanied by a relaxation of tensions, allows for a gradual detachment on the part of the viewer and actor from the workaday world and from the specific problem focused upon in the dramatic ceremony. As the frame of reference is expanded it leads, paradoxically, to a consciousness of the void as well as of the filled, of the created and the uncreated, the concrete and abstract, being and nonbeing, the one and the many. It is at this stage of the initiation that the viewer begins to understand the significance of what Bharata called *rasa* ("savor" or "taste"), that dynamic principle which gives immediate perception into the essence or inside of the dramatic ritual and the "innate architecture" of the artistic creation.[12]

Shakuntala is in keeping with the Hindu concept of dramatic arts as well as with the Hindu alchemical tradition. For both the Hindu dramatist and the alchemist, man is his own god, the instrument of his own development and final liberation from perpetual transmigrations. Introverted by nature, he dwells within to seek and find fulfillment. In keeping with this psychological fact, altars in Hindu temples are placed from six to eight feet underground, a concrete manifestation of a spiritual quest. The occidental, in contrast, is extroverted; he is dependent upon God and the religious institutions with which he identifies for his salvation. Occidental man exteriorizes himself to find God; he humbles and punishes himself in order to be able to unite with this divinity.[13]

Reality for the Hindu—which includes stage reality—is comparable to the westerner's unconscious. Consequently, thought, nightmares, fantasies, and colors are considered empirical truths by the Indian; they enable him to become integrated into the All. Tibetan, Buddhist, and Hindu gods are "archetypal form/thoughts," projections of man's mind which nevertheless exist in the empirical world. In direct contrast is the occidental view of thought and the thought processes: these are considered to be abstractions which possess no concrete reality; they are and remain illusions.[14]

The goal of Indian disciplines, whether they be dramatic, religious, or alchemical, is to teach man more about himself so that he may perfect his spiritual and physical essence, deepening his sense world and allowing him to comprehend more fully why he is required to experience samsara. Such instruction encourages him to objectify, to refrain from identifying with objects and people in the phenomenological world where the nonilluminated live out their existences, and to search out ways to transcend the sphere of illusion and reach *samadhi* (absorption in Self). The dramatic ritual, alchemy, and certain religious disciplines such as yoga instruct man in ways of enlarging his scope of being; they provide him with the ability to experience himself in the uniqueness of his individuality as well as in the collective nature.[15]

Artha: *Solutio*

In keeping with the traditional Indian alchemical practice of establishing laboratories in areas far from the corruption and pollution of worldly society, *Shakuntala* opens on a forest scene. The King is hunting.

We learn that the King is Siva's earthly counterpart. Alchemically, he represents mercury which Indian alchemists call the "semen of Siva." According to the Kubjikamata Tantra, if exhausted mercury is incinerated with six times its weight in sulfur it is revitalized.[16] A generating principle, mercury was equated with the elixir of long life as well as with that element which empowers vile metals to become transformed into gold. The powers inherent in mercury were considered to be so powerful that the fourteenth-century Vedantic sage Madhava called alchemy "the science of mercury." When making such a statement, however, he was not endowing the metal per se with extraordinary virtues (though these were also implicit in its essence), but rather alluding to its spiritual being: it had become a virtual hierophany. Mercury, when properly distilled, enabled man to find liberation from perpetual reincarnations. The mercurial system was, concluded Indian alchemists, capable of strengthening the body as well as the spirit; it paved the way for increased knowledge leading directly to man's reabsorption in Brahman.[17]

Unlike Siva, who with his wife Sakti was a total being, the King was incomplete. The "quintessence of Siva," according to Hindu scriptures, contains the female principle or ovum; it within him brings about immortality, and the "glorified body" or godly being comes into existence.[18] Devoid of the energetic principle in life that is the female force, the King had developed only one side of his personality, the patriarchal, masculine consciousness which manifested itself in aggressive acts. He had not experienced a profound relationship with a woman as yet and, therefore, felt isolated, experiencing the female principle only in a most limited way. A balance between the patriarchal and matriarchal spheres had to be created if the King, the archetypal man or the ruling consciousness of political and social order, was to evolve spiritually and psychologically. That the King was hunting in the forest implies that he was actively searching for some prey in the matriarchal sphere. Metaphysically, it indicates that the one (King) would have to become two (male and female), thus creating a dynamic or state of tension which would bring into being the next step of the evolutive process.

At the outset of *Shakuntala*, the Charioteer tells the King: "You are like Siva on a deer hunt:/Bow and arrow in search of the antelope."[19] Like the divinity identified with *linga*, the phallus or procreative force in nature, so the King was in search of his Sakti, or *yoni*, the female element with its rounded and containing features.[20] Hunting, which indicates a quest on both the physical and metaphysical levels, also represents the beginning of the alchemical process. Although the head of the social and spiritual world of his kingdom and the possessor of great riches and beautiful, gracious wives, the King experiences a void because he has never known love. He does not yet possess what Jung calls the "treasure hard to attain," that is, the feeling or relating principle which would allow for fluidity and malleability within the psyche.

The forest, with its uncontrolled and uncultivated flora and fauna and various minerals—the domain of the Great Mother—is the focus of the King's attention. Animals, aquatic plants, and trees mirror nature's fertile aspects; they also create a liquid atmosphere. The encounter the King will experience in this elemental realm where instincts roam free will enable him to develop that "diamond body," that Golden Essence which will lead to his spiritual salvation by enlarging his worldly experience. Symbolically, the King will gain entry into his own subliminal depths and arouse those still untapped forces, thereby putting his whole physical and spiritual mechanism in tune with cosmic rhythms and tensions. Siva, as the "Lord of Beasts and Prince of Yogis,"[21] will lead the King to the source of these nourishing forces, thus creating balance where imbalance reigned, drawing an ego-centered individual into the pleromatic sphere of cosmic consciousness.

The King suddenly grows annoyed because the antelope he is hunting outruns his arrows. He asks the Charioteer to catch up to his prey.

> They excel even the gods.
> This speed is a miracle, it plays tricks with my eyes—
> Small objects put on size, the crooked becomes straight.
> I seem to be nowhere and everywhere.
>
> (P. 13)

The deer may be associated with Buddha's so-called Deer Park Sermon, the first he preached at Benares (now Varenase) which treated the subject of causation and illusion.[22] He said that all entities, both manifest and unmanifest, may be likened to a mirage, to the moon visible in water, or to an echo: they are neither real nor unreal. Buddha made the distinction between the terrestrial, personal, and subjective condition of the ego-centered or unenlightened being, preoccupied mainly with worldly desires, with the moment rather than with the eternal and pure spirit (*purusa*), and the trans-cosmic plane (in Buddhist parlance, the nonbreath or nirvana stage). That the antelope was running at high speed underscores the King's preoccupation with the moment, rather than the "eternal"; the individual instead of the collective, ego-centeredness rather than Self-centeredness. The notion of celerity comes into being in the world of duality (empirical domain); where polarities as such pave the way for tension. The fact that the King was drawn into the world of the particular and that he was concentrating on his prey served a cosmic purpose, however. It awakened a dynamic principle within him which served to counteract inertia. It is his destiny to act as he does, to hunt for something which he needs for completion. It is also important that he is the product of his past incarnations; as such he is part of the process whereby potentials are lived out and finally consummated in keeping with karmic law. Only after all such experiences have become manifest can it be said that man has "awakened"; only with such illumination can he be, paradoxically, annihilated and nirvana be realized.[23]

The element of speed depicted on stage brings an interplay of opposites into view, leading to the drama's action and "savor."[24] In keeping with this vitalism, the text mentions animals, grasses, flowers, and a speeding chariot, evoking the continuous circuit of organic and inorganic life which plunges the protagonists and viewers directly into mythical time, where past, present, and future cohabit with an eternal present. The transient exists only as measured by the eternal; the perishable is juxtaposed to the immortal in infinite cycles.

The yogi-alchemist meditates to experience deeper levels of consciousness. In like manner, the King hunts for his antelope and thereby enters a new category in the time-space continuum. No longer limited to the surface or outward configurations of objects, animals, or plants, his senses see them as dilating, expanding, altering forces, dynamic principles inhaling and exhaling in an active universe. As the yogi/alchemist enters the world of nonduration through physical and spiritual disciplines, so the King, dazzled by the speed of his chariot, disoriented by the novelty of his new experience, "burns" temporal time, annihilates history, divests himself of the "blackness" and "ignorance" of inherited lives—and glimpses nontime.[25]

Both Kalidasa's visual images and his use of metaphors underscore the world of duality on stage and the tensions to which it gives rise: the deer which leaps into the air like a woman, breathing freely and gracefully; the plants and seeds of all types altering in form, consistency, and temperament. The notion of freedom, of an unconstructed and unobstructed sphere of existence, emerges. The subtle elements of air, breath, and wind also come into play. Chinese alchemists spoke of *k'i* ("breath"); Indian alchemists mention Vayu, the god of the wind, and frequently call him "vital breath," that force which dominates bodily functions. Hatha-yogic treatises such as *Rasarvana* pay particular attention to breath, because practitioners believe that the body may remain alive for an indefinite period of time if the control of such a vital force is properly learned and used in conjunction with mercury.[26]

As the governing principle of both terrestrial and spiritual worlds, the King begins his initiation into another modality of being. In keeping with his karma or universal causality, he has to experience the world of illusion—that is, life with all of the pains and joys involved. Conflict, which alchemists translate as the process of triturating and dismembering metals, leads to knowledge, thus enabling the practitioner of such spiritual devices to pass beyond the artha condition and be awakened to the kama stage of development.

Kama: *Coagulatio*

When the King hears voices cry out, "The sacred stag!" (p. 13), he immediately stops hunting. The stag must not be harmed. For Buddhists, the Golden Stag is the prototype of all stags; it is a Bodhisattva, the Savior, a hierophany enabling man to become liberated from worldly passions. Jainism, which arose at the same time as Buddhism, forbids all killing. Instantly, therefore, the King knows that he is approaching a sanctuary, the dominion of divinity. When entering a sacred zone, one severs oneself from the temporal sphere. The ashram represents, symbolically, the heart or center of divine being. Sages and the devout who withdraw into such consecrated ground spend their time in protracted disciplines which enable them to contact transcendent spheres and find their own spiritual centers.[27] The King puts away his bow and arrow, for he has left the external world of matter, with its sports and the ardor associated with them, to enter the internal domain of the ascetic where the inner flame and fire is kindled. In hatha and tantric yoga, the hierophant's rituals are so arduous that "sweat" and "heat" are forced up through the body at all levels. So powerful is the control over the bodily functions of certain practitioners of these religious rituals that they are able to walk or lie on burning coals without suffering injury. The "inner heat" produced via tantric techniques coincides with the "mystical heat" of the alchemists.[28]

The King, featured as the hunter at the outset of the scene, has thus far lived his life peripherally, only through the excitation aroused by the sport he practiced. In that he has a bow and arrow, he may be considered the incarnation of Siva. Another god, however, was also incarnated in the King: Kama, the Indian counterpart of Cupid. Kama carried the "flower-bow" and shot the "flower-arrows" in Hindu cosmology. He activated heart, feeling, and desire and was therefore looked upon as the promulgator of the arts, love, and passion. It was said that early in his life Kama had been ordered by Indra, the king of the gods, to aim his arrow at Siva, considered the "master yogi and archetypal ascetic-solitary" within the Hindu pantheon. Once Siva's meditation was halted, he was filled with love for the divine daughter of the Himalayan king, the female principle, an externalization and concretization of his own energy as projected onto nature. Siva, in his new condition, had to contend with this force in the outer world; he had to recognize its existence and learn to deal with it. Thus aroused from the "timeless contemplation of his innermost supernal luminosity," Siva was so angry that flames shot out from his third eye, reducing Kama instantly to ashes. In desperation, Kama's wife, Rati, begged Siva to return her husband to her. He could not reproduce him physically but did incarnate him as a force known henceforth as Ananga. It is Kama—in his invisible and nonmaterial presence—who brings love into being.[29] It is he, the unseen protagonist, who propels the twists and turns, pirouettes and sensual gyrations, which follow in the drama.

An atmosphere of serenity, relaxation, and inactivity now reigns in the ashram. The "fruit lies rotting," the grain remains untouched, "the deer gaze nonchalantly" about, and the "paths and pond are wet" (p. 15). The Great Mother is at rest; she awaits the King, thus setting the Great Wheel in motion.[30]

As the King approaches the ashram he suddenly feels his arm trembling, which he recognizes as a "strange omen." He wonders why, in this sacred area where discipline and tranquility reign and where ascetics endeavor to experience the quiet stillness of life in its anonymous and eternal aspects, he should feel such tension. In moments he realizes that he is not to blame, but that "fate has doors everywhere" (p. 15), that Brahma's omnipresence may be experienced in infinite ways. The King apologizes to the sages for having hunted in the sacred territory. After blessing him, one of them tells the King that he is gathering sticks for "the sacrificial fire," a ritual which enables mortals to experience divinity. Sacrifice, one of the most important concepts in Hindu and Buddhist thought, is at the heart of all ascetic and alchemical operations. It was sacrifice that allowed man to become immortal;[31] it is sacrifice that will enable the King to further his cosmic evolution.

Fire, for the Hindu and Buddhist as well as for the alchemist, is an element of that "secret force" which "lies asleep in the umbilical region." If one learns how to kindle this element so that all parts of the body may experience its ardor and warmth, then man transcends his human limitations. In kundalini and tantric yoga, the initiate believes that a "divine power" (Sakti) inhabits his being and remains dormant within him in the form of a coiled serpent (Kundalini). Through specific meditative practices and physical techniques, he is able to unlock the door and allow this energetic force to be aroused and lured upward as "heat," capable of stirring the "fire" of feeling within whatever area he chooses to activate. The female element stands for the "fiery energies of all gods."[32] Kundalini, then, may be regarded as a manifestation of Agni, the fire god, Surya, the sun god, and Indra, the atmospheric deity; these are manifested on earth as fire, sun, and thunder. For the Indian alchemist as well as for Kundalini and Tibetan tantrists, inner fire, created either through the body itself or by artificial means (in the athanor), reduces subtle matter to ashes, the impure to its pure state.

Two alchemical elements are at work in the ashram: the spiritual fire of the ascetics and the water of the flora and fauna. The lush vegetation produces its own heat and this, mixed with the dampness of the enclosed area, creates vapor. The stage happenings take on an intangible quality: solids seem to vanish as the distillation process becomes activated. Solids are made volatile, transformed into impalpable essences. The atmosphere is conducive to the reception of Kama's darts, to love.

Despite the ashram's surface serenity—nothing is budging and quietude and gentility reign—the King notices that in this "Forest of Penance," his arm still trembles. "Fate has doors" (p. 15), he declares; mysteries exist which man cannot understand. In Tibetan meditative practices, doors symbolize the hierophant's passage from one sphere of consciousness to another. In this context, the ashram is a type of door which the King must experience, not only in the visible realm, but within his own psyche, his own spiritual center. Important, too, is the fact that ashrams have been compared to mandalas, those circles and squares which represent, psychologically, man's impulses toward wholeness. Metaphysically, they are meditative devices used by initiates to concentrate their energies on a central point. The initiate sets his gaze on the outer circles or squares of the mandala images which represent the polarities in life: life and death, attraction and repulsion, and all of the other forces which are involved in the life process. Sometimes mandalas have four cardinal points depicting terrifying demons, "guardians of the doors," whose task it is to protect the meditator from the intrusion of disruptive forces ready to distract him from his discipline. These monsters aid the initiate to overcome inner pollution, the yielding to fearful and destructive thoughts and sensations which emerge from his subliminal world and diffuse his powers of concentration. To find one's own center indicates an integration of opposites and a coordination of every aspect of the spiritual and physical organism. The ashram/mandala may open the door to new experiences and dimensions heretofore unknown to the King.

He is told that the head of the ashram, the sage Kanva, is away "on a pilgrimage to ward off the evil eye from his daughter" (p. 14)—in reality his foster daughter, Shakuntala. Eyes, associated with luminaries such as the sun and moon and also with Siva's third eye, are organs for inner sight. As disruptive forces, eyes may destroy, reducing everything in sight to ashes; as positive forces, they enable illumination. Kanva's attempt to ward off the evil eye and the fact that demons have invaded the ashram since his departure indicate that the creative center—the point which brings equilibrium in a mandala image and by extension within the religious retreat—has been diffused. Imbalance now exists.

Shakuntala enters with two friends. Her foster father had asked her before his departure to water the plants. Obedient and gentle in all ways, she carries out the requirements of her sex and class. Associated with water from the very outset of the play, Shakuntala becomes a source of nourishment, an embodiment of nature's fertile aspects. She is a diminutive of the Great Mother, a symbol of fecundity and of life in its most rudimentary form: a world *in potentia*. The Chandogya Upanishad says, "Only this water in solidified form are this earth, the atmosphere, the heavens, the mountains, plants and trees, wild animals, even to worms, flies and ants—they are all only this water in solidified state."[33]

The King is immediately captivated by Shakuntala. He observes her every motion as he stands protected behind a clump of trees. For the Hindu and Buddhist, trees are sacred. It is said that Buddha gained illumination under a bo tree, and he is frequently represented as a tree. The tree is often used in forested areas when altars are unavailable. The tree may also represent the world axis: its roots are Brahma, its trunk is Siva, and its branches are Vishnu; thus it encompasses all cosmic spheres. That the King stands near a clump of trees implies that he is immersing himself in the divine and, therefore, collective sphere; he is no longer acting as an individual mortal but assuming the stature and countenance of a divinity.

The King is fascinated by Shakuntala, the anima figure, and is mesmerized by her countenance. He compares her to earthly and celestial spheres, to matter and spirit, to the lotus and the moon: "The lotus is lovely though filth-covered/The moon prettier for her dark spot" (p. 16). The lotus is important in Indian thought. It represents the female principle because of its rounded form and its watery environment.[34] It is used for meditative purposes because of its shape. If concentrated upon in the proper manner, the initiate may experience "the heart of the lotus" or his own inner radiance—his supernal point. The eight-petaled lotus symbolizes cosmic harmony and is frequently featured in Hindu iconography with Vishnu asleep on the surface of the flower or "causal ocean," the aquatic element in nature. For the Buddhist, the lotus represents Buddha-nature: the center of this flower remains unbothered by the muddied environment, implying that samsara in no way detracts from its eventual absorption in nirvana. In the Bhagavad Gita, the lotus is a manifestation of Brahman.[35] As the smooth and oily surface of the lotus leaves lets the mud slip from its petals, so should the human being allow life's vicissitudes to detach themselves from his being.

Shakuntala will become that lotus image upon which the

meditator focuses his attention in order to experience superior centers of being where time becomes timeless and the microcosm unites with the macrocosm. In her lotus association, Shakuntala will develop her levels of experience and, in so doing, evolve from the two to the four to the six to the eight to the sixteen-petaled lotus, until she becomes that thousand-petaled lotus which has passed through all the other phases of existence. Like Sakti, who, having fulfilled her potential, transcended her previous incarnations and joined with Siva in the creation/dissolution ceremony, the lot of all who exist in the empirical world, so Shakuntala will be drawn to the King.[36]

That the King compares Shakuntala to the lotus also indicates that her presence has given birth to another dimension within his universe. The cosmic waters from which the mystical lotus grows have allowed the previously dormant "radiant sun" or Golden State to emerge. For the alchemist, gold and the lotus both represent immortality. As gold is associated with divinity and spirit, so the lotus also coincides with that force within man which seeks to liberate him from material existence, from perpetual transmigrations. Before moksa can come into being, however, gold must be absorbed; it must be fixed with mercury, maintains the Indian alchemist. "Gold is to be melted over fire and mixed with an equal quantity of incinerated mercury. . . . Gold leaves are reduced to ashes, if they are smeared with one-fourth their weight of incinerated mercury."[37]

The spiritual/alchemical atmosphere has been prepared for the King's meeting with Shakuntala. The two are the earthly counterparts of Siva and Sakti. As the future thousand-petaled lotus, Shakuntala will become "the door" or the "womb," the "mouth" through which universal waters flow. She will participate in the creation of that incorruptible gold, the highest form or aspect of Mother Earth, "Goddess of Moisture," the procreative and maternal manifestation of the Absolute.[38] In her water/lotus aspects, Shakuntala will be the bestower of beauty, purity, and happiness. The vaporous condition created at the outset of the scene couples with the ardent fire of spiritual growth within the atmosphere and is transformed into the burning sensations of passion.

The King again compares Shakuntala to natural forces, a fitting background to this radiant virginal figure.

Her lips glisten like new leaves,
Her arms are shoots
And her youth sprouts a glory of glittering flowers.

(P. 16)

The King will experience her as he does a flower, absorbing her essence, inhaling her feelings, and taking in her beauty. According to tantric belief, man must not only accept nature as it is, but also use it well and not divest himself of it. The Kularnava Tantra states: "As one falls into the ground, so one must lift oneself by the aid of the ground." Passion is very much part of the earth experience. "Every function is part of the Divine Action (sakti) in Nature." When a man "eats, drinks or has sexual intercourse, he does so not with the thought of himself as a separate individual satisfying his own peculiar limited wants, an animal filching as it were from nature the enjoyment he has, but thinking of himself in such enjoyment as Siva."[39] Mortals, therefore, experience themselves as gods and, in so doing, accomplish their destiny. Thus matter is thoroughly absorbed, experienced in order to be surpassed so that the metauniverse may become a reality. Intellect (*buddhi*), an aspect of the empirical world, aids in the process of gaining autonomy over oneself—in becoming that smooth leaf from which all cares slip.

The frequent repetition in *Shakuntala* of water images to describe vegetation of various kinds coincides with the Indian alchemists' extensive use of drugs and medicines. These they extract from nature's own storehouse in order to remedy a condition of imbalance or sickness in the body. Lotus juice, they believed, had magical powers. Alluded to frequently as "soma" (a personification of the divinity Soma), it was capable of restoring health and improving longevity. A gift of the gods brought to man by an eagle, soma enabled mortals to communicate with divinity: it brought on the state called "divine drunkenness."[40] To imbibe soma, as the King was doing visually and emotionally, was to pave the way for the *coagulatio* operation, the emotional condition favorable to the reception of Shakuntala.

Soma, then, "awakened" the King from his strictly patriarchal activities and laid the groundwork for the Golden Essence to come. The Avatamsaka Sutra (150–350 A.D.) says that the drug called hataka may also prepare for the purest of conditions. "One *liang* of it [hataka] will turn a thousand *liangs* of bronze into pure gold." In the *Mahaprajnaparamitopadesa*, Nargarjuna, the great second- or third-century A.D. Buddhist teacher, alchemist, and magician, wrote: "By drugs and incantations one can change bronze into gold. By the skillful use of drugs silver can be changed into gold, and gold into silver."[41]

By visually imbibing the juice from the lotus or soma plant in the form of Shakuntala, the King triggered a whole new interplay of emotions and relationships. A fresh chemistry within his being set his libido ablaze, as the alchemist's athanor flames when fed wood and coal. The inner heat he now experienced brought about a redistribution of particles within the King's physical and emotional system, altering substances and powers and transforming inertia into kineticism. Shakuntala, as the all-embracing unsullied natural principle, became the focal point of the King's meditation; as such she gained magical power over him, transmuting him into malleable metal, into a loving and gentle soul. The same operations used in alchemy to alter the consistency and powers of metals are used in tantrism and yoga, where they are called the "force of *samādhi*."[42]

The King felt "pulled" toward Shakuntala (p. 17). Kama, the world of desire, form, and impulse, was being activated. Buddhist alchemists consider the drawing of one individual toward another to be the effect of magnetism, and it is likened to a burning fire which must be experienced so that it may be extinguished. Only when one has felt the heat of passion may an awakening be experienced and the Buddhist know detachment.[43] The King, experiencing the universal law of karma and kama, allows himself to be allured. By experiencing the ardor of passion, he can step out of life and encounter Self in the unprovoked, detached manner of the most evolved ascetic.

Shakuntala shoos a bee away. The bee in this context could be considered a person inebriated with the pollen of life, flitting from one source of nourishment to another, extracting the sacred juices of life from all the beautiful flowers. Unable to remain still or silent, the King emerges from his hiding place behind the tree. He reproaches Shakuntala and her friends for disturbing the peace of the ashram with their chatter and childish games. They have not violated any rituals or rites, they retort. Then they welcome the stranger. The King, however, hides his identity and introduces himself as one of his own officers.

Kama's power has made itself known to Shakuntala as well. Her ultrasensitive nature seems suddenly troubled; she cannot understand her new feelings. A desire which neither plant nor animal can satisfy has entered her world for the first time. She is disturbed and disoriented because her sexual longings have been awakened. Kama, the begetting power, is pursuing his course, and therefore Shakuntala will be the instrument through which matter, abundance, and multiplicity will make itself known, as distinguished from the nonmanifest cosmic realm of Brahman.[44]

Alchemical forces are at work. The King, as mercury, is associated with Siva's semen; Shakuntala, as sulfur (Sakti), coincides with the earth/body and earth/fire (Agni) principle, the combustive element in nature. In the Kamasutra, the "book of rules" for lovers and courtesans written in the third or fourth century A.D., love and sexuality are not treated as sinful or relegated to hushed or hidden areas. On the contrary, in tantric mystical disciplines, sexuality is vitally important. It is when uniting sexually that man and woman transcend their mortal condition and become archetypal forces: man is Siva (lingam, phallus), while the woman is Sakti (yoni, vagina). As sulfur and mercury, they will unite to make gold, thereby transforming the polarities of the empirical world into the oneness of the nonmanifest domain. The fusion of male and female as universal principles is understood in Hindu scriptures as the welding of thought and breath, spirit and matter.

When the King first entered the Forest of Penance, the hermits were preparing for his sacrificial fire ritual, a prelude to the King's initiation into his kama phase. The King, in keeping with alchemical recipes, will have to endure burning sensations, trituration, and a kind of dismemberment so that the vulgar or earthly male-female condition may be transmuted into its aristocratic and golden equivalent. As the practitioners of tantric and hatha yoga attempt to absorb the earthly counterpart of the solar force—their Golden Essence—into their systems through breathing techniques, fasting, and muscular discipline, so the King will also attempt to purify his emotions, to absorb that spiritual metal into his system.

The yoga's work, as well as that of the alchemist, is designed to control, direct, and channel bodily impulses into higher visions. When the King first saw Shakuntala, a fire glowed within him. The more he observed her, the more fire blazed within him, going beyond the physical domain and flowing forth into the cosmos, focusing on the mineral sphere. He says, "This is not fire, but a gem:/I must make her mine" (p. 20). In keeping with alchemical tradition, the King seeks to metamorphose Shakuntala. As does the minerologist and alchemist, he will take this gem in its elemental state, dark from the blackness of the surrounding earth, cut her to size, polish her, concentrate the fire of his energies upon her, and transform her into the sparkling diamond or adamantine essence.

The *coagulatio* operation has begun. No longer hunting at random or filling his days with frivolities and pastimes, the King concentrates his vision and life force on Shakuntala, his luminous center. He gives her a ring with the royal seal ostensibly to free her from her obligations to friends. (It seems she owes them a plant.) Representing infinity, the Eternal Wheel of Buddhism, and Brahman's void, the ring is a bond, a link between sulfur and mercury, sun and moon, woman and man. As an earthly counterpart of an infinite process, it is subject to creation and dissolution, to the vicissitudes of life. With this gift, the King begins his circular trajectory, his initiatory procedure, his cosmic dance, reminiscent of Siva's tandava, when he united space and time with duration and brought forth the creative act.

Voices are heard offstage. The King's "horses are kicking up brown dust which settles like a film of locusts on the ashrama trees"; an "elephant is scattering the deer" and "is lunging at the trees"; because "he is blinded by torn creepers, he is charging into the holy huts" (p. 21). The atmosphere of play and frolic, at the outset of the scene has now given way to turmoil. In the Rig-Veda, the horse is associated with Agni, a fiery, impetuous, and valorous steed, one "nobly born." Indra, the atmospheric god, became associated with stallions, accounting for traumatic situations, eruptions of instinctuality, and searing and fiery forces in the world. The elephant, a sacred animal identified either with Buddha because of its stability and immutability or with the forces of chaos and disruption when driven mad, is also identified with Siva. It often wears a gem on its forehead, a parallel to Siva's third eye, which sparkles with wisdom and enlightenment, but which, under certain conditions, can also incite and destroy. That the animals were now wreaking havoc in the ashram, uprooting trees and shrubs in their fury, implied that the energy which had been provoked, were it to remain unchanneled, could bring chaos and not cosmos to the couple.

Dharma: *Calcinatio*

Dharma, the god of justice, ushers in the reign of individual and collective order on both terrestrial and cosmic levels. According to the Dharmasutra ("the book of laws") written allegedly by Manu, who was the prototype of man and a legendary figure, certain regulations and rituals must be followed if evolution into higher spheres of being are to be known. The King, in the dharma phase of his life, will conform to the strictures imposed upon him and, in so doing, will experience the *calcinatio* condition.

The King now speaks to the Jester, who complains of his physical discomfort because the King insists that they camp out in the forest rather than return to the palace. A subtle psychologist, the Jester also listens to the King as he talks of his love for Shakuntala. The King maintains that she looked at him "out of the corner of her eyes." He muses on the lightness of her step and the grace of her stance and is surprised at her "quick anger." He confesses, as he attempts to articulate his feelings:

> Words are poor things.
> God made her as beautiful as a painting.
> She is flawless, created out of whatever is
>   lovely, precious, and simple. . . .
> She is a virgin flower, a serene leaf,
> An uncut diamond, untasted honey.

(P. 26)

Again the image of the diamond is used: "flawless," she represents perfection in an unpolished state. As an "uncut diamond," she is still part of the earth principle, the *prima materia*. In such a condition, she is still "ungraspable," an impersonal force rooted to the *nigredo* or black earth; living ferment sprouts from her natural habitat, awakening a force within the King. Though buried in darkness, she is light; bright, although opaque; radiant and sparkling, although identified with matter.

The diamond—the mystic's "luminous center"—is that area within each individual where spiritual riches are stored. Only through protracted attention and discipline can this creative point be experienced. To reach it, the initiate must shape, pare, smooth, and fashion the unripe and blackened carbon and transmute it into the luminescent and dazzling gem that it is once its potential has come to the fore. According to Indian alchemists, such transmutation on a physical as well as a spiritual plane has parallels in the poetic or artistic process, when the amorphous idea is transmuted onto paper or canvas. The diamond, identified with the Philosopher's Stone, represents immortality, that inalterable, invincible, immutable spiritual substance known as Buddha Nature. Buddha's throne under the bo tree was said to have been made of a single diamond. The adamantine world buried within matter, as yet unmanifested, lives *in potentia* in Shakuntala, the female, sulfuric force within nature. In conjunction with mercury, the unfulfilled Shakuntala, living in the sacred protective atmosphere of the ashram, will evolve into her next phase of development.

The King questions the Jester about the best method to enter the ashram so that he may captivate and capture Shakuntala. The Jester suggests he introduce himself as the King and tell the ascetics he is there to collect taxes. Aghast at such an idea, the King replies: "Their payment is more precious than gold" (p. 27). They pray and do penance; they practice the disciplines which lead to self-mastery and autonomy. It is important to break the bonds that enslave spirit to the world; therefore, the King seeks the Philosopher's Gold and not the metal, the powers invested in this purest of essences and not merely funds to keep his government wealthy.

Two young hermits enter the scene. They inform the King that demons have been harassing their ashram since their guru, Kanva, departed to do penance in the forest. Demons or monsters are frequently found in myths and legends which feature ascetics attempting to renounce the world in order to conquer themselves. The demon or monster, representing an instinctual force which lies buried in the unconscious or in the universal void, may symbolize a fear, an impulse, or some unresolved latent content with which the conscious mind has not yet coped. During an initiation period, whether in oriental or occidental disciplines, the initiate must experience death followed by rebirth, chaos leading to cosmos. That the ashram, the seat of man's spiritual world, is set in elemental nature, the heart of the Great Mother, and that it is being invaded by demons indicates that some spiritual sickness has overcome the area. As supreme monarch, the archetypal governing principle, the King is called upon to expel the demons and purify the area.[45]

The King has come to a turning point in his life. The world

of multiplicity is upon him. The hermits insist he remain with them to lead them in the absence of Kanva. They are not strong enough to pursue their holy work without the protection of a temporal figure. The King, on the other hand, receives an urgent message from the Queen Mother, demanding that he return to the palace to celebrate "the Fast of the Son's Homage," which is to take place in four days. He is torn between his head (the mother and the society and government offices she represents, the obligations to his other wives, and so forth) and his heart (his love for Shakuntala, the Earth Mother as manifested in her pristine form).

The Jester advises the King to "stand in the middle" (p. 29). Hindu and Buddhist ascetics use this term to mean abstention from extremes. To cling to any mode of action for selfish or personal aims indicates an enslavement to what this point of view represents. The middle path was the Way of Gautama Sakyamuni (Buddha), who warned of extremes and the nefarious results such attitudes brought in their wake—domination by the senses rather than liberation from them. The King's mother's calling him back to the palace was an attempt to test her power over him. It is she who forces him to act, to take a stand, to become conscious of the depth of his feelings. Kama, the spokesman for the bride, has plunged his arrow deep into the King's heart, thus paving the way for life's continuous circuit. Dharma will now see to it that disciplines are maintained, not only solidifying the liquidity of the first encounter, but also causing tension and friction to reach an incandescent state.

The King decides to send the Jester, whom the Queen Mother has always treated as a son, to the palace in his stead. His governmental obligations, therefore, are considered lighter—almost clownish—in comparison with his feelings. The King remains in the forest. As the generative principle, the mercurial life force, he focuses and fixes his emotions on Shakuntala. The heat of his passion burns all peripheral pastimes: only the pure flame remains. Worthy of attention is the fact that immediately after the King's decision to remain in the ashram, the novices inform him that he has worked magic and that the demons no longer plague the serenity of their sacred domain.

Shakuntala has withdrawn for the night. Alone, the King sighs for his beloved in an apostrophe to the moon.

O Moon, how many of the lovesick you deceive!
Your arrows are not flowers, nor is moonlight cold.
It burns, and the arrows are as sharp as rock.

(P. 30)

He has called upon the moon goddess, symbol of nature's immortal and regenerative forces, universal rhythms and time cycles, to help him measure his own course. In tantric rituals a parallel is made between lunar and feminine forms. Complex analogies are also drawn in hatha yoga between luminaries and various body parts, including arteries, genital organs, heart, stomach, liver, and more. The goal of these practices is to find the harmony between man's bodily centers—that is, the seat of bodily rhythms and transcosmic forces and energetic impulses. If such a fusion does take place, an absorption in primal unity may occur at least temporarily.[46]

The moon is also identified with water, dew, and tears, those fluids which circulate about the universe in the form of sap, milk, and blood, and which nourish creatures as does the god-given soma. In the same way, the divine waters of the Ganges rehabilitate and purify those who bathe within it. Tender and understanding at certain periods, the moon lightens man's way through the dismal spheres of primeval life; it fosters dreams; it refreshes from the intense heat of summer and the harshness of daylight. The Brihadaranyaka Upanishad says:

The moon is honey for all beings, and all beings are honey for this moon. The intelligent, immortal being, the soul of this moon, and the intelligent, immortal being, the soul in the individual being—each is honey to the other. Brahman is the soul in each; he indeed is the Self in all. He is all.[47]

Illuminated by those forces symbolized by the moon, the King walks to the cane bower and there, in the enclosed, protected, and womblike area, finds Shakuntala, surrounded by flowers and resting on a bed of stone. At peace with nature, she becomes the living incarnation of its nutritive forces: the honey, water, and milk of life. The King overhears Shakuntala speaking to her friends of her love. She scratches a love poem with her nails onto a lotus leaf described "as soft as a parrot's breast." The lotus is referred to in the Upanishads as "the lotus of the heart"; it is not surprising that she should have chosen it to articulate her feelings. Overjoyed by the knowledge that his love is reciprocated, the King will no longer remain passive. His mercurial nature will emerge. "The god of love gave me sorrow, but he can heal it too,/Like black clouds that burst in rain" (p. 32). The King tells Shakuntala of his love for her. Although he "cannot break tradition" and repudiate his other wives, he will marry her and declare her his favorite. He offers to marry her according to Gandharva rites. Gandharva, the heavenly musician, believed that marriage could be contracted by an exchange of garlands between the couple and that no other ritual, either religious or civil, was necessary. Such a love union was recognized according to the Laws of Manu as one of eight kinds of marriages acceptable to the society of the time. The husband was given specific obligations and responsibilities: dharma.

The marriage takes place, and the King leaves shortly thereafter for the palace. Shakuntala will join him later. However, her joy is so great that she neglects to pay proper homage to Durvasas, an ascetic who comes to visit at the ashram. He curses her angrily and declares that her husband will forget her until such time as she returns the ring he gave her. Meanwhile, Shakuntala's foster father, Kanva, returns to the ashram. He has been told of Shakuntala's marriage and of her pregnancy. He realizes that she can no longer remain in the ashram and must join her husband. A painful parting is enacted between father and daughter and between Shakuntala, her friends, the animals she has raised in the forest, and the plants she has always tended. The protective, paradisiac world of the young girl will disappear and give way to the harsh collective sphere of wife and mother. Before her departure, the hermits bring Shakuntala gifts of grain, flowers, and tree branches. "You deserve diamonds and golden bracelets," they tell her. A holy sage asks her to circle the sacrificial fire they have just lit in her home, in this way purifying her of all of her iniquities. "May your sins dissolve in the fragrance of these sacred offerings" (p. 42).

Terrified and pained at the prospect of her voyage into the world, Shakuntala experiences disorientation for the first time, the vertigo which arises from the unknown. Nature mirrors Shakuntala's distress: the deer no longer munch the grass, the peacocks have given up their dance, the dew falls on the branches like crystalline tears, and Shakuntala's pet fawn follows her sadly down the path. When the shriek of the chakravaka sounds in the forest— strident and terrified because she cannot find her mate—an ominous atmosphere descends upon the scene (p. 44).

In the palace, the King sits in court busying himself with

affairs of state. He is told that hermits and a young girl wish to see him. He receives the visitors. Shakuntala stands before him veiled. Strangely enough, though he neither recognizes nor remembers her, he is drawn to her. The curse has taken effect. The hermits are aghast at this turn of events. Shakuntala, deeply pained, laments her lot. "I am lost. He can't even remember what happened" (p. 51). Disgrace is heaped upon her. The hermits insist that Shakuntala remain in the palace despite the King's denying ever having married her or even having seen her. As a last resort, Shakuntala remembers the ring. She will show it to him and he will certainly recognize it and remember he gave it to her. She makes the gesture of taking the ring off her finger when she realizes that it has been lost. When she was bathing in the Ganges prior to her visit to the palace, it must have slipped off.

That Shakuntala has lost her golden ring implies that her quest for mystical union, in the alchemical sense, has been thwarted; the single focus or central meditative point which the ring represented has vanished, dispersed in the world of multiplicity. Fragmented spiritually and psychologically, she lacks the power to pursue her quest. Gold, the mystical body representing sacrosanct words and feelings, absolute truth, the purest of principles, has been lost amid the sacred waters of the Ganges: her own unconscious. In the depth of her sorrow Shakuntala accepts the fact that "Fate has intervened" (p. 51). The fire of pain sears her. In vain she repeats certain conversations she has had with the King when walking together in the forest; in vain she attempts to help him recall a past which no longer exists for him. A sage now intervenes and predicts that the King's "first son will be blessed with a circle in his palm." If Shakuntala's child "has this sign, take her as your queen. If not, send her back to the ashrama"(p. 53). The King agrees. Shakuntala will remain in the palace until the birth of her child.

Memory, for the Hindu and Buddhist, is of prime importance. Whenever the gods lose their memory temporarily, it indicates a fall from the divine condition. An inability to recall personal events is equated with an inability to remember previous existences; thus it is a loss of perspective toward eternity, the gods, and oneself. Only with a perfect memory can one reach "the beginning of time" and thereby transcend it. For Buddha, memory was knowledge; it represented illumination, man's most precious faculty. To make use of memory, to develop its power through concentration, was advocated by the Buddha. To allow this vital instrument to weaken is to yield to dispersion, distraction, and ignorance. Memory enabled the Indian to recall, recognize, and develop that sacred zone within him, the central point where Nonbeing and Absolute Reality may be discovered. The Isha Upanishad states: "Let my life now merge in the all-pervading life. Ashes are my body's end. OM. . . . O mind, remember Brahman. Remember thy past deeds."[48]

The King's loss of memory is symptomatic of his lack of equilibrium. Without perspective, unable to differentiate or distinguish one situation from another, he is devoid of any scale of values. Shakuntala's pain heightens. She longs for "the earth" to "swallow" her up, to moisten her heated countenance, to extinguish the fire of life. She leaves the King. Shouts are heard offstage. A priest enters. He recounts a strange happening he has just witnessed. "Suddenly a white light in a woman's form swooped out of nowhere and picked [Shakuntala] up and took her into the sky" (p. 54).

A policeman enters. He is castigating a fisherman, accusing him of having stolen a royal ring. The fisherman claims to have caught a fish, cut it open, and found the ring in its belly. The ring is brought to the King, who recognizes it immediately. The curse's poison is annulled and he remembers Shakuntala, his marriage, and his passion for her. It is too late, however. Shakuntala has been taken to heaven, to her mother's abode; her mother, the audience learns, was a nymph who had stayed on earth only long enough to give birth to her. Grieving over Shakuntala's disappearance, the King is visited by the fire of hurt and the blackness of remorse. "She was a dream, an incantation, a breath of lovely air./Such things don't come back" (p. 61).

Moksa: *Sublimatio*

During the moksa phase of spiritual evolution, the hierophant attempts to find release from worldly entanglements and to experience an "emancipation of the soul." Having fulfilled his potential on earth, he reaches what alchemists term the *sublimatio* condition. The metaphysical meaning of this spiritual release has been summed up by the sixteenth-century philosopher Vijnanabhiksu: "Just as the statue, already existing in the block of stone, is only revealed by the sculptor, so the causal activity only engenders action by which an effect manifests itself, giving the illusion that it exists only in the present moment."[49] The King, now in a state of depression, is catalyzed by Indra, the atmospheric god, who asks the King to help him fight his enemies. The battle takes place and the god is victorious. The King is seen on stage in Indra's chariot, a singular honor for a mortal, earning him the admiration of his people, who have now erected monuments and written songs in his honor.

Indra's Charioteer takes the King to higher regions, where he will gain insight and perspective into cosmic matters. Indian alchemy speaks of a fifth element—*akasa*, which has been identified with Aristotle's ether—in addition to the four recognized by occidental alchemists. Akasa, or the "soniferous ether," can only be heard and not experienced by the other senses. It is composed of unchanging and infinite atoms. Some mystics consider it to be the *prima materia* out of which the other elements were born. The Upanishads say:

From the Atman [the universal soul or Brahman] arose akasa, from the akasa the wind, [from wind, fire, from fire, water, from water, earth]. When this earth shall pass away, the reverse order of changes will take place, earth to water, water to fire, fire to air, air to akasa, akasa to Brahma.[50]

The moment the King accepted Indra's invitation to participate in divine wars and pursue his course in the god's chariot, he broke with the mundane world; like the yogi who claimed to be able to levitate and thereby experience cosmic spheres, so the King reaches akasa and the *sublimatio* condition. The Charioteer stops at a celestial ashram. The King notices that

> The bathing water is golden with the pollen of lotuses.
> Meditation is practiced on heaps of gems,
> Here there is self-discipline near bewitching girls.
> Other sages practice austerity for gain:
> Here they scorn it.
>
> (P. 69)

All here is pure and golden in essence and substance.

Suddenly the King's arm begins to throb, as it had before he first met Shakuntala. He cannot understand, amidst these marvels, why he should experience such discomfort. He sees a little boy teasing a lion cub. Little girls, wearing the dresses of the hermitage, look at the boy with annoyance. They see the King and ask him to intervene. As the King looks at the boy, he experiences a sensation of emptiness: he has no son. He looks more closely and notices the sign of royal birth on the boy's hand. Certainly the boy is his son, he thinks. He questions the girls, who tell him that the boy was born in this celestial palace and that his mother is related to a heavenly nymph. The King picks up an amulet which has just fallen from the boy's wrist and returns it to him. The girls look at the King in horror. Anyone except his parents who touches his amulet, which was given to the boy at birth, will die. It contains a rare herb called aparajita, which turns into a poisonous snake. Nothing happens to the King, however, indicating that he is the boy's father. They embrace.

Meanwhile, a young lady wearing a saffron-colored robe, her hair tied in a hermit's knot, approaches when she sees a stranger embracing her son. The boy runs to her and tells her that this stranger calls himself his father. The King recognizes her as Shakuntala and his joy knows no bounds. He asks her forgiveness in the gentlest terms. She murmurs her happiness.

> Be still my heart.
> My fate pities me, having done its worst.
> This is my husband.
>
> (P. 72)

She begins weeping as she tells her son: "My son, a star is dancing?" (p. 73). The King falls to his knees before her.

> Forget the sad past of separation, my beautiful wife.
> Delusion filled my mind.
> To a blind man a garland is a snake.
>
> (P. 73)

The King knows the feeling of freedom which comes with fulfillment. The *sublimatio* or vaporous atmosphere in these celestial regions has allowed him to experience a transcosmic sphere of life without impediment. Not oblivious to the rigors of existential conditions, he has earned moksa through the disciplines imposed upon him in the feeling domain by Shakuntala, in the governmental sphere by his duties as monarch, and in the military area by his battles. All facets of his earthly stay have now been integrated.

Only one more thing remains to be desired. When a sage comes offering Indra's blessing, he asks the King whether he wants anything else. The King answers:

> May the lord of the earth seek the good of my subjects.
> May the wise be honored.
> And may I be released from further lives.
>
> (P. 74)

The King has lived out his karma. The seeds of his destiny, present in his former incarnations as well as in the acts dramatized in Kalidasa's play, have now germinated. Artha, kama, and dharma have transformed unconscious contents which had lain dormant within the King into the deeds of his life, the incidents which shaped his future. By activating feeling and sentiment, vital factors in Sanskrit drama, the King has earned release from the entanglements of life. Mercury, contained within Siva's semen as incarnated in the King, united with sulfur, or Sakti's ovum, as represented by Shakuntala. A son was born from this *complexio oppositorum*, thus insuring humankind's future existence. In the *sublimatio* condition, the King and Shakuntala transcended the law of time. No longer bound by temporal rhythms or earthly matters, they existed in a "deconditioned" state leading to Nonbeing or Absolute Reality as adamantine essences.

Although the King and Shakuntala disappeared from earthly view, the savor of those precious moments spent in the empirical domain linger. In the Brihadaranyaka Upanishad one may read:

> As a lump of salt when thrown into water melts away and the lump cannot be taken out, but wherever we taste the water it is salty . . . so . . . the individual self, dissolved, is the Eternal—pure consciousness, infinite and transcendent. Individuality arises by identification of the Self, through ignorance, with the elements; and with the disappearance of consciousness of the many, in divine illumination, it disappears. Where there is consciousness of the Self, individuality is no more.
>
> This it is, O my beloved, that I wanted to tell you.[51]

Conclusion: The Eternal Quest

The many and varied approaches to the arts in general and to the theatre in particular include alchemical, linguistic, psychological, semiotic, structuralist, and historical views. Each method is valid for the one who finds that it answers an intellectual and emotional need; each is meaningful if it deepens the understanding of the work under scrutiny and broadens the horizons of the critic explicating it. Whatever the approach, it must be catalytic, stimulating and exciting to those involved in the pursuit of knowledge and encourage them to develop their potential.

Alchemists used both the operational and the theoretical approaches to their alchemical work. The former has been defined as the strictly scientific work undertaken in the laboratories, the actual experimentation. This aspect of alchemy does not concern me here. It was superseded by the study of chemistry in the seventeenth and eighteenth centuries in Europe, owing in great part to the work accomplished by Robert Boyle, Hermann Boerhaave, George Stahl, and Antoine Lavoisier, to mention but the most notable. *Theoria,* however, calls for speculation, association of ideas, images, sensations, observation, and meditation; alchemy in this sense is still alive today. It is not only used both actively and effectively by Jungian psychiatrists and psychotherapists in an attempt better to understand the human personality, but is, as Antonin Artaud suggested, in a general sense also implicit in the process of creating and staging a play, in the formation of the actor, and as the catalyst for the critic.

Theoria, or esoteric alchemy, is that transformatory process which takes place within the human psyche, that dynamic interchange between subject (alchemist) and objects (*prima materia*). It is this energetic factor which triggered certain charges within the alchemist's unconscious as he peered into the vials, retorts, and pelicans before him, as he heated and cooled, sublimed, fixated, and coagulated his elements. When he pondered over the "miraculous" transformations he was observing and fostering and attempted to comprehend the mysteries of matter, he noted his findings in cryptic riddles and other types of signs which only those initiated into these arcana could decode. During his quest for answers, the alchemist allowed his feelings to fire, ferment, fuse, distill, dilate, and finally structure themselves in iconographic representations—veritable maps and charts of his inner world, delineations of his spiritual and psychic climes.

The dramatist experiences a similar transformation ritual; so too does the actor and the critic. The dramatist is his own *prima materia;* it is from his soma and psyche that he molds his work in accordance with the disciplines and recipes required by the alchemist—*mortificatio, calcinatio, separatio, solutio, coagulatio, fixatio,* and *coniunctio*—expressed in a variety of ways, depending upon the nature of the experiments involved. In like manner, the actor uses his own being, both physical and spiritual, to flesh out his role and breathe life into an amorphous vision. Such a feat of magic requires arduous initiation, as does the work of the critic who uses the play as an energizer, a force irritating and arousing unknown and untried entities within his unconscious, which then dilate, radiate, and explode, flowing in spectacular array.

During the experimental period the alchemist combined and recombined his metals, creating amalgams, expelling refractory forces from hiding, compelling or cajoling them to come into play and collide, conflict, triturate, flay, and dismember one another, thus forcing contact and friction. So the dramatist, actor, and critic also extract and eject certain factors within their collective unconscious and entice them out of the chiaroscuro of their *nigredo* domain. Once the light of consciousness or *albedo* condition becomes apparent to them, their work takes on a luminosity of its own; it acts and reacts, revealing aspects of their temperament and spiritual world which would otherwise have remained inaccessible. Their Golden Essence may cohabit with their silvery moonlight or magical qualities, or usher in ironlike characteristics which may corrode and rust; leaden attributes may become visible in heavy and poisonous situations in which miasmic and polluted elements of the personality emerge. Acids may vitiate the atmosphere, eating away at all attempts to sublime the sequence; stasis may foster putrescence; airlessness may force the stifling and stilled climate of *mortificatio* to clothe the scene. Sublimation and purity may also come into existence as the air grows rarified; the particles take on prismatic overtones and glow in the bluish-white radiance of celestial spheres. The fire of passion, of will, of energy, may cause friction, urging the *rubedo* condition to succeed by searing and sucking out all that defiles and contaminates. It is what lies in waiting behind the mask, the curtain, the artifice such as the opacity of a smile, and all of those other protective devices people manufacture, whether consciously or not, to hide their real selves, but which the dramatist, actor, and critic seek to reveal through the fluidity of the transformatory ritual implicit in alchemy.

Artaud writes about the drama of creation, which he compares to "the theatrical operation of making gold."[1] Play-writing is the dramatist's Philosopher's Stone: his spiritual gold, his created act, a decanted essence of himself. He is the process. It is his soma and psyche that he warms, nurtures, disciplines, and encourages to yield the miracle which is the play. During the rite of passage from the idea to the written word, the playwright learns how to purify his drama, to rid his work of extraneous elements which detract from the central theme. The dramatist's task is difficult as was that of the alchemist. He may experience periods of *mortificatio* during the creative process, when the pain of creation will crush and macerate his being and death will seem to be close at hand; of *calcinatio,* when burning, bruising sensations may drive him to agonize; of *solutio,* when he is flooded with incongruous and disparate elements which may either blend into *aqua permanens,* allowing him to view his work from a variety of angles and perspectives, thus making solvent that which had previously resisted correction, or he may drown in the task, his unconscious deluging his conscious mind with cascading images, symbols, and ideations of all types; of *coagulatio,* when the fluid characters and temperaments he is bringing into existence take on consistency, permitting confrontations, flagellations, and flayings; of *fixatio,* when scenes, sequences, entrances, and exits experience dimensionality and become operational and when the flow of emotions grow, become encrusted in words, and implanted in visualizations, amalgamating in the intricacies of plot; of *separatio,* when the cutting and objectifying process encourages the dramatist to evaluate his work, to look upon the complex in a more detached manner, considering each facet, nuance, conversation, and theatrical convention as an individual entity as well as in its polysynthetic condition. Once the dismembering ritual has allowed the adamantine essence to come into being and the play crystallizes in its own fire, the *coniunctio* or welding stage has molded heretofore disparate forces into an inextricably powerful whole.

The play—the dramatist's Philosopher's Stone—is born. It no longer belongs to its creator. The umbilical cord has been severed; it is neither his double nor his appendage. It has taken on a life of its own and struggles to maintain itself in the mainstream of existence. It becomes a catalyst, a force that stimulates and provokes all those who approach it. Purveyor and conveyor of emotions and conceptualizations, the play, now having taken on a reality of its own, possesses the capacity to charge, electrify, thrill, or shock all those within its orbit.

The play nurtures, feeds, and warms the beings of the critic and the actor. A symbiotic relationship is fostered; impulses are aroused, instincts awakened, and these must also become purified in order to take on consistency of their own. These feelings or conceptualizations must be put through the seven alchemical operations in order to transform them into ordered and sequential ideas. As the alchemist and playwright project contents of their unconscious onto their work and in so doing make amorphous feelings palpable, so the actor and critic attempt a similar transformation. During the process, each in his own fashion expresses his metaphysical, psychological, and aesthetic reactions to the mysteries hidden in the dramatic text. Remaining after the distillation process is the trial by water and fire (the actor as he ushers his character into being and the critic as he completes his work) that are quintessential elements, vital to the performer and critic and to the culture from which they emerge. These facets, rooted in the play, take on a fresh existence in this new context. Disrobed and robed, these works of art take on the shadings of eternity.

In this, the first book devoted to an alchemical approach to theatre, the plays under analysis reveal powers at work: this book follows that trajectory which takes one from a world *in potentia* to one of actuality, from the domain of unlimited possibilities to the sphere of defined realities. The ancient alchemists used to say that the statue lies hidden within the block of marble. It is, therefore, up to the artist to carve it as he sees fit.

A Dream Play takes the audience directly into Strindberg's subliminal realm and there, amid a plethora of fantasy figures, we are made privy to an *albedo/sublimatio* condition. These heavenly spheres where spiritualized attitudes exist in an undifferentiated state, however, suddenly come to an end. Indra's Daughter, the mediator between spirit and matter, God and man, is sent to earth to review man's worldly condition. During the *separatio* process— that is, in her incarnated condition—she will be compelled to experience, along with humankind, the agonies of life. As she goes through the routine of existence, she will be tortured, submerged, dissolved, and entangled, and in the process will take on the stature of an Earth Mother, attempting all the while to revivify what is putrescent. Her task is difficult, and in accomplishing it she goes through the *nigredo/mortificatio* operation, during which time she endures the hostility of the people around her. Her inward journey allows her to experience previously unknown emotions; stifling religious attitudes also lacerate her with guilt, remorse, and sorrow. These fire her anger, debilitate her sense of justice, and inundate her with spleen. The foul elements are splashed away in the *solutio* stage of *A Dream Play,* which then concludes with her return to celestial climes and her refusal to reveal to humanity (which she considers unprepared and immature) the mystery of creation. The chrysanthemum bud which bursts into bloom at the top of the castle indicates a *renovatio,* that is, hope in the future, but not necessarily an ascension. It does, however, encourage man in his quest for *sublimatio.*

Ghelderode's *Escurial* depicts the *mortificatio* state of development. Hope is invisible; a condition of putrescence reigns. The play is set in what Ghelderode considered the most reactionary and oppressive era in Spanish history, the reign of Philip II; subtle parallels are drawn between the protagonists' world and the vices and cruelties of contemporary man. The *nigredo* condition delineated on stage casts a tenebrous cloud over the proceedings: a prophetic vision of things to come. *Escurial* represents the end of an empire and a way of life founded on vilification, autocracy, theocracy, and madness. Ghelderode's alchemical drama features a king who feeds on fungus, and the monstrous apparitions which ambulate on stage are iconographic representations of his protagonists'—or rather antagonists'—subliminal domain. His fantasies take on dimension and depth, proliferating wildly as they cackle and screech and sink ever more deeply into the mire.

Claudel's *Break of Noon,* one of the most sensual and erotic of dramas, is an exteriorization of the tension existing between an ultraspiritual attitude far beyond the dramatist's own reach and his own earthbound and passionate temperament. Claudel's archetypal creatures, who incarnate his inner troubles, were forever yearning for peace and harmony, for the *sublimatio* condition. They went through the alchemical trials and disciplines during the theatrical ceremonies, but Claudel's leaden creatures were never sublimed. The *solutio/albedo* experience, forever mentioned and desired, was not really achieved. Failure (or perhaps near failure) resulted: flesh needs and feeds on flesh and not on the aerated, tasteless, colorless, and invisible particles which make up the celestial spheres.

Yeats's protagonists in *The Only Jealousy of Emer* take the audience from *separatio* to *coagulatio* conditions. Each of his characters attempts to see and live beyond his differentiated earthly condition; each longs for spiritual harmony and to this end rearranges and reevaluates circumstances and reblends behavioral patterns, thereby bringing fresh alloys and amalgams into existence. The three anima figures in Yeats's play represent three aspects of the female principle: the earth wife in her mundane existence, the *femme inspiratrice* as the object of a fleeting affair, and the Eternal Feminine, that all-powerful, all-pervasive woman who fights a never-ending battle to dominate and captivate her prey. The subtle *separatio* sequence which divides these female entities parallels a similar severing within the hero's psyche and represents Yeats's own battle to balance the elements. Although a *renovatio* is offered at the conclusion of the drama, an ascension does not occur. Whereas rebirth is considered a hopeful sign in *A Dream Play,* in Yeats's cosmology a return to earthly existence leads to more suffering and *mortificatio*. The Wheel of Life turns again, forcing mortals into another period of trituration and dismemberment rather than allowing a reintegration into the Anima Mundi.

Witkiewicz's *Water Hen* reduces everything to the *solutio* condition. A restatement of the Puer Aeternus myth, Witkiewicz's drama features a protagonist who refuses to grow up and rejects the struggle which is the lot of all those who seek to enter maturity. The water condition, expressed in the title, suits the protagonist's temperament: it dissolves and disperses the solid, renders the seen invisible, and allows consistencies to alter and float about in a fragmented and faceless state. The antihero of *The Water Hen* is in fact antithetical to alchemical dicta. The alchemists believed in man's evolution from a leaden to a golden state if the proper disciplines and rituals were followed. Witkiewicz's protagonist slumbers in his own inconsistencies and narcissism. Stunted in his growth, he represents the aborted chemical experiment leading to *mortificatio*: death by suicide, a physical replica of a psychological condition.

Villiers de l'Isle-Adam's *Axël* fixates on gold: both the spiritual essence and the metal and the moral values associated with both. This *fixatio*—an unproductive, stayed metaphysical condition in which the metal gold seems to be of utmost import—characterizes humankind invested with lust, greed, and perversity. Gold, in its more refined and sublimed condition, reveals the emergence of a *separatio* condition, when the powers of discrimination, evaluation, and understanding function and finally lead to the *sublimatio* conclusion. During the fourfold alchemical operation as dramatized in *Axël,* the protagonists divulge feelings ranging from acerbic to corrosive; they murder, incarcerate, and dismember each other both spiritually and physically. Only after the protagonists have sacrificed their worldly condition, having annihilated the fleshly concerns which they feel are forever in conflict with their spiritual growth, can the *summum bonum* be attained. Then the king and queen—mercury and sulfur—become one, leading to fulfillment and beatitude.

The Dybbuk, by Shloyme Ansky, may also be viewed as a religious mystery, but of a different nature than that in *Axël.* It represents an artistic replica of the abrasive spiritual condition the Jews knew for centuries during oppression and persecution in Russia and Poland. *The Dybbuk* dramatizes a love which cannot be broken even in death, that of the alchemical bridegroom and bride, the eternal couple whose embrace is divested of matter and whose emotions know no earthly ties or linear dimensions. Particularly moving because of the tenderness of the relationship between the boy and girl, *The Dybbuk* is also a mystical document. The kabbalistic "White Fire on Black Fire" leads to the *mysterium coniunctionis* at the play's finale.

Alchemical interpretations of the Japanese Noh drama *Matsukaze* and the Sanskrit play *Shakuntala* allow for comparisons between occidental and oriental approaches to theatre and life. The outer world, for the oriental and the Hindu, is merely an expression of the transient aspect of phenomenological existence. Humankind's inner realm and the secrets which lie buried within it are extracted by the dramatist and presented on stage in miniature, via a mask, a screen, a gesture, a sigh. Nature plays an all-important role in both *Matsukaze* and *Shakuntala*. The protagonists are not severed from the world about them. On the contrary, they partake in the richness of its substance; they are attuned to life forces such as a tree, a lake, or a flower. Yet, paradoxically, they are detached from the world about them and live comfortably both in their capacity as individuals and as part of a flowing and eternal cosmos. The alchemical operations experienced in *Matsukaze* and *Shakuntala* are, in varying degrees, integrated into Buddhist, Shinto, Taoist, Hindu, and related beliefs. Each is wedded to a particular spiritual way; each replicates the fusibility of metals and their glowing purity, both emotionally and religiously, and brings integration to the protagonists with their acceptance of karma.

Alchemy—not the science, but the method, not the *operatio* but the *theoria*—offers no solutions to the dramatist, the actor, or the critic, but opens a way for the examination of the work of art. It allows the individual who participates in its operations to experience the impact of a play perhaps more profoundly than would another approach, by broadening his horizons, ordering the chaotic, and rectifying what needs amending. But here, too, the effect depends upon the sensibilities of those involved. The alchemist believed in man's ability to ascend the hierarchy of values to the Golden State, to purify what was sullied within his own soul. He may be said to have had a Promethean point of view. His idea of transcending earthly wretchedness by finding the Philosopher's Stone is certainly indicative of hubris. Yet similar views are implicit in the investigations undertaken by today's doctors, cosmologists, physicists, mathematicians, philosophers, and men of religion, as well as by the creative artist. All ostensibly work for the betterment of humanity as well as for their own edification; all seek to make their impress on eternity; all consciously or unconsciously have a mission.

Alchemy, wrote Jung, "was one of the great human quests for the unattainable." It is an example of an instinctive activity within man which cannot be explained rationally, any more than can genius or talent. Alchemy projects "an inner psychic experience into chemical substances that seemed to hold out mysterious possibilities, but nevertheless proved refractory to the intentions of the alchemist."[2] So the play also allows one to reach beyond one's limited field of vision toward the Infinite. Theatre may be looked upon as operational alchemy.[3] The *vas Hermetis* of the alchemist is the play for the dramatist, actor, and critic, the font or vessel in which the participants immerse themselves as they experience their individual transformation rituals. The activity which entices emotion and awakens sensation must also evoke thought, which then leads to evaluation, discrimination, and the sifting of material. The work of art is born.

Let us add to the alchemical dictum *Solve et coagula* one of Solomon's proverbs, written over 3,000 years ago: "Take fast hold of instruction; let her not go; keep her; for she is thy life" (Prov. 4:13).

The quest continues . . .

NOTES

Introduction

1. Antonin Artaud, *The Theatre and Its Double*, trans. Caroline Richards, p. 48.
2. C. G. Jung, *Collected Works*, trans. R. F. C. Hull, 14:555.
3. Quoted in Julian Franklyn, ed., *A Dictionary of the Occult*, p. 8.
4. Serge Hutin, *L'Alchimie*, p. 7; translation mine.
5. Ibid., p. 31.
6. Franklyn, ed., *Dictionary of the Occult*, p. 5.
7. Jung, *Collected Works*, trans. R. F. C. Hull, 13:148.
8. Ibid., 12:34.
9. Hutin, *L'Alchimie*, pp. 62–73.
10. Plato, *Timaeus*, trans. Francis M. Cornford, p. 62.
11. Alice Raphael, *Goethe and the Philosophers' Stone*, p. 98. See also Jung, *Collected Works*, 12:220.
12. Raphael, *Goethe and the Philosophers' Stone*, p. 12; Jung, *Collected Works*, 12:220; 13:105, 171, 346–48.
13. Bettina L. Knapp, *Antonin Artaud Man of Vision*, p. 87.
14. Goethe, *Faust*, trans. Philip Wayne, 2:83.

Chapter One

1. August Strindberg, *A Dream Play*, trans. Evert Sprinchorn, p. 10. All quotations from *A Dream Play* are from this edition.
2. August Strindberg, *Inferno, Alone, and Other Writings*, trans. Evert Sprinchorn, p. 121.
3. Ibid., p. 62.
4. Ibid., p. 121.
5. Gunnar Brandell, *Strindberg in Inferno*, pp. 26, 84.
6. Strindberg, *Inferno, Alone, and Other Writings*, p. 228.
7. Quoted in Brandell, *Strindberg in Inferno*, p. 168.
8. Ibid., p. 169.
9. Strindberg, *Inferno, Alone, and Other Writings*, p. 87.
10. Wilhelm Ganzenmüller, *L'Alchimie au moyen âge*, p. 104; translation mine.
11. Strindberg, *Inferno, Alone, and Other Writings*, p. 112.
12. John Maxon Stillman, *The Story of Alchemy and Early Chemistry*, p. 70.
13. Quoted in Jung, *Collected Works*, 14:432.
14. Ibid., p. 80.
15. Marcelin Berthelot, *Les Origines de l'alchimie*, pp. 39–40; translation mine.
16. Jung, *Collected Works*, 14:197.
17. Quoted in Brandell, *Strindberg in Inferno*, p. 174.

18. Ibid., p. 175.
19. Ibid.
20. Quoted in Jung, *Collected Works*, 14:194.
21. Frida Uhl Strindberg used to refer to her husband as the Flying Dutchman when he made a grand entrance in his dashing cape and high hat (Strindberg, *Inferno, Alone, and Other Writings*, p. 21).

Chapter Two

1. Michel de Ghelderode, *Seven Plays*, trans. George Hauger, p. 69. The quotation from *Christopher Columbus* appears on p. 174.
2. Michel de Ghelderode, *Théâtre*, 1:84. All quotations from *Escurial* are from this edition; translation mine.
3. Ghelderode, "The Ostend Interviews," in *Seven Plays*, p. 14.
4. Mircea Eliade, *The Forge and the Crucible*, p. 31.
5. C. G. Jung, "Transformation Symbolism in the Mass," *Eranos Yearbooks*, trans. R. F. C. Hull, 2:292.
6. Eliade, *Forge and the Crucible*, p. 32.
7. Jung, "Transformation Symbolism," p. 328.
8. Ibid., p. 320.
9. Jung, *Collected Works*, 12:295.
10. Quoted in Titus Burckhardt, *Alchemy*, p. 101.
11. Jung, "Transformation Symbolism," p. 301.
12. John Read, *Prelude to Chemistry*, p. 47.
13. Ibid., p. 63.
14. Read, *Prelude to Chemistry*, pp. 243, 158.
15. Eliade, *Forge and the Crucible*, p. 41.
16. Ibid., p. 56.
17. Jung, *Collected Works*, 13:227.
18. Ibid., p. 147.
19. George Ferguson, *Signs and Symbols in Christian Art*, p. 15.
20. Jung, *Collected Works*, 14:6.
21. Julien Tondriau and Roland Villeneuve, *Dictionnaire du diable et de la démonologie*, p. 93.
22. Quoted in Jung, *Collected Works*, 14:145.
23. Quoted in Mircea Eliade, *Rites and Symbols of Initiation*, p. 81.
24. Ghelderode, *Seven Plays*, p. 6.
25. Jung, *Collected Works*, 14:474.
26. Wylie Sypher, *Comedy*, p. 194.
27. Marie Louise von Franz, *Aurora Consurgens*, trans. R. F. C. Hull and A. S. B. Glover, p. 57.

Chapter Three

1. Paul Claudel, *Partage de Midi*, p. 11. All *Break of Noon* references are to this edition; translation mine.
2. Quoted in Herbert Silberer, *Hidden Symbolism of Alchemy and the Occult Arts*, p. 122.

3. Paul Claudel, *Oeuvres en prose,* p. 1469; translation mine.
4. Ibid., p. 1010.
5. Quoted in Jacques Madaule, *Le Drame de Paul Claudel,* p. 139; translation mine.
6. Harold A. Waters, "Claudel's *Partage* Desacralized," *L'Esprit Créateur* (Spring 1973), p. 19.
7. Paul Claudel, *Oeuvre poétique,* p. 432; translation mine.
8. Ibid., p. 91.
9. For further references to the sun, see Claudel, *Oeuvre poétique,* p. 68.
10. Ibid., p. 99.
11. Jung, *Collected Works,* trans. R. F. C. Hull, 8:456.
12. Bettina L. Knapp, *Dream and Image,* p. 246.
13. Ferguson, *Signs and Symbols in Christian Art,* p. 178.
14. Quoted in Silberer, *Hidden Symbolism of Alchemy and the Occult Arts,* p. 123.
15. Paul Claudel, *Mémoires improvisés,* p. 225; translation mine.
16. Jung, *Collected Works,* trans. R. F. C. Hull, 9:50–51.
17. Claudel, *Oeuvre poétique,* p. 54.
18. Quoted in Silberer, *Hidden Symbolism of Alchemy and the Occult Arts,* p. 161.
19. Quoted in Stillman, *Story of Alchemy and Early Chemistry,* p. 243.
20. Burckhardt, *Alchemy,* p. 103.
21. Stillman, *Story of Alchemy and Early Chemistry,* p. 70.
22. Hutin, *L'Alchimie,* p. 103.
23. Arthur E. Waite, *Alchemists through the Ages,* p. 29.
24. Claudel, *Oeuvre poétique,* p. 100.
25. Quoted in Stillman, *Story of Alchemy and Early Chemistry,* p. 414.
26. Quoted in Read, *Prelude to Chemistry,* p. 27.
27. Quoted in Silberer, *Hidden Symbolism of Alchemy and the Occult Arts,* p. 129.
28. Stillman, *Story of Alchemy and Early Chemistry,* p. 216.
29. Burckhardt, *Alchemy,* p. 101.
30. Ferguson, *Signs and Symbols in Christian Art,* p. 23.
31. Quoted in Read, *Prelude to Chemistry,* p. 208.
32. Quoted in Burckhardt, *Alchemy,* p. 188.
33. Ibid., p. 146.
34. Quoted in Burckhardt, *Alchemy,* p. 185.

Chapter Four

1. Leonard E. Nathan, *The Tragic Drama of William Butler Yeats,* p. 21.
2. William Butler Yeats, *Memoirs,* p. 216; Jean Brun, *Héraclite,* p. 126; translation mine.
3. Charles Berryman, *W. B. Yeats,* p. 117.
4. Eric Bentley, *In Search of Theatre,* p. 302.
5. Quoted in Nathan, *Tragic Drama of William Butler Yeats,* p. 157.
6. Robert Graves, *The White Goddess,* p. 75.
7. "Celtic Mythology," *New Larousse Encyclopedia,* p. 232.
8. William Butler Yeats, *Eleven Plays of William Butler Yeats,* ed. A. Norman Jeffares, p. 114. All quotations from *The Only Jealousy of Emer* are from this edition.

9. Quoted in Read, *Prelude to Chemistry,* p. 186.
10. Quoted in Stillman, *Story of Alchemy and Early Chemistry,* p. 411.
11. Ibid., p. 243.
12. John Rees Moore, *Masks of Love and Death,* p. 35.
13. Plato, *Timaeus,* p. 49.
14. Read, *Prelude to Chemistry,* p. 113.
15. Ibid., p. 141.
16. Quoted in Berryman, *W. B. Yeats,* p. 32.
17. Jung, *Collected Works,* 14:520.
18. Rajan Balachandra, *W. B. Yeats,* p. 98.
19. Edward Edinger, "An Outline of Analytical Psychology," p. 10.
20. Quoted in Nathan, *Tragic Drama of William Butler Yeats,* p. 160.
21. Graves, *White Goddess,* p. 101.
22. Ibid., p. 272.
23. Jung, *Collected Works,* 14:520.
24. Balachandra, *W. B. Yeats,* p. 98.
25. Ibid., p. 98.
26. William Butler Yeats, *A Vision,* p. 135.
27. Jung, *Collected Works,* 14:272, 240, 131, 130–32.
28. Yeats, *Vision,* pp. 135, 90–100.
29. Quoted in Nathan, *Tragic Drama of William Butler Yeats,* p. 523.
30. Jung, *Collected Works,* 14:352.
31. Ibid., p. 252.
32. Quoted in Read, *Prelude to Chemistry,* p. 138.
33. Ibid.

Chapter Five

1. Quoted in Read, *Prelude to Chemistry,* p. 132.
2. Stanislaw Ignacy Witkiewicz, *Insatiability,* trans. and with an introduction by Louis Iribarne, p. xi.
3. Ibid., p. xx.
4. Daniel Gerould, ed., *Twentieth-Century Polish Avant-Garde Drama,* p. 31.
5. André Breton, *Arcane 17,* p. 105; translation mine.
6. André Breton, *Manifeste du surréalisme,* p. 64; translation mine.
7. Quoted in Massimo Carra, Caroline Tisdall, Edwald Rathke, and Patrick Waldberg, *Metaphysical Art,* p. 87.
8. Witkiewicz, *Insatiability,* p. xxi.
9. Quoted in Czeslaw Milosz, *Emperor of the Earth,* p. 38.
10. Gerould, ed., *Twentieth-Century Polish Avant-Garde Drama,* pp. 484, 491.
11. Bernard F. Dukore and Daniel C. Gerould, eds., *Avant-Garde Drama,* p. 9. Translation of *The Water Hen* by Daniel C. Gerould and C. S. Durer; all quotations from *The Water Hen* are from this edition.
12. Quoted in Jung, *Collected Works,* 14:432.
13. Ibid., p. 473.
14. Ibid., p. 229.
15. Ibid., 13:78.

16. Ibid., p. 73.
17. Marie Louise von Franz, *Puer Aeternus,* pp. 15–25.
18. Jung, *Collected Works,* 13:70, 72.
19. Ibid., p. 87.
20. C. G. Jung, *The Visions Seminars,* p. 486.
21. Eliade, *Forge and the Crucible,* p. 153.

Chapter Six

1. Franz, *Aurora Consurgens,* p. 158.
2. The rose and the cross are supposed to have originated from the Latin *ros* ("dew") and *crux* ("cross"), indicating that the alchemical dew of the philosophers was the chemical that was the most "powerful dissolvent of gold." The cross represents light. Others believe that the rose was crucified when placed on the cross. *The Chymical Nuptials of Christian Rosencreutz* (1616) further elaborated the mysteries of the alleged founder of the Brotherhood of the Rosy Cross.
3. Villiers de l'Isle-Adam, *Axël,* pp. 48–50. All *Axël* references are to this edition; translation mine.
4. Franz, *Aurora Consurgens,* p. 166.
5. Ibid., pp. 72–73.
6. Stillman, *Story of Alchemy and Early Chemistry,* p. 44.
7. William T. Ferjie, *The Occult and Curative Powers of Precious Stones,* p. 248.
8. Jean Chevalier and Alain Gheerbrant, *Dictionnaire des symboles,* p. 273.
9. Marie Louise von Franz and Emma Jung, *The Grail Legend,* trans. Andrea Dykes, p. 255.
10. Quoted in Stillman, *Story of Alchemy and Early Chemistry,* p. 239.
11. Franz and Jung, *Grail Legend,* p. 165; see also chap. 1, n. 3 above.

Chapter Seven

1. Gershom Scholem, *Major Trends in Jewish Mysticism,* p. 344.
2. Shloyme Ansky, *The Dybbuk,* trans. Henry G. Alsberg and Winifred Kazin, pp. 18–19. All quotations from *The Dybbuk* are from this edition.
    In 1734 the Baal Shem descended from his mountain retreat and revealed his holiness to the masses of oppressed Jews. Wherever he traveled, his reputation preceded him as a healer and comforter. He attracted scholars and admirers to his home at Medziobozh. His most notable disciples were the rabbis Jacob Joseph of Polnoye and Dov Baer the Maggid ("preacher") of Mezerich. For further information, see Epstein, *Kabbalah;* Scholem, *Major Trends;* and Gershom Scholem, *The Messianic Idea in Judaism.*
3. Perle Epstein, *Kabbalah,* pp. 108–16.
4. Scholem, *Major Trends,* pp. 69, 74–75, 77.
5. The following two paragraphs are based on Scholem, *Major Trends,* pp. 281–84.
6. *Encyclopaedia Judaica,* 3:34. During World War I he helped organize relief committees for Jewish war victims. In 1917 he was elected to the All-Russian Constituent Assembly and helped organize the Vilna community. In 1909

Ansky moved to Warsaw and undertook the founding of the Jewish Ethnographic Society.

7. See Mendel Kohansky, *The Hebrew Theatre: Its Fifty Years,* pp. 32–34. Although the production was successful, as were those in the United States, Germany, France, and elsewhere, the most memorable performance was given by the Habima Players in Moscow on January 31, 1922. Eugeny Vakhtangov, the director of the Habima Theatre and a pupil of Constantin Stanislavsky, spent three years preparing it. The Yiddish Art Theatre production took place in New York in 1922; the Neighborhood Playhouse production of 1925–26 was directed by David Vardi, who had assisted in the Habima production. A Yiddish film version was made in Poland (1934); a Hebrew version translated by Chaim Nachman Bialik was made in Israel (1968). The opera *Il Dibbuk,* composed by Ludovico Rocca and with a libretto by Renato Simoni, premiered at La Scala in 1934; another opera, composed by Michael White, opened in Seattle, Washington, in 1963. There are also two ballets based on *The Dybbuk:* choreographed by Max Ettinger (1947); choreographed by Harold Robbins, music by Leonard Bernstein (1974). In 1977 the play was directed by Joseph Chaikin at the New York Public Theatre.
8. Scholem, *Major Trends,* p. 267.
9. Gershom Scholem, *Kabbalah,* p. 372.
10. Marie Louise von Franz, *Number and Time,* trans. Andrea Dykes, pp. 33, 53.
11. Scholem, *Messianic Idea,* p. 348.
12. Scholem, *Major Trends,* p. 132.
13. Stillman, *Story of Alchemy and Early Chemistry,* p. 56.
14. Gershom Scholem, *Sabbatai Sevi,* p. 306.
15. Gershom Scholem, *Kabbalah and Its Symbolism,* p. 49.
16. Ibid.
17. Ibid.
18. Epstein, *Kabbalah,* p. 59.
19. Esther Harding, *Psychic Energy,* p. 8.
20. Scholem, *Kabbalah and Its Symbolism,* p. 43.
21. Ibid., p. 49.
22. Scholem, *Major Trends,* p. 341.
23. C. G. Jung, "The Interpretation of Visions," *Spring* (1964), pp. 23–32.
24. Harding, *Psychic Energy,* p. 323.
25. Jung, *Collected Works,* 8:309.
26. Scholem, *Major Trends,* pp. 228–30.
27. Marie Louise von Franz, *Creation Myths,* p. 197.
28. Jung, *Collected Works,* 8:279.
29. Esther Harding, *Woman's Mysteries,* p. 59.
30. Jung, *Collected Works,* 14:461.
31. Esther Harding, *The Way of All Women,* pp. 37–39.

Chapter Eight

1. *Matsukaze,* trans. Royall Tyler, in Donald Keene, ed., *Twenty Plays of the Nō Theatre,* p. 32. All quotations from *Matsukaze* are from this edition.
2. Jung, *Collected Works,* 12:324.

3. Joseph Needham, *Science and Civilisation in China,* vol. 5, pt. 2, p. 83; Nathan Sivin, *Chinese Alchemy,* p. 5; Laurence G. Thompson, *Chinese Religion,* p. 93.
4. Sivin, *Chinese Alchemy,* pp. 147, 150.
5. See Emma Hawkridge, *The Wisdom Tree,* pp. 445–47.
6. Needham, *Science and Civilisation in China,* vol. 5, pt. 2, p. 83.
7. Thompson, *Chinese Religion,* p. 89.
8. Erwin Rousselle, "Spiritual Guidance in Contemporary Taoism," *Eranos IV,* p. 66.
9. Ibid.
10. William Bruce, *Religions in Japan,* p. 45.
11. Daisetz T. Suzuki, *An Introduction to Zen Buddhism,* pp. 9, 95.
12. Daisetz T. Suzuki, *Zen and the Japanese Culture,* p. 111.
13. Ibid., p. 26.
14. Elizabeth A. Behnke, "The Dimensions of Nothingness," *Main Currents in Modern Thought* (Jan.–Feb. 1974), p. 101.
15. Suzuki, *Zen and the Japanese Culture,* pp. 27, 28.
16. Ibid., p. 378.
17. Yasuo Nakamura, *Noh,* p. 30.
18. *New Larousse Encyclopedia of Mythology,* "Japanese Mythology," p. 409.
19. Ezra Pound and Ernest Fenollosa, *The Classic Noh Theatre of Japan,* p. 278.
20. Daiji Maruoka and Tatsuo Yoshikoshi, *Noh,* trans. Don Kenny, pp. 99–106.
21. Akhtar Qamber, *Yeats and the Noh,* p. 51.
22. Maruoka and Yoshikoshi, *Noh,* p. 125.
23. Pound and Fenellosa, *Classic Noh Theatre of Japan,* p. 280.
24. Maruoka and Yoshikoshi, *Noh,* p. 119.
25. Nakamura, *Noh,* p. 158.
26. Maruoka and Yoshikoshi, *Noh,* p. 119.
27. Nakamura, *Noh,* p. 30.
28. Behnke, "Dimensions of Nothingness," p. 102.
29. Ibid.
30. Quoted in Eliade, *Forge and the Crucible,* p. 112.
31. Needham, *Science and Civilisation in China,* vol. 5, pt. 2, p. 9.
32. Ibid., p. 92.
33. Hawkridge, *Wisdom Tree,* p. 444.
34. Needham, *Science and Civilisation in China,* vol. 5, pt. 2, p. 85.
35. Quoted in Hawkridge, *Wisdom Tree,* p. 446.
36. Quoted in James R. Ware, *Alchemy, Medicine, Religion,* p. 279.
37. See Needham, *Science and Civilisation in China,* vol. 5, pt. 2, pp. 98–100. The quotation is on p. 92.
38. Ibid., pt. 3, p. 58.
39. Sivin, *Chinese Alchemy,* pp. 169, 170.
40. Suzuki, *Zen and the Japanese Culture,* p. 393.
41. Quoted in Ware, *Alchemy, Medicine, Religion,* p. 62.

Chapter Nine

1. Keith A. Berriedale, *The Sanskrit Drama,* p. 161.
2. Nath Seal Brahendra, *The Positive Sciences of the Ancient Hindus,* p. 175.

3. For a description of the four aims, see Heinrich Zimmer, *Philosophies of India,* pp. 33–42.
4. Mircea Eliade, *Yoga,* pp. 282–83.
5. Heinrich Zimmer, *Myths and Symbols in Indian Art and Civilization,* pp. 140–48.
6. Paul Younger, *Introduction to Indian Religious Thought,* p. 55.
7. *The Upanishads,* trans. Swami Prabhavananda and Frederick Manchester, p. 60.
8. See René Daumal, *Bharata,* pp. 8–30.
9. Ibid., p. 66.
10. *Upanishads,* pp. 60–62.
11. Daumal, *Bharata,* pp. 27, 15.
12. Ibid., pp. 15–27.
13. Jung, *Collected Works,* trans. R. F. C. Hull, 11:480, 482, 490.
14. Ibid., p. 480.
15. Ibid., pp. 480–82.
16. Bhudeb Rasa-Jala-Nidhi Mukherjee, *Ocean of Indian Chemistry and Alchemy,* 5:xlvii.
17. Eliade, *Forge and the Crucible,* p. 128.
18. Ibid.
19. P. Lal, ed., *The Great Sanskrit Plays,* trans. P. Lal, p. 3. All quotations from *Shakuntala* are from this edition.
20. Eliade, *Yoga,* p. 355.
21. Ibid.
22. Joseph Campbell, *The Masks of God,* p. 169.
23. Eliade, *Yoga,* p. 34.
24. Zimmer, *Philosophies of India,* p. 450.
25. Eliade, *Yoga,* pp. 83, 185.
26. Ibid., p. 283.
27. Thomas J. Hopkins, *The Hindu Religious Tradition,* p. 12.
28. Eliade, *Yoga,* p. 108.
29. Zimmer, *Philosophies of India,* p. 141.
30. Ibid., pp. 158–60.
31. Eliade, *Yoga,* pp. 244–49.
32. Ibid., p. 246.
33. Quoted in Stillman, *Story of Alchemy and Early Chemistry,* p. 108.
34. Zimmer, *Philosophies of India,* p. 96.
35. *The Bhagavad Gita,* trans. Geoffrey Parringer, p. 31.
36. Zimmer, *Philosophies of India,* pp. 584–85.
37. Mukherjee, *Ocean of Indian Chemistry and Alchemy,* 5:246–49.
38. Zimmer, *Myths and Symbols in Indian Art and Civilization,* pp. 91–96.
39. Zimmer, *Philosophies of India,* pp. 576–77.
40. Eliade, *Yoga,* pp. 278–80.
41. Ibid., p. 279.
42. Ibid., p. 280.
43. Zimmer, *Philosophies of India,* p. 472.
44. Ibid., p. 143.

45. Eliade, *Yoga*, p. 223.
46. Mircea Eliade, *Patterns in Comparative Religion*, p. 179.
47. *Upanishads*, p. 90.
48. Ibid., p. 28.
49. Quoted in Eliade, *Yoga*, p. 23.
50. Quoted in Stillman, *Story of Alchemy and Early Chemistry*, p. 110.
51. *Upanishads*, p. 88.

Conclusion

1. Antonin Artaud, "Le théâtre alchimique," *Oeuvres complètes*, 4:62; translation mine.
2. Jung, *Collected Works*, 13:108.
3. Artaud, *Oeuvres complètes*, 4:58–63.

SELECTED BIBLIOGRAPHY

Ansky, S. *The Dybbuk*. Translated by Henry G. Alsberg and Winifred Katzin. Preface by Chaim Zhitlowsky. New York: Liveright, 1971.

Artaud, Antonin. *Oeuvres complètes*. Vol. 4. Paris: Gallimard, 1964.

———. *The Theatre and Its Double*. Translated by Caroline Richards. New York: Grove Press, 1958.

Balachandra, Rajan. *W. B. Yeats*. London: Hutchinson University Library, 1965.

Behnke, Elizabeth A. "The Dimensions of Nothingness." *Main Currents in Modern Thought,* Jan.–Feb. 1974, pp. 99–105.

Bentley, Eric. *In Search of Theatre*. New York: Vintage Books, 1954.

Berriedale, Keith A. *The Sanskrit Drama*. London: Oxford University Press, 1964.

Berryman, Charles. *W. B. Yeats*. New York: Exposition Press, 1967.

Berthelot, Marcelin. *Les Origines de l'alchimie*. Paris: Georges Steinheil, 1885.

Bhagavad Gita, The. Translated by Geoffrey Parringer. New York: E. P. Dutton and Co., 1975.

Brahendra, Nath Seal. *The Positive Sciences of the Ancient Hindus*. Delhi: Moti Lal Barnasi Dass, 1958.

Brandell, Gunnar. *Strindberg in Inferno*. Cambridge: Harvard University Press, 1974.

Breton, André. *Arcane 17*. Paris: 10/18, 1965.

———. *Manifeste du surréalisme*. Paris: Gallimard, 1963.

Bruce, William. *Religions in Japan*. Tokyo: Charles E. Tuttle Co., 1970.

Brun, Jean. *Héraclite*. Paris: Seghers, 1969.

Burckhardt, Titus, *Alchemy*. Baltimore, Md.: Penguin Books, 1974.

Chevalier, Jean and Gheerbraut, Alain. *Dictionnaire des symboles*.

Campbell, Joseph. *The Masks of God: Oriental Mythology*. New York: Viking Press, 1974.

Carra, Massimo, Tisdall, Caroline, Rathke, Edwald, and Waldberg, Patrick. *Metaphysical Art*. New York: Praeger Publishers, 1971.

Claudel, Paul. *Mémoires improvisés*. Paris: Gallimard, 1969.

———. *Oeuvre poétique*. Paris: Pléiade, 1967.

———. *Oeuvres en prose*. Paris: Pléiade, 1965.

———. *Partage de Midi*. Paris: Gallimard, 1949.

Portmann, Adolf, and Ritsema, Rudolf, eds. *Color Symbolism*. Zurich: Spring Publications, 1972.

Daumal, René. *Bharata*. Paris: Gallimard, 1970.

Dukore, Bernard F., and Gerould, Daniel C., eds. *Avant-Garde Drama*. New York: Thomas Y. Crowell, 1976.

Edinger, Edward. *Ego and Archetype*. New York: Putnam's Sons, 1972.

———. "An Outline of Analytical Psychology," unpublished.

———. "Psychotherapy and Alchemy." *Quadrant*, vol. 2, no. 2 (Summer 1978), pp. 5–37.

Eliade, Mircea. *The Forge and the Crucible*. New York: Harper Torchbooks, 1971.

———. *Patterns in Comparative Religion*. New York: New American Library, 1974.

———. *Rites and Symbols of Initiation*. New York: Harper Torchbooks, 1958.

———. *Yoga*. Princeton, N.J.: Princeton University Press, 1973.

Epstein, Perle. *Kabbalah: The Way of the Jewish Mystic*. New York: Doubleday and Co., 1978.

Ferguson, George. *Signs and Symbols in Christian Art*. Oxford: Oxford University Press, 1973.

Ferjie, William T. *The Occult and Curative Powers of Precious Stones*. Blauvelt, N.Y.: Rudolf Steiner Publications, 1973.

Franklyn, Julian, ed. *A Dictionary of the Occult*. New York: Causeway Books, 1973.

Franz, Marie Louise von. *Aurora Consurgens*. Translated by R. F. C. Hull and A. S. B. Glover. New York: Pantheon Books, 1966.

———. *Creation Myths*. Zürich: Spring Publications, 1972.

———. *Number and Time*. Translated by Andrea Dykes. Evanston, Ill.: Northwestern University Press, 1974.

———. *Puer Aeternus*. New York: Spring Publications, 1970.

———, and Jung, Emma. *The Grail Legend*. Translated by Andrea Dykes. New York: G. P. Putnam's, 1970.

Ganzenmüller, Wilhelm. *L'Alchimie au moyen âge*. Verviers, Belgium: Bibliothèque Marabout, 1974.

Gerould, Daniel, ed. *Twentieth-Century Polish Avant-Garde Drama*. Introduction by Daniel Gerould. Ithaca, N.Y.: Cornell University Press, 1977.

Ghelderode, Michel de. *Les Entretiens d'Ostende*. Paris: L'Arche, 1956.

———. *Seven Plays. Theatre*. Translated by George Hauger. Vol. 1. New York: Hill and Wang, 1969.

———. *Théâtre*. Vol. 1. Paris: Gallimard, 1950.

Goethe, Johann W. von. *Faust*. Translated by Philip Wayne. 2 vols. Middlesex, England: Penguin Books, 1959.

Graves, Robert. *The White Goddess.* New York: Farrar, Straus and Giroux, 1974.

Harding, Esther. *Psychic Energy.* Princeton, N.J.: Princeton University Press, 1973.

————. *The Way of All Women.* New York: Harper and Row, 1975.

————. *Woman's Mysteries.* New York: G. P. Putnam's Sons, 1971.

Hawkridge, Emma. *The Wisdom Tree.* Boston: Houghton Mifflin Co., 1945.

Hillman, James, *Suicide and the Soul.* Zurich: Spring Publications, 1976.

Hopkins, Thomas J. *The Hindu Religious Tradition.* Encino, Calif.: Dickenson Publishing Co., 1971.

Hutin, Serge. *L'Alchimie.* Paris: Presses Universitaires de France, 1971.

Jung, C. G. *Collected Works.* Vol. 8. Translated by R. F. C. Hull. Princeton, N.J.: Princeton University Press, 1969. Vol. 9. Translated by R. F. C. Hull. Princeton, N.J.: Princeton University Press, 1968. Vol. 11. Translated by R. F. C. Hull. New York: Pantheon Books, 1963. Vol. 12. Translated by R. F. C. Hull. London: Routledge and Kegan Paul, 1953. Vol. 13. Translated by R. F. C. Hull. Princeton, N.J.: Princeton University Press, 1967. Vol. 14. Translated by R. F. C. Hull. New York: Pantheon Books, 1963.

————. "The Interpretation of Visions." *Spring,* 1964, pp. 97–138.

————. "Transformation Symbolism in the Mass." *Eranos Yearbooks.* Vol. 2. Translated by R. F. C. Hull. Princeton, N.J.: Princeton University Press, 1955.

————. *The Visions Seminars.* New York: Spring Publications, 1976.

Keene, Donald. *Japanese Literature.* New York: Grove Press, 1955.

————, ed. *Twenty Plays of the Nō Theatre.* New York: Columbia University Press, 1970.

Knapp, Bettina L. *Antonin Artaud Man of Vision.* New York: Avon Books, 1971.

————. *Dream and Image.* Troy, New York: Whitston Press, 1977.

Kohansky, Mendel, *The Hebrew Theatre: Its Fifty Years.* Jerusalem: Israel University Press, 1969.

Lal, P., ed. *The Great Sanskrit Plays.* Translated by P. Lal. New York: New Directions, 1964.

MacKenzie, Norman. *Dreams and Dreaming.* New York: Vanguard Press, 1965.

Madaule, Jacques. *Le Drame de Paul Claudel.* Paris: Desclée de Brouwer, 1964.

Maruoka, Daiji, and Yoshikoshi, Tatsuo. *Noh.* Translated by Don Kenny. Osaka, Japan: Joikusha Publishing Co., n.d.

Milosz, Czeslaw, *Emperor of the Earth.* Berkeley: University of California Press, 1977.

Moore, John Rees. *Masks of Love and Death*. Ithaca, N.Y.: Cornell University Press, 1971.

Mukherjee, Bhudeb Rasa-Jala-Nidhi. *Ocean of Indian Chemistry and Alchemy*. Vol. 5. Calcutta: J. N. Dey, 1938.

Nakamura, Yasuo. *Noh*. Tokyo: Weatherhill-Tankosha, 1971.

Nathan, Leonard E. *The Tragic Drama of William Butler Yeats*. New York: Columbia University Press, 1965.

Needham, Joseph. *Science and Civilisation in China*. Vol. 5, pts. 2 and 3. Cambridge: Cambridge University Press, 1974 and 1976.

Plato. *Timaeus*. Translated by Francis M. Cornford. New York: Bobbs-Merrill Co., 1959.

Pound, Ezra, and Fenollosa, Ernest. *The Classic Noh Theatre of Japan*. New York: New Directions, 1959.

Pronko, Leonard. *Guide to Japanese Drama*. Boston: G. K. Hall, 1973.

Qamber, Akhtar, *Yeats and the Noh*. New York: Weatherhill, n.d.

Raphael, Alice. *Goethe and the Philosophers' Stone*. New York: Garret Publishers, 1955.

Read, John. *Prelude to Chemistry*. New York: Macmillan Co., 1937.

Rousselle, Erwin. "Spiritual Guidance in Contemporary Taoism." In *Eranos IV*, edited by Joseph Campbell. Princeton, N.J.: Princeton University Press, 1970, pp. 59–101.

Scholem, Gershom. *Kabbalah*. New York: New York Times Book Co., 1974.

———. *Kabbalah and Its Symbolism*. New York: Schocken Books, 1969.

———. *Major Trends in Jewish Mysticism*. New York: Schocken Books, 1961.

———. *The Messianic Idea in Judaism*. New York: Schocken Books, 1971.

———. *Sabbatai Sevi*. Princeton: Princeton University Press, 1975.

Seigen, Morton Irving, *William Butler Yeats: The Poet as a Mythmaker 1865–1939*. East Lansing, Mich.: Michigan State University Press, 1962.

Senior, John. *The Way Down and Out: The Occult in Symbolist Literature*. New York: Greenwood Press, 1968.

Silberer, Herbert. *Hidden Symbolism of Alchemy and the Occult Arts*. 1917. Reprint. New York: Dover Publications, 1971.

Sivin, Nathan. *Chinese Alchemy: Preliminary Studies*. Cambridge, Mass.: Harvard University Press, 1968.

Smith, Daniel H. *Selections from Vedic Hymns*. Berkeley, Calif.: McCutchan Publishing Corp., 1968.

Stillman, John Maxson. *The Story of Alchemy and Early Chemistry*. 1924. Reprint. New York: Dover Publications, 1960.

Strindberg, August. *A Dream Play*. Translated by Evert Sprinchorn. Introduction by Jacques Chwat. New York: Avon Books, 1974.

————. *Inferno, Alone, and Other Writings*. Translated by Evert Sprinchorn. New York: Anchor Books, 1968.

Suzuki, Daisetz T. *An Introduction to Zen Buddhism*. Foreword by C. G. Jung. New York: Grove Press, 1964.

————. *Zen and the Japanese Culture*. Princeton: Princeton University Press, 1973.

Sypher, Wylie. *Comedy*. New York: Doubleday, Anchor Books, 1956.

Tain, The. Translated by Thomas Kinsella. London: Oxford University Press, 1975.

Thompson, Laurence G. *Chinese Religion: An Introduction*. Belmont, Calif.: Dickenson Publishing Co., 1969.

Thorndike, Lyn. *A History of Magic and Experimental Science*. Vol. 2. New York: Columbia University Press, 1923.

Tondriau, Julien, and Villeneuve, Roland. *Dictionnaire du diable et de la démonologie*. Paris: Marabout Université, 1963.

Upanishads, The. Translated by Swami Prabhavananda and Frederick Manchester. New York: Mentor, 1957.

Villiers de l'Isle-Adam, J.-M. *Axël*. Paris: Le Courrier du Livre, 1969.

Waite, Arthur E. *Alchemists through the Ages*. Blauvelt, N.Y.: Rudolf Steiner Publications, 1970.

Ware, James, R. *Alchemy, Medicine, Religion*. Cambridge, Mass.: MIT Press, 1966.

Witkiewicz, Stanislaw Ignacy. *Insatiability*. Translated and with an introduction by Louis Iribarne. Urbana, Ill.: University of Illinois Press, 1977.

Yeats, William Butler. *Eleven Plays of William Butler Yeats*. Edited by A. Norman Jeffares. New York: Collier Books, 1973.

————. *Memoirs*. New York: Macmillan Co., 1973.

————. *A Vision*. New York: Macmillan Co., 1938.

Younger, Paul. *Introduction to Indian Religious Thought*. Philadelphia: Westminster Press, n.d.

Zimmer, Heinrich. *Myths and Symbols in Indian Art and Civilization*. Princeton, N.J.: Princeton University Press, 1974.

————. *Philosophies of India*. Princeton, N.J.: Princeton University Press, 1974.

INDEX

Abbess (*Axël*), 141, 143

Actors: the four elements and, 14–15; in Noh drama, 199–201

Adam, 157

Adam Kadman, 157, 162, 163, 165; fire and, 160

Agnes (*A Dream Play*): *citrinitas* and, 25; *separatio* and, 26–27

Air: as alchemic element, 7–8; Cuchulain and, 92–93; the dramatist and, 14; fermentative spirit of, 79; Leah as personification of, 176; *Only Jealousy of Emer* and, 95, 98; *sublimatio* and, 11; wind and, 74

Akasa, 246

Akropolis (Wyspianski), 115

Albedo, 48, 184, 250; ashes and, 39; *Break of Noon* and, 87; the dramatist and, 13; *A Dream Play* and, 23–24; psychological aspects of, 9; silver and, 107; Song of Songs and, 167

Alchemy: in ancient Egypt, 3, 5, 80; Arab tradition and, 4; astral influences and, 86; author's use of term delineated, 2–3; Babylonians and, 5; character traits in practitioners of, 6–7; in China, 4; contamination and, 163; dance and, 56; death and, 54, 88, 112; as Double, 1; the dramatist and principles of, 250–52; esoteric, 249–50; etymology of, 4; fluidity and, 203–4; goal of, 5–6; Hindu, 4, 6, 223, 224, 229, 235–36, 246; in Japan, 191, 202–3, 206; Jung on, 6, 257; man's earthbound state and, 143; metaphysical aspects of, 2, 5–6, 15, 137, 191; music and, 35; sacrifice and, 47; secrecy and, 6; Songs of Songs and, 166–67, 177; Strindberg's experiments in, 20–22; Taoism and, 214; theoretical base of, 4–5; Yeats and, 90

Amalric (*Break of Noon*): fire/water and, 70–71; name analyzed, 65–66;
as sulfur principle, 73–74; wind and, 74

Anaximander, 5

Anima figures: defined, 105; Eve as, 139; Leah as, 167–68, 169, 186; in *Only Jealousy of Emer,* 105–10, 254; Sara as, 151; Victoria as, 31; Water Hen as, 120, 129, 130, 131

Anima mundi, 47, 153; Yeats and, 89, 93

Animals, 8; antelope (stag), 227, 228, 229; birds, 81, 82, 97–98, 212; the cow, 76; dogs, 52–53, 54, 76, 147; elephants, 238; fish, 29, 96–97, 105–106; the goat, 51; the horse, 75, 100, 238; the lamb, 27; in man (Claudel), 75; religious function of, 64; Sanskrit drama and, 219; Strindberg and, 22–23

Ansky, Shloyme, 154, 255; background of, 158

Antibarbarus (Strindberg), 22–23, 37

Aqua permanens, 5, 9, 60, 132, 150, 251. *See also* Water

Aquinas, Saint Thomas, 56

Aristotle, 219

Arms, symbolism of, 99–100

Arnold of Villanova, 29, 96, 118

Artaud, Antonin, 1, 15, 47, 114, 249, 251

Artha, 219; phase of *Shakuntala,* 225–29

Asch, Sholem, 112

Ashes, symbolism of, 39

Ashram, symbolism of, 229, 232

Axël (Villiers de l'Isle-Adam): act 1 of, 139–44, 255; act 2 of, 145–48; act 3 of, 148–51; act 4 of, 151–53; structure of, 137–38; as transformation process, 137

Axël (*Axël*): Rosicrucians and, 145, 146, 149–50; sulfur personification, 145–46

275

Bettina L. Knapp was educated at Lake Erie College, Barnard College, the Sorbonne, and Columbia University, from which she received the Ph.D. in 1956. Since 1960 she has been professor of Romance languages and comparative literature at Hunter College and the Graduate Center of the City University of New York. She is the author of many previous books, among them *Antonin Artaud Man of Vision, Jean Genet: An Analytical Study, Jean Racine: Mythos and Renewal in Modern Theatre, Dream and Image, The Prometheus Syndrome,* and *Gérard de Nerval: The Mystic's Dilemma,* and of scores of articles, reviews, and other writings.

The book was designed by Gary Gore. The typeface for the text is Century Schoolbook, based on the original cuts by Linn Boyd Benton in collaboration with T. L. De Vinne in 1894. The display face is Korinna.

The text is printed on S. D. Warren's 1854 text paper, and the book is bound in Holliston Mills' Kingston black linen over binder's boards. Manufactured in the United States of America.

1495

ϕ

$\sqrt{6}+ / \sqrt{6}-$

OP

$\sqrt{H}$

EQ

dramacii